CW01637750

The Uses of Social Science

The Open University

The Uses of Social Science

Edited by Mark Banks and Clive Barnett

The Open University Walton Hall, Milton Keynes MK7 6AA

First published 2012.

© 2012 The Open University

All rights reserved. No part of this publication may be reproduced, stored in a retrieval system, or transmitted in any form or by any means, electronic, mechanical, photocopying, recording, or otherwise without either the prior written permission of the publishers or a licence permitting restricted copying issued by the Copyright Licensing Agency, 90 Tottenham Court Road, London W1P 0LP. This material may not be lent, resold, hired out or otherwise disposed of by way of trade in any form of binding or cover other than that in which it is published, without the prior consent of the Publishers.

Edited, designed and typeset by The Open University.

Printed and bound in the United Kingdom by Bell & Bain Ltd, Glasgow

ISBN 978 1 8487 3474 6

1.1

MIX
Paper from responsible sources
FSC® C007785

Contents

Introduction 1
Clive Barnett and Mark Banks

Chapter 1 Describing childhood intimacies 15
Kesi Mahendran

Chapter 2 Quantifying intimate lives 53
Peter Redman

Chapter 3 Understanding shadow work 99
Gabe Mythen

Chapter 4 Theorising the value of leisure 139
Mark Banks

Chapter 5 Forecasting the future of transport 183
George Revill

Chapter 6 Contesting the place of music 225
Jason Toynbee

Chapter 7 Enacting elections 267
Richard Heffernan

Chapter 8 Giving people a voice 307
Vicki Squire

Conclusion 347
Clive Barnett and Mark Banks

Acknowledgements 351

Index 355

Introduction

Clive Barnett and Mark Banks

1 Using social science

Social science is used in all sorts of different ways. For example, it is used to generate evidence about children's educational achievements, to explain the causes of homelessness, to understand the nature of poverty, to help people give up smoking and to calculate rates of inflation. In all of these areas and in many others, social scientists seek to enhance living standards, improve people's health and well-being, increase economic efficiency, pursue social justice, and develop more sustainable ways of living and working.

The chapters in this book will show you how social science is used to make sense of all sorts of private troubles and public issues. It is used to make sense of the most intimate aspects of our lives, our relationships with family and friends. It is used to make sense of people's working lives and leisure time, whether they work in factories or in offices, or at home looking after children, or in dangerous occupations that exist in the shadows of public life. It is used to make sense of how the places we live in are tied to all sorts of faraway places, through flows of mobile commodities, information and people. And it is used to make sense of how people participate in all sorts of activities, by taking part in elections or community life, in the attempt to exert some control over their lives.

What is it that social scientists actually do? This is the question that the chapters in this book respond to, as they investigate a range of topics. If we think of the word 'science' as meaning the systematic investigation of phenomena as well as the resulting body of organised knowledge, then 'social science' can be thought of as the systematic investigation of social worlds. The term 'science' might bring to mind an image of experiments, large data sets and equations. Well, as you will discover in this book, social scientists can use large data sets and they do use experiments to investigate social worlds. Social science, however, also uses other methods as well. Social scientists undertake in-depth interviews, organise focus groups, and even immerse themselves in other people's lives to observe them (an approach known as 'ethnography'). You will learn in the chapters that follow that different quantitative and qualitative methods enable social science to be used in all sorts of ways.

Social science is often organised into disciplines: these are distinct subject areas, such as social anthropology, economics, human geography, politics, psychology, social policy, and sociology. There is often considerable overlap between these disciplines, and there is also a wide range of interdisciplinary fields of social science investigation, such as development studies, educational studies, urban and regional studies, media and communication studies, and women's studies. Rather than focusing in turn on one discipline after another, this book is organised around four topics – *intimacy*, *work*, *mobility* and *participation* – approached in an interdisciplinary way. These topics have been selected because each is studied by social scientists from various disciplines, often working collaboratively. The emphasis in the chapters in this book is, then, very much on interdisciplinary social science – on areas of investigation that draw on the insights, methods, concepts and theories of a number of fields, and that are defined not by disciplinary specialisation but by a shared focus on a common topic area or object of analysis.

The chapters in this book are arranged in order to introduce and develop a particular framework with which to analyse what social scientists do and how social science is used. This framework sees social science as doing three closely related things – it *describes*, *understands* and helps to *enact* social worlds (‘*the DUE framework*’, for short). This introduction outlines this framework. As you read through the book, you might want to refer back to this introduction occasionally, to remind yourself about the relationships between the three different elements of the framework.

2 Describing, understanding and enacting social worlds

The DUE framework is meant to help you understand the different aspects of social science, by identifying distinct elements of the whole enterprise of doing social science, and looking at each one in detail. The topics dealt with in each chapter of the book have been chosen to provide material and case studies through which you will learn about what is involved in social science description, understanding and enactment. The topics are all examples of some of the varied issues and themes studied by social scientists across a range of disciplines, but their treatment in these chapters is shaped by the aim of helping you apply the DUE framework to think about how social science is both useful and is used.

The DUE framework is meant to serve as an analytical device to help you identify the different aspects of doing social science. As such, it helps to break up and pick out the constituent activities involved in doing social science, so that you can see what is involved in each one, and so that you might better appreciate how the different aspects all fit together in practice. The terms description, understanding and enactment might already bring to mind particular meanings, so it is helpful at this stage to clarify how they are used in the DUE framework and throughout this book.

Description

The most obvious sense of the word 'describe' is to write down, record or give an account of something. It has a neutral sound to it – describing what you had for breakfast or how you get to work in the morning appears to be a matter of recounting some facts, without having to justify or explain why you did this or did that. In the DUE framework, description refers to the outcome of all the processes through which social scientists produce data, evidence and information about the social world. There are two aspects to this. First, social science makes use of various methods and techniques to collect, gather and generate such materials: social scientists conduct surveys, interview people, analyse official statistics and observe people's everyday activities. Second, on the basis of these methods, social scientists generate accounts of the social world – for example, descriptions of what people think about issues, of patterns of behaviour across society, or of particular practices.

In the chapters in this book, 'description' therefore refers to the linkages between social scientists' accounts and representations of the social world, and the *methods* they use to generate the *data*, *evidence* and *information* presented in those accounts and representations. With that in mind we can say that social science description involves techniques and practices of investigating, observing, selecting, collecting, recording, surveying, mapping and measuring. It also involves various analytical practices that are applied to data and information, such as documentary analysis, experimentation and calculation.

Importantly, all of those techniques and practices involve an element of translation. No matter how accurate or reliable a description is, it is not the same as the thing described – just as a description of your breakfast is not the same thing as the breakfast itself. For example, a census provides a thorough description of a national population – its size, its composition in terms of age, gender and ethnicity, and its geographical distribution. But actually generating this description of a national population takes a lot of work: designing census forms, collecting the data, recording and presenting it. And a census inevitably captures only some aspects of the characteristics of a population, not others. In any approach to social science, this element of selectivity has consequences for the uses made of social science.

Social science description is, then, a process that actively generates data, evidence and information of a factual sort by translating the complex and messy goings on of life into presentable form – into tables of data, percentages, or detailed written descriptions. An important emphasis in discussing social science description, therefore, is the idea that this is a means by which social science is used to *make visible* certain phenomena – patterns of inequality, for example, or the intimate dynamics of family life.

Understanding

'Understanding' refers to the comprehension, interpretation and explanation of phenomena. If social scientific descriptions provide us with accounts of the social world, then, at its simplest, the next stage in the DUE framework refers us to the understandings to which those descriptions give rise. In the DUE framework, social science understanding is defined as the process through which social scientists seek to further analyse, and then interpret and explain the social world.

Our ability to understand the social world depends crucially on accurate and reliable descriptions of it. However, things are not quite as straightforward as that might make them sound. Social scientific descriptions do not necessarily lead to social scientific understandings in a simple or straightforward fashion. There are two main reasons for this. First, the findings generated by the process of social scientific description have to be interpreted, or made sense of: facts rarely speak for themselves. Different interpretations can often be made of the same findings, giving rise to competing understandings of what those findings mean. Second, description itself is not a neutral activity. The questions that social scientists ask about the social world and what they see when they are investigating it are shaped by their prior understandings of what the social world is like or should be like. Although such prior understanding will often be modified by what social scientists find, it nevertheless shapes the descriptions they generate. So, while there can be no understanding without prior description, there can be no description without prior understanding either.

Social science understanding therefore refers to the skills and techniques of interpretation, analysis, explanation, modelling and imagining. You will see in the chapters in this book that a central part of social science understanding is the use of *concepts* to make sense of data, evidence or information. For example, you will read about the ways in which different social science concepts of work are used to develop markedly different understandings of the dynamics of labour markets and the pleasures and distractions of leisure time. An important emphasis of social science understanding is the idea that *facts don't speak for themselves*; concepts are important devices when picking out what is relevant about a social science description, and when making sense of the patterns they may reveal. In turn, social science understanding also involves the deployment of *values* in mediating the relationship between descriptions and understandings. For instance (and to stick with the example of concepts of work), feminist social science uses the concept of gender to bring into view the range of activities traditionally undertaken by women but often ignored in definitions of work and labour. In so doing, they transform the description of work, certainly, by making use of a specific concept – gender – but they do so from a perspective of seeking to challenge unequal power relations between men and women with a view to further realising the important value of equality. Social science understanding combines concepts and values, often in distinctive *theoretical frameworks*, in order to *make sense* – to provide an explanation, a contextual background or an interpretation that gives new meaning or significance to what is described.

Enactment

Enactment may seem a slightly archaic word, bringing to mind acts of legislation or the judgments of a court. The suggestion that social science helps to enact social worlds highlights the ways in which social science has effects on the phenomena and processes it investigates – that is, the ways in which social science *makes a difference* to social worlds. In the DUE framework, then, enactment refers to the idea of making something happen, and it is used to draw attention to the ways in which social science descriptions and understandings are always undertaken for a purpose. These descriptions and understandings have broader, often public reference points, addressing important issues or concerns and hoping, at least, to make a difference by bringing new issues to light (through better descriptions) or by changing how they are addressed (through better understandings). In one sense, this is the most obvious way in which we can see social science being used – it is used to *inform and influence debates* about what to do about some issue, whether action is taken by policy makers, corporations or ordinary people. And in so far as social science does have any influence in this way (for good or ill, one might add), it is clear that it also has a role in *shaping social worlds*. For example, if social science research informs public debate about the causes of obesity, perhaps pointing to the relationship between health, food and income level, then this might well lead to specific policy initiatives to improve nutritional levels among particular groups of people. This would be an example of social science both informing and shaping social worlds, since those policy initiatives would change the opportunities, experiences and practices of targeted populations.

Social science is used to help enact social worlds through processes of intervening, evaluating, supporting, challenging and legitimising. In these ways, social science helps to shape who we are and what we can be. The chapters in this book illustrate both senses of enactment, showing the ways in social science informs or influences debates and policies, and how it also has an active role to play in shaping social worlds too. In the first sense, social science is used to inform through such activities as contributing to public debates or policy making, or providing evidence that is used by various groups, organisations and institutions – schools, hospitals, companies, governments or campaign groups. At the same time, social science enacts by shaping social worlds – perhaps by redefining our own sense of identity. For example, by measuring and mapping social behaviour, social scientists produce descriptions of 'average' social behaviour. These descriptions can become powerful norms that orientate people's expectations and ambitions, in turn helping to shape how social behaviour develops and evolves over time.

Each element of the DUE framework refers to a range of activities that social scientists engage in when trying to:

make visible social worlds

make sense of patterns and behaviour

make a difference to how social worlds work in practice.

Throughout the book, social science will be shown to make social worlds visible in public arenas through practices of description, and to identify processes of causality, responsibility and persuasion through which social worlds are formed and change through practices of understanding. In turn, these two uses of social science will be shown to be important in recognising how social science helps to inform and shape (and is informed and shaped by) social worlds – how it helps to enact them.

As you read through the chapters, each element of the DUE framework is being elaborated through the detailed consideration of a substantive topic. But you should try to bear in mind that even while you are learning about one particular element of the DUE framework, there are likely to be links and connections to the other two elements. This relationship between the elements, and the feedback between the three elements, will be drawn out as you move from chapter to chapter, and we shall return to it in the conclusion to the book.

3 Doing things with social science

The DUE framework which you have just read about might seem, at first sight, to be rather abstract. As you read through this book, however, you will see that each aspect of the framework is developed in detail, before moving on to another aspect. To help you start thinking about how the DUE framework is developed in the course of the book, it might be helpful to summarise how the framework is developed chapter by chapter.

Chapters 1 and 2 both focus on the substantive topic of *intimacy*. They explore this topic in order to introduce a set of tools and techniques that enables social scientists to describe social worlds. In Chapter 1, Kesi Mahendran discusses the role of social science in debates about the possible effects of media on family life, children's development and personal behaviour. She shows how social scientists have adopted various methods – including experimental approaches, in-depth interviews and focus groups – to make visible how people make use of media technologies in their everyday lives. This chapter introduces the distinction between quantitative and qualitative methodologies, and considers some of the uses of each approach.

In Chapter 2, Peter Redman also looks at how social science has been used to make intimate practices into objects of public debate. In this case, he considers the extent to which the survey method has helped to make visible the range and scale of different sexual practices among large national populations. As in Chapter 1, the example of sex surveys throws into relief questions about what any single methodology is best used for, and what its limitations are.

In both Chapters 1 and 2, you will also learn that the focus on intimacy as a substantive topic is particularly helpful in drawing out some of the issues that arise in all social science *description* – for example, questions about what weight should be given to how people themselves describe their own social worlds, or how to establish whether observed patterns of behaviour can be generalised beyond the particular example under investigation.

In Chapters 3 and 4, the substantive focus shifts away from 'private' worlds of family and sexuality, towards public worlds of *work* and leisure. In Chapter 3, Gabe Mythen looks at various forms of paid work that are hidden, that take place in the shadows as it were. This includes the work undertaken by illegal migrants, which is often poorly paid and very risky, and the work involved in providing sexual services in exchange for money. In terms of the DUE framework, Chapter 3 aims to move you beyond looking primarily at social science description, towards thinking about how description is related to *understanding*. In this chapter, in particular, the idea that facts don't speak for themselves is introduced, in order to underscore that, for a piece of information to count as social science evidence, it has to be made into evidence by being placed into a wider explanatory or interpretative framework of concepts and theories.

In Chapter 4, Mark Banks develops this idea that facts don't speak for themselves. He looks at social science that investigates practices that seem to be the very opposite of work – leisure activities: from going on holiday to going to the gym after work to relax and recharge. You will read here about different theories, including economic theories of rational choice, sociological theories of individualisation, theories of class and theories of gender. And he raises the question of how far different patterns of work and leisure reflect people's choices or are influenced by factors beyond their control – a question which, as you will see, is not answered simply by reference to data and evidence, but requires some degree of conceptual interpretation.

In showing how facts don't speak for themselves, how concepts are used to understand social worlds and how values are deployed in different theories, Chapters 3 and 4 begin to draw into focus the degree to which social science investigation is always likely to lead to disagreement. This is not because social scientists cannot agree on a single method, robust explanation or cast-iron technique of measurement; it is because the things that social scientists investigate are themselves often highly contentious, hotly debated and subject to multiple and competing interests and interpretations.

If these Chapters 3 and 4 introduce the importance of social science understandings, then Chapters 5 and 6 develop further the idea that social science understandings are always *contested*. These two chapters focus on the topic of mobility, looking at the ways in which people, things and information are able to move around the world and the conflicts and tensions this generates.

Chapter 5 looks at the role of social science in contested public issues, using the example of debates about large transport infrastructure development in the United Kingdom. Social science has long been involved in attempts to forecast future patterns of mobility and provide the infrastructure of roads and railways that these forecasts seem to demand. It is often assumed that this sort of use of social science contributes to gains in economic efficiency and personal mobility that are to the benefit of all. In Chapter 5, however, George Revill shows that social science is also used to challenge the presumed benefits of major transport decisions, and becomes embroiled in contested public issues in support of alternative scenarios.

In Chapter 6, this same theme of contested understandings is developed by Jason Toynbee, using the example of music cultures to explore how social science makes sense of the ways in which music is used by ordinary people to negotiate the power relations that infuse their own everyday lives. This chapter explores in detail the qualitative and quantitative techniques used by social science, in both academic and commercial settings, to establish what music actually means to people. Chapter 6 concludes with a discussion of how social science is implicated in the making of music markets. In this case, social science does not just describe and understand mobile forms of music, but plays an important role in the commodification and circulation of music.

The idea that social science helps to *enact* social worlds in this way, the third element of the DUE framework, is further developed in the last two chapters of the book. The notion of enactment carries two related senses here, both of which are elaborated in Chapters 7 and 8. The first is the idea that social science is used to inform and influence public debates, institutional practices, and policy interventions around a wide range of issues and problems. The second is the idea that social science actively shapes both social worlds and the subjects of those worlds – ordinary people, experts, professionals and others. Both of these aspects of enactment are discussed in Chapters 7 and 8, which focus on the substantive topic of *participation* to illustrate the ways in which social science is involved in making a difference to the activities through which individuals are able to take part in wider society.

In Chapter 7, Richard Heffernan discusses social science studies of elections and voting, showing how social science contributes to public debates about the meaning of these practices, the most formal types of political participation. Elections generate lots of raw data, and social science helps to give meaning to the results by describing who voted and why, and by seeking to understand why people vote as they do. The theories of voting behaviour that social scientists have developed are shown to inform and influence public debates about the virtues of voting, changing patterns of political participation, and evolving trends of partisan support.

In Chapter 8, the final chapter of this book, Vicki Squire broadens the idea of enactment to include both informing debates and practices, and the active shaping of social worlds. She discusses participatory social science, a range of approaches that seeks to actively involve research subjects in the design and dissemination of social science investigations for the explicit purpose of helping those people 'have voice' in the public realm. The chapter discusses the tradition of social science known as participatory action research (PAR), showing how this style of social science seeks to enact social worlds in two ways: first, to inform institutional policies and practices; and, second, to shape social worlds by working collaboratively with participants in research to seek to transform structures of power. PAR illustrates the ways in which social science descriptions depend on the participation of non-social scientists, and how social science understandings often draw on the understandings that ordinary people already have about their lives and experiences.

If the chapters in this book make clear the range of uses to which social science is put, Chapter 8 leaves you with the question of what social science *should* be used for. Some of the uses discussed in these chapters depend on the claim that social science provides rigorous, objective data and reliable, generalisable explanations of phenomena. These uses are often justified in the name of making things better, improving people's lives, or solving problems. Some of the uses of social science that you will read about depend on stronger claims that social science can act as an advocate of the disempowered or as a medium for social justice, by listening to and helping to represent the perspectives of the most disempowered members of society. These uses also draw on the idea that social science should not just be useful, but used to make things better, to improve things.

Taken as a whole, then, this book invites you to think about three things: how social scientists try to make visible, make sense and make a difference to the social phenomena they investigate. It provides you with an analytical framework through which to analyse and assess how social scientists go about these tasks, one which focuses on how social science is used to describe, understand and enact social worlds.

Chapter 1
Describing childhood intimacies

Kesi Mahendran

1 Introduction 19
1.1 Structure of the chapter 22
1.2 Aims of the chapter 22
2 Investigating the effects of television on young people 23
2.1 Defining the public issue 23
2.2 Using experiments to identify causal relationships 27
2.3 Making use of experimental social science 30
2.4 Alternative approaches: controlled experiments and qualitative methods 32
3 Debating the sexualisation of children 37
3.1 Sexualisation as a public issue 37
3.2 Sluts and whores: describing young people's social worlds 39
3.3 Interpreting qualitative interview evidence 44
4 Conclusion: researching childhood innocence and desire 49
4.1 Chapter summary 50
References 52

1 Introduction

In this opening chapter you will be introduced to two social science methods: **quantitative** experiments and **qualitative** interviews. The chapter uses the example of debates about childhood 'innocence' to explore how each of these methods is used to generate distinctive forms of social science *description* of intimate practices of family life, sexuality and personal identity.

Quantitative methods make use of numerical data and forms of analysis which draw on mathematics and statistics. They are effective in describing patterns and for studying extensive causal processes.

Qualitative methods include unstructured or semi-structured interviews, focus groups and life histories, textual and documentary analysis, participant observation, and ethnography. They are effective in bringing to light participants' perspectives on their actions, and for studying causal processes in detail.

As a way of introducing the main topic of this chapter, let us begin with two short observations on the significance of children consuming products produced by the adult-entertainment company Playboy. In both of these comments, mention is made of the famous Playboy bunny logo, the profile of a rabbit head with a bow tie first used by Hugh Hefner for the cover of his magazine *Playboy* in 1953. The logo has now become a feature of all sorts of merchandise, including children's clothing and stationery.

The first observation (Reading 1.1) comes from a news report in a leading national newspaper in the UK.

Reading 1.1

Playboy bunny T-shirts and pop music videos to blame for sexualisation of children, expert warns

Provocative clothes and explicit music videos are increasing the sexualisation of children, according to the director of a centre for rape victims.

Dr Catherine White said the number of young people being seen at the Sexual Assault Referral Centre in St Mary's Hospital in Manchester had risen in recent years.

She claimed the increasing use of adult images in youth culture is changing what teenagers see as unacceptable behaviour.

Dr White, the clinical director of the centre, said: 'We have to look more fundamentally at what's happening. There's an increasing sexualisation of children. When you see a little girl wearing a T-shirt with a Playboy bunny, that's wrong isn't it?

'I've seen another that said "Porn star in the making".' She went on: 'Music videos are extremely influential. I think it's all

> subconscious and there's a drip, drip, drip effect. It might not be one thing but all together it's having an effect on values, on what is acceptable and not acceptable.'
>
> (Source: Beckford, 2009)

The second observation is taken from a social science research report on the same issue. It is an extract from a response by one of the participants in a **focus group** which is a particular kind of qualitative interviewing.

A **focus group** is a qualitative method used to obtain opinions and experiences from a small number of people (e.g. up to about 12–15), who participate in a group discussion organised around a specified range of topics.

Reading 1.2

Sexualised goods – a mother's view

'You don't want to force them to think about things that they're innocently thinking [is] a nice pink bunny. ... Just allow them to be children for that bit longer. You don't always want to be the one that's coming in spoiling it and making them think of the bigger issues. There are times they ... don't need to worry about who they're offending on their T-shirt. They don't need to maybe think about the moral issues of absolutely everything that they do, like what clothes to put on in the morning' (Mother, FG4).

(Source: Buckingham et al., 2010, p. 50)

Readings 1.1 and 1.2 present two contrasting views on the sexualisation of children. The first is put forward as an expert opinion; the second as an example of ordinary, or lay, thinking.

Take a few moments to reflect on your own opinions on this issue. Do you tend to agree more with Dr White in Reading 1.1, or with the mother in Reading 1.2? Are these two opinions incompatible?

This chapter will look at how different sorts of descriptive evidence are used by social scientists to inform and engage in arguments and debates about childhood innocence and sexualisation. The vulnerability of children to media images and popular culture, and the degree of protection that they should be accorded from the 'effects' of these, has been an important topic of public debate to which social scientists from fields such as sociology, social psychology, education and media studies have contributed.

As you read the chapter, you will find out how social scientists go about assessing the issues associated with childhood, media and consumerism illustrated by Readings 1.1 and 1.2. They do so by generating descriptions of various sorts, using methods which produce evidence that is then presented as supporting particular understandings of these issues. You will read about two examples of social science being used to inform debates about childhood and popular culture. In the first example, the focus is on the role of social science in debates about *the effects of television on the young*, which began in the 1950s, when more and more households in the UK were installing televisions in their homes. This was a period when there was widespread public concern about what effects sitting passively in front of the television might have on children's emotional and social development. In the second example, the focus is on more contemporary debates about *the sexualisation of children*, which we have already touched on.

These two examples are closely related. The debates which started in the 1950s have continued and developed, and both concerns might be thought of as examples of how social science is involved in mediating between private troubles and public issues. The idea that children are exposed, in the privacy of the home, to external influences of adult and commercial culture which threaten to undermine patterns of family life or social order is a long-standing public issue. And it relates to some of the most personal and intimate of private troubles – anxieties about parenting and about child development.

In looking in more detail at these debates, the chapter aims to investigate how social scientists have studied the potential impact on children of television and popular culture. In particular, it focuses on the methods that social science uses to produce *descriptions* of the social world. It looks at the relationship between two broad approaches to generating social science descriptions: quantitative approaches (in this case, the use of experimental methods) and qualitative approaches (in this case, the use of interviews). These approaches can, depending on how they are used, generate very different *understandings* of issues concerning childhood and popular culture. The relationship between quantitative and qualitative approaches in social science is a theme that you will return to in subsequent chapters.

1.1 Structure of the chapter

Section 2 of this chapter starts by discussing how concerns about the effects of television on the young have been addressed by social scientists who use quantitative experiments to identify 'cause-and-effect' relationships between different aspects of social life. The section then introduces you to another means of generating descriptions, data and evidence about television's effects: the qualitative interview. Section 3 explores further the role of qualitative interviews in relation to a contemporary debate about intimate practices, namely concerns about the dangers of the premature sexualisation of children in popular culture. Section 4, the conclusion, reviews the two approaches to social science *description* that have been outlined in the chapter, and considers some questions which their use raises in terms of how we *understand* public issues and how social science helps to *enact* social worlds.

1.2 Aims of the chapter

This chapter aims to:

- examine the role of social science in responding to public issues generated by concerns about children's relationship to popular culture
- examine social science approaches to generating descriptions of the relationships between childhood and watching television or consuming commercialised popular culture
- introduce the quantitative experimental method as one of the main approaches for describing cause-and-effect relationships in social science
- introduce the qualitative interview as one of the main approaches for describing people's own opinions, perspectives and beliefs about social relationships
- review the principal differences, combinations and uses of each approach.

2 Investigating the effects of television on young people

In 1958 the social psychologist Hilde Himmelweit and her colleagues published what would come to be seen as a ground-breaking report, entitled *Television and the Child: an Empirical Study of the Effects of Television on the Young* (Himmelweit et al., 1958). In the report, they drew an explicit analogy between social science research and research in the natural sciences: 'Like research in the natural sciences, social research depends for its value on continuity and on systematic progress towards a deeper understanding of each problem' (Himmelweit et al., 1958, p. xv).

This section looks at how Himmelweit's research developed this sense of systematic understanding by making use of a particular approach to generate social science descriptions, namely an experimental method that aimed to identify cause-and-effect relationships between different variables. The report published in 1958 was not, however, a merely 'academic' enterprise. It would lead to the introduction of one of the defining features of British public culture in the second half of the twentieth century, and one which still shapes decision making and debate in twenty-first century media environments – the so-called '9 o'clock watershed'. This is a rule that governs programming decisions, based on the assumption that before 9pm there are likely to be children watching television, so broadcasters should schedule programmes with this fact in mind. After 9pm it is assumed that children's viewing is the responsibility of their guardians and so programmes can contain more adult content.

2.1 Defining the public issue

The introduction of the watershed, and the use of social science in the development of this example of public policy, grew out of debates in the early 1950s about the effects on children, family life and society of a 'new' technology that was fast expanding into the most intimate space of social life, the home: television. In the context of these public debates, in 1954 the Audience Research Department of the British Broadcasting Corporation (BBC) proposed to the Nuffield Foundation, a leading non-governmental funder of social science research in the UK, that it should sponsor an inquiry into the impact of television on children and young people. The foundation agreed, and it appointed the social psychologist Dr Himmelweit to direct the television inquiry.

Figure 1.1 Hilde Himmelweit

Investigations into the relationships between children and television had begun a few years earlier in the United States. The Boston-based psychologist Eleanor Maccoby, in a study entitled 'Television: its impact on school children', published in 1951, had conducted **open-ended interviews** with the mothers of 622 children, comparing children who watched television with children who didn't (Maccoby, 1951). Interestingly, in this study Maccoby found that television *increased* the amount of time that families spent with each other, by displacing time spent reading, playing both indoors and outdoors, and listening to radio.

In an **open-ended interview**, questions are posed and the interviewee can respond freely. Where questions are described as 'closed', the interviewee is given a set of alternative responses and they must choose one.

Table 1.1 reproduces an original table from Maccoby's paper. You will see that the verbal answers she received to the question 'What happens when the children are watching TV and supper is ready?' are coded into categories, ranging from 'No problem' to 'Not ascertained'.

Table 1.1 Maccoby's study of the impact of television viewing on children's behaviour: 'What happens when children are watching TV and supper is ready?'

No problem	Children not watching TV at supper time (including families who have changed their supper hour)	15%
No problem	Children come to table without pressure	26%
No problem	Mother doesn't care, children do as they wish	23%
	Parent gives a command (or comes in and turns off the set), children comply without open resistance	13%
Conflict	Children beg to be allowed to finish program; usually, parent wins, but often there is some compromise, or child is allowed to eat meal in front of set.	20%
Not Ascertained		3%
		100%

Source: Maccoby, 1951, p. 429

In order to generate statistical data of this sort, Maccoby could have used what is called a 'closed' response approach, in which respondents either fill in a structured questionnaire or survey with a prescribed range of permissible answers, or perhaps indicate the extent to which they agree with a set of pre-determined statements. This kind of approach is now used in all sorts of fields, not just social science – you have probably come across this sort of questionnaire in newspapers or magazines, or in marketing surveys carried out over the phone or on the street.

However, it is interesting that in this early study of children and television Maccoby used an approach to questioning that is now more associated with qualitative approaches, in that it was designed to open up or elicit a range of relatively unstructured responses, rather than seeking to identify patterns of choice from a pre-determined range of categories or statements. But while Maccoby would have received rich verbal responses to her open-ended questions in the interviews, you can see that she did not present the mothers' individual comments directly, as examples of how her respondents felt about or interpreted the issue, as one might in a qualitative study. Instead, she used a coded summary of their collective responses in order to identify and statistically aggregate some general patterns and broad categorical differences.

In effect, we might say that Maccoby applied a quantitative style of analysis to some qualitative data, in order to provide descriptive patterns and generalisations about the relationship between television and children's behaviour. One thing this early study helps us see, by using open-ended interviews to generate quantitative descriptions, is the role of the social scientist in actively shaping those descriptions.

Maccoby's research was among the first attempts to 'scientifically' describe the effects of television on young people. At the time that the Nuffield study was commissioned, however, there had still been no *large-scale systematic* quantitative research into the effects of television on children and young people. Himmelweit and her colleagues were the first to undertake such research. Their inquiry was conducted at a particular historical moment, when television was spreading rapidly, but it was still possible to compare the behaviour of children from homes with television with that of children who had no access to television. However, the inquiry also faced the problem of trying to know what sort of effects the researchers should be looking for:

> We faced the difficulty that the effects of television could manifest themselves in almost every aspect of children's lives. To find out what to measure and where to draw the line, we therefore turned to the many opinions that had been expressed about the effects of the medium. Not surprisingly, such opinions tended to be heavily influenced by personal attitudes, and were often contradictory.
>
> (Himmelweit et al., 1958, p. 2)

The stated aim of the inquiry, therefore, was intentionally very broad: it sought to find out '[h]ow television affects different types of children in different aspects of their lives, at different points in time, and according to different viewing circumstances' (Himmelweit et al., 1958, p. 2). How might a social scientist go about investigating the relationships between something quite specific (watching television) and something potentially quite disparate ('effects' which are diverse and differentiated and dispersed)? In this example, Himmelweit and her colleagues made use of formal experimental methods to establish, test and assess *causal* relationships between television and its effects on behaviour.

2.2 Using experiments to identify causal relationships

Himmelweit's research provides an example of social science which uses an experimental approach. Experiments are used to establish the relationship between one set of factors and another – in this case, between watching television on the one hand, and attitudes, emotions and behaviour on the other. Social scientists often use experiments when their chief objective is to identify relationships of cause and effect – that is, to identify whether an effect can be explained by a hypothesised cause: in this case, again, whether certain sorts of behaviour, such as children being unruly or disobedient at mealtimes, can be said to be caused by television.

As already noted, since there was little research on television at this time, the type of experimental approach that Himmelweit and her colleagues adopted did not follow the model of a laboratory experiment, in which most of the **variables** are under the control of the researcher. In some areas of social science, experiments are carried out in laboratory conditions; research by social psychologists into the effects of television does sometimes adopt this model. Himmelweit and her colleagues, however, chose to conduct their research in a real-world setting, in this case in schools in London, Portsmouth, Bristol, Sunderland and Norwich. This decision was taken in order to ensure that the researchers could learn more about the range of influences on young people and their viewing habits as they emerged from observing real-world activities and situations.

A **variable** is a factor or influence that can vary or change in the course of investigation.

As we have already seen, the aim of the Nuffield inquiry into television that Himmelweit directed was to investigate possible relationships of cause and effect between television and attitudes, emotions and behaviour. At its simplest, an experimental approach seeks to identify a causal relationship by examining the effect that one variable has on another, by manipulating the first variable and then measuring change in the second. The variable that is manipulated is called the **independent variable.** The variable that is measured is known as the **dependent variable**.

The **independent variable** is the variable factor or influence that will be manipulated in an experiment.

The **dependent variable** is the variable factor or influence that will be measured in an experiment.

In the case of the Himmelweit study, the amount of television watched was one of the independent variables. In other words, variations in the amount of television that children watched were identified as potential causal factors in shaping children's attitudes, emotions and other behaviours, with these 'effects' serving as the dependent variables.

In cases where there are likely to be a number of different effects, a researcher may seek to measure more than one dependent variable. For example, it might be supposed that watching television (the independent variable) affects concentration, sleep and aggression. A comprehensive study would therefore measure each of these three dependent variables.

So in the Himmelweit study, concerned as it was with the effects of television, television viewing was the independent variable: the potential cause of various effects. The key question examined by this inquiry was what effects television viewing had on a range of dependent variables.

As we have already seen, Himmelweit and her team were in a good position in the mid-1950s to carry out an experiment using television as the independent variable. As they observed in their report, 'in many ways we had an experimental set-up in a real-life situation [since] at that time less than half the population owned a television' (Himmelweit, et al., 1958, p. xiv). Because of this, they were able to conduct research with two clearly defined groups: an **experimental group** (those with television) and a **control group** (those without television). This is a common feature of experimental design. It involves two groups or conditions: one where the independent variable is present (the experimental condition), and one where it is absent (the control condition).

The **experimental group** is a group where the independent variable is present.

The **control group** is a group where the independent variable is absent.

We have also already mentioned that at the time of this study there was relatively little research on this topic, so the research team did not know exactly what likely effects television might have. Contemporary opinions suggested television viewing might affect all sorts of things, such as sleep, eyesight, levels of aggression and/or passivity, and concentration. It had also been suggested that there could be displacement effects, where watching television reduced a child's willingness to perform other tasks or activities, such as household chores or reading. Because of the scale of the study commissioned, Himmelweit and her team were able to measure all of these dependent variables. They used a series of questions to measure different potential *causes*, or independent variables (for example, hours of television watched and the content of programmes viewed), as well as possible *effects*, or dependent variables (such as concentration, levels of aggression, hours of sleep, tiredness at school).

The strength of the experimental method in social science is that once a significant relationship has been established this can be used to predict future relationships which involve the same variables. The causal relationships established by well-conducted experiments can then be used to inform efforts to manipulate either independent or dependent variables. As we shall see, this is exactly how the television study directed by Himmelweit was used. It is important to note that experiments are used to make claims about general patterns or processes that are applicable beyond the particular circumstances of the study itself. In the case of an experimental approach such as that directed by Himmelweit, experiments are used to provide descriptions of causal relationships which are assumed to be applicable and generalisable across wider populations, once all contextual variables have been taken into account. Underpinning the authority of experimental approaches in social science, then, is the idea that they can generate widely applicable, objective and accurate knowledge about the social world that is similar to the sorts of knowledge associated with the natural sciences.

There is one final point worth noting about the use of the experimental approach in the social sciences. Social scientists using this approach take great care to select accurate samples, and to control and measure variables. You will learn more about some of these methodological issues in the following chapter. Nevertheless, however carefully they seek to establish valid cause-and-effect relationships, it is virtually impossible to be 100 per cent certain that a particular effect has been caused by one variable impacting on another. There is always the possibility that the effect in question (for example, aggression) is caused not by the independent variable (in this case, television viewing), but by another variable – perhaps by a child's personality, parental influences, or other factors. As a result, social scientists rarely claim that their findings 'prove' this or that relationship. They are more likely to talk in terms of a **significant relationship** between two variables. This idea of significance suggests there is a likelihood that variables are meaningfully linked, but it leaves open the possibility of making further revisions and refinements as new knowledge is generated in the course of further research. In this respect, then, social science research which uses experimental methods is like the natural sciences after all, in the sense that its findings are considered to be *fallible* – that is, open to change or revision – rather than absolutely certain and final.

A **significant relationship** is a highly probable relationship between two variables.

Keeping in mind this idea that experiments can provide insight into significant relationships of cause and effect, it is now time to turn our attention to the ways in which the Himmelweit study of television and children was used to inform or enact policy decisions.

2.3 Making use of experimental social science

The Nuffield inquiry offered a number of significant findings that both challenged and confirmed some of the prevailing opinions and assumptions around the causes and effects of viewing television. For example, and contrary to expectations, it was found that time spent in front of the television did not make a difference to children's performance in tests. Equally, television viewing was not found to have an adverse effect on levels of tiredness and concentration. In these cases, social scientific description challenged opinions about television's negative social effects. The study did confirm assumptions that images of violence and aggression had measurable effects. However, it found that verbal acts of aggression, reprimand or ridicule, if they occurred in real-life scenarios (e.g. when shown on sports programmes or panel shows), sometimes caused more discomfort than scenes containing physical violence in the form of, for example, a gun fight in a Western. Himmelweit's study also established the beginnings of an understanding of what it termed 'addiction' to television, and the idea that children found comfort in the regular appearance of familiar characters. In confirming some opinions about the effects of television, and challenging others, the Himmelweit report provided a series of descriptions of the activities surrounding television viewing that laid the basis for future research.

The final report also made key recommendations to parents, producers and policy makers. It contained two central findings that led to action by the BBC. First, it found that children often continued to watch television up until 9pm, with a small number of them watching right through to the end of broadcasting, which at that time was 11pm. The second finding, which in many ways corroborated public concerns, was that children did demonstrate certain fears and anxieties based on what they had seen on television.

The report's large-scale systematic description of the times of day during which children were watching television provided evidence that led the BBC to enact its recommendations. The report suggested that 6pm to 9pm should be considered 'family viewing' time, and recommended that broadcasters should take some responsibility for ensuring that programmes viewed during those hours were suitable for children. The Independent Television Authority, which had been established in the 1950s to regulate all broadcasting in the UK (both public service and commercial services), commissioned a report in 1959, published by May O'Conor in 1960, which took forward Himmelweit's recommendations. It agreed that broadcasters must take into account the younger audience watching television before 9pm. After that time, responsibility for viewing laid with parents.

It was, then, from these social science research projects that the policy of the 9 o'clock watershed became established on British television, and remains in place today. Based on the principle that all programmes broadcast before then should be suitable for a general audience, which includes children, the watershed means that broadcasters need to consider the balance of programming and the representation of sex and violence in both factual and non-factual programming before 9pm. The watershed has become established as a feature of television culture in the UK (see Figure 1.2). For our purposes here, the most significant point to bear in mind is that this policy arose out of the descriptions generated by a particular sort of social science – one which described what, when and how children viewed television programmes, and which also described the relationships between television viewing and other activities and behaviours. These *descriptions* informed the development of particular *understandings* of the effects of television, and these in turn informed the *enactment* of quite specific policy recommendations in terms of public and commercial television in the UK.

Figure 1.2 The 9 o'clock watershed is now a taken-for-granted part of British culture

To summarise, the importance of the Himmelweit study was to establish the range and complexity of relationships which social scientists interested in the effects of television could investigate, and to establish the usefulness of quantitative experiments in doing so. Research into television and other media has, since the pioneering work of the 1950s, gone in different directions, reflecting different methodologies and informing different arguments about how social science descriptions and understandings can and should inform policy and decision making.

2.4 Alternative approaches: controlled experiments and qualitative methods

While the Maccoby and Himmelweit studies that you have looked at were examples of experiments conducted in the 'real world' – that is, respondents were studied outside of formal laboratory conditions – a range of more 'controlled' experimental studies of television's effects on children were developed in the 1960s. These included experiments conducted in the 1960s by Albert Bandura at Stanford University, California, which are known generally as the 'BoBo doll' experiments. Unlike Himmelweit, Bandura decided to conduct his studies in controlled laboratory conditions. In his series of experiments, children aged between 3 and 6 years old viewed an adult acting out a series of aggressive actions on a BoBo doll. (The Bobo doll is an inflatable toy about five feet tall, designed to spring back upright when knocked over.) Each child was then taken into a second room and given an opportunity to play with some toys, including a BoBo doll.

Bandura's experiments had four variations. In the first, the adult was in the same room as the children, acting aggressively towards the BoBo doll. In the second, the adult was seen on television acting aggressively towards the doll. In the third, children watched on television an adult dressed as a cartoon cat who, though acting in a more cat-like manner, performed the same acts of aggression on the much-beleaguered BoBo doll. Finally, in the fourth variation, children directly watched an adult playing with the BoBo doll, but no aggressive words or acts were aimed at it. After each scenario was enacted, the children were left in another room with a similar doll, and their behaviour towards it was observed.

In this experiment, then, the dependent variable was the aggressive behaviour displayed by children, and the independent variables were the different scenarios of aggressive behaviour the children were exposed to before playing with the toys themselves.

Bandura found that in all three of the experimental conditions where the children had watched aggressive behaviour, they displayed an increase in aggressive behaviour when they played with the toys in the second room (Bandura et al., 1963). These findings helped to establish a widely held understanding that there was a *direct* relationship between aggression on television and aggression in children. In short, this type of experimental design seemed to support the idea that watching aggression on television directly caused children to be aggressive.

Figure 1.3 Images from the BoBo doll experiments. The middle and bottom rows contain images of child participants replicating the behaviour of the adult shown in the top row.

It is worth emphasising again that the descriptions generated by Bandura in these studies depended on the use of a controlled experimental design, unlike the earlier studies of the 1950s. In principle, this allowed a much tighter relationship between cause and effect to be established, without the various 'interferences' that might creep into a more open-ended approach. Bandura's use of the experimental method appeared to demonstrate that television viewing had direct, unmediated effects on children's behaviour.

Other strands of social science research into television viewing and children's behaviour have adopted *non*-experimental methods. These have generated very different sorts of descriptions of the relationship between media and behaviour, and have informed different understandings of the dynamics of this relationship.

Two of the most prominent UK-based researchers in this area have been the media educationalist David Buckingham and the social psychologist Sonia Livingstone. In both Buckingham's and Livingstone's research, the idea that television viewing has direct, unmediated and predictable effects on children is called into question. Their research tends to emphasise that the same television programme will be viewed by different children in different ways. This is partly because one child's private preoccupations will lead it to interpret a programme in one way, while another child's private preoccupations will lead it to interpret the same programme differently. But just as importantly from a social science perspective, the differing *social contexts* in which children view television programmes will shape how those children interpret them (Buckingham, 1996; Livingstone, 1998). Influences such as class, gender, ethnicity, age, family structure and nationality all affect how media are made sense of by children, as well as by adults. These issues of social context and structure are a key feature of social science inquiry, and you will learn more about them in later chapters.

In contrast to Bandura's 'controlled' experiments, where children were taken out of their social context and assessed in laboratory conditions, the research strategies developed by Buckingham and Livingstone adopted an approach specifically designed to investigate and assess the socially situated and context-specific relationships between television and its young audiences. Buckingham encouraged people to talk about what they feel and think about a topic – in this case, how they think and feel about television programmes and other media.

The descriptions generated by research of this sort challenge the linear model of viewing that is implicitly shared by the different experimental approaches of Himmelweit and Bandura. In the experimental research, a model of 'sender–message–receiver' is at work (see Figure 1.4).

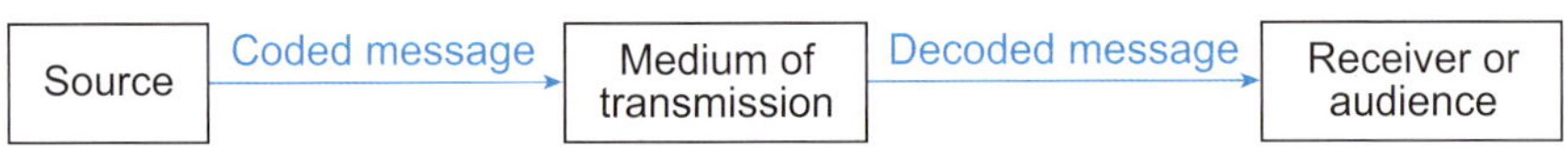

Figure 1.4 A sender–message–receiver model

This model assumes that a single, uniform meaning is transferred directly from the programme to the child sitting passively in front of the television screen (Livingstone, 1998, p. 71). The research developed by Buckingham and Livingstone does not just generate different descriptions – it also challenges the understandings of the relationships between television and its viewers as established in experimental approaches. The meanings that television programmes convey are thought of as much more diverse than the 'sender–message–receiver' model suggests. Just as important, this research emphasises the viewers, including children, as 'active' interpreters of meanings rather than 'passive' receivers of messages. Interestingly, Livingstone (1998) combines both qualitative and quantitative methods in developing the concept of the *resourceful viewer*. As she explains, audiences 'bring with them expectations, knowledge, interests and understandings' to the act of interpretation (Livingstone, 1998, p. 102). For Buckingham and for Livingstone, the messages conveyed by television permit more than one interpretation; and the receivers of those messages – the audience, even the childhood audience – are reasonably resourceful in interpreting the meanings offered to them.

Rather than observing 'behaviours', this research starts by allowing participants to present the meanings they take from various media – sometimes by asking them about this in interviews or focus groups; sometimes by observing them 'ethnographically' in everyday situations; sometimes by asking them to select attributes from pre-determined lists. You will recall that an example of this sort of research was used at the start of this chapter, in the Introduction – which began with a quote from a participant in a focus group, published in a report co-authored by Buckingham. That quote is presented as an opinion that is valid and interesting in its own right, but it also provides an example of a lay understanding of an 'active' interpreter.

This section has begun to show how different methods can be used for different purposes in social science. Qualitative approaches tend to seek to get 'inside' social worlds, by eliciting accounts of what things mean to people, or how they make sense of situations and relationships. Quantitative approaches are more concerned with identifying patterns, trends and relationships from the 'outside', as it were, across wider populations, and so are much less concerned with specific or individual meanings and experiences. These two approaches are not necessarily incompatible, as we shall see. However, it is important to recognise that they tend to produce different descriptions of social phenomena, and can support different understandings of social processes.

These differences in understanding become clear when you consider that the experimental approach discussed in Section 2.2 tends to describe television and its effects in terms of stimuli, messages and behaviour. It lends itself to a view of children as being shaped by television in relative isolation. It can generate descriptions of shared patterns of response, but is less good at telling us what children themselves think and feel about the television they watch. By contrast, qualitative approaches seek to restore a sense of the broader context in which children engage with television, whether this is in terms of who they watch and talk about television with, or in terms of their family background, ethnicity or gender (for example). And these approaches are much more concerned with giving proper weight to the thoughts and feelings of children as viewers themselves.

The differences between quantitative and qualitative approaches are, then, often related to uses to which social science is being put. Embedded within the descriptions that social scientists produce are different understandings of what the world is like, and how it is made and remade. For instance, much of the experimental work on television – a quantitative approach – implies that children's worlds are determined by external influences that affect them. Much of the more qualitative work, in contrast, implies that children actively contribute to making their own worlds. As already noted, this does not mean the two approaches are necessarily incompatible. Livingstone's work, which has been important in establishing the idea of active audiences and engaged viewers, uses both approaches. It is not that one approach is 'better' than the other. It does mean, though, that you should keep in mind that different approaches can be used to generate different outcomes, in terms of the *descriptions* they present, the *understandings* they support and the practical *enactments* they recommend.

3 Debating the sexualisation of children

The previous section concluded by introducing the role of qualitative descriptions in generating and reorienting understandings of television and its effects on children, in contrast to the types of understanding developed on the basis of experimentally based, quantitative descriptions. In this section, you will explore in more detail what is perhaps the most common qualitative method by which social scientists seek to describe how people give meaning to their actions: the in-depth interview. You will learn about the use of interviews to generate qualitative interpretations in the context of a different, but related, controversy associated with our understandings of childhood 'innocence' and intimacy: contemporary debates about the sexualisation of childhood.

3.1 Sexualisation as a public issue

Although public concern about children and sex has a long history, more recent debates centring on children's claimed 'sexualisation' go back to the 1980s and 1990s. For example, writing in *The Independent* newspaper in 1992, Dr Fay Hutchinson of the London Brook Advisory Centre identified the problem of the 'explicit sexualisation of children' in which 'we allow them adult clothing and adult things' (quoted in Duschinsky and Barker, forthcoming 2012). Anxiety about sexualisation really started to take off in the first decade of the twenty-first century, however. For instance, in a report published in 2003 by the policy think-tank the Australia Institute, the academic social scientist Michael Flood and the institute's chief executive, Clive Hamilton, synthesised a wealth of evidence in support of their claim that childhood in western societies is becoming increasingly sexualised. For the authors, that term encompasses a wide range of phenomena, including the earlier onset of puberty, a fall in the age when young people first have sexual intercourse, the increased exposure of children and young people to sexually explicit media content, and the mainstreaming of images shaped by a pornographic aesthetic – a process sometimes referred to as 'pornification' (Flood and Hamilton, 2003). Three years later the Australia Institute published a second report, by social scientists Emma Rush and Andrea La Nauze (2006), which went so far as to endorse the notion of 'corporate paedophilia' as a way of suggesting that the commercially driven sexualisation of children amounted to a form of child abuse.

Around the same time, the influential American Psychological Association (APA) organised a task force to report on the sexualisation of girls. Its report defines sexualisation in the following terms:

> There are several components to sexualization, and these set it apart from healthy sexuality. Sexualization occurs when (1) a person's value comes only from his or her sexual appeal or behaviour, to the exclusion of other characteristics; (2) a person is held to a standard that equates physical attractiveness (narrowly defined) with being sexy; (3) a person is sexually objectified – that is, made into a thing for others' sexual use, rather than seen as a person with the capacity for independent action and decision making; and/or (4) sexuality is inappropriately imposed upon a person.
>
> (American Psychological Association, 2007, p. 1)

More recently, in the UK, a series of reports on sexualisation commissioned by various government departments culminated in 2011 in the Bailey Review into the commercialisation and sexualisation of childhood. The report produced by this inquiry opened by arguing that the pressure on children to grow up 'takes two different but related forms: the pressure to take part in a sexualised life before they are ready to do so; and the commercial pressure to consume the vast range of goods and services that are available to children and young people of all ages' (Bailey, 2011, p. 6).

There are two important things to note about these examples of public concern over sexualisation, and in particular the concern about its effect on girls and young women. First, the definitions of sexualisation are actually quite varied. For instance, the APA's definition makes no reference to commercial pressures or childhood; Flood and Hamilton's definition includes physiological factors (the earlier onset of puberty); Rush and La Nauze's definition identifies sexualisation as a form of child abuse. The differences between those definitions suggest that the single term 'sexualisation' is being used to refer to a range of different phenomena, and that different descriptions and understandings are at play in these debates.

Second, you may also have noticed that all of these authors seem to assume that the forces which they identify as having an impact on children's and young people's lives will shape those lives in *predictable* ways. There is an understanding of commercial popular culture at work here that is similar to the one you saw in the previous section's discussion of experimental research on television's effects: the understanding that social science can help predict the *causal* relationships between (for example) sexual imagery in advertising, and the behaviours and beliefs of children.

The previous section ended by introducing you to approaches that adopt more qualitative ways of perceiving such issues, by seeking to describe the meanings that children and young people and their parents ascribe to the media messages that critics of sexualisation focus on. One of the main methods adopted for that purpose is the qualitative interview. It is a method that allows researchers to generate descriptions based on what people think about issues of sexualisation and how they go about making sense of the media environments they live in. In this section, you will learn more about how this approach is used to inform public debates about the sexualisation of children.

3.2 Sluts and whores: describing young people's social worlds

Qualitative methods are a means by which social scientists try to enter into the social worlds inhabited by the people they study. Qualitative interviews are relatively open-ended, and they seek to allow interviewees to talk about their lived realities, their decision-making processes, and the meanings, values and beliefs that shape their lives.

Interviews can be carried out in different ways. They can be conducted over the phone, over the internet, face-to-face, in focus groups, or as part of a longer-term process in which the researcher becomes immersed in a particular social world, often for many months at a time (an approach called ethnography). Sometimes the researcher will use a fully open-ended or 'unstructured' interview, where the interviewer seeks to create as much space as possible for interviewees to speak at length about a given topic or their biographical experiences. Occasionally the interviewer will pose questions, to encourage the interviewee to go deeper into specific areas, but he or she will not plan too many questions in advance. Instead, the interviewer will let the interviewee talk freely and in his or her own terms, following up on leads suggested by what the interviewee says. Sometimes they will use a less open-ended or 'semi-structured' interview approach, in which a schedule of questions and prompts is used to ask more or less the same sorts of things to different participants. These sorts of interview methods are intended to elicit lots of talking by participants or, in the case of group interviews or focus groups, between participants, without seeking to standardise answers. By contrast, questionnaires or survey interview research, which you will learn more about in Chapter 2, are intended to elicit answers to a prescribed range of questions that can be aggregated into general patterns. Qualitative interviewing is less concerned with patterns, and more interested in gaining insight into the processes and practices through which people make sense of their social worlds.

To illustrate how qualitative interviewing is used in social science, let's explore an extract from a research project conducted by a sociologist of education, Jessica Ringrose (Ringrose and Barajas, 2011). This study investigated the ways in which teenagers, aged between 14 and 16, deployed sexuality in their use of online social networking sites such as Bebo and Facebook. Part of the purpose of the study was to understand how young people make sense of the sexual meanings or messages conveyed to them by the media and by such things as branded goods and merchandise. In the course of her study, Ringrose carried out group and individual interviews with twenty-five girls and boys in schools.

Reading 1.3 is an extract from this study. It is a transcript of a qualitative interview with a 14-year-old girl called Denise, who explains why she and her friends describe each other as 'sluts' and 'whores' on a social networking site.

As you read the transcript, focus on the reasons Denise gives as to why she and her friends use the words 'slut' and 'whore'.

Reading 1.3

Interview with Denise

Denise:	We have this little thing, like she's my slut, I'm her whore. Because loads of people used to call us it, so we just thought whatever, we'll just be them then. And like one day we just found a [digital] background like it, and we were like, oh, that's quite nice. And people are like, why have you got slut … and it's like, I don't mean it like that. But 'cos I didn't know, like if you read it if you'd be thinking, 'Oh my god!'
JR [Jessica Ringrose]:	So you mean that people used to say that you were a slut, what do you mean by that?
Denise:	Well, 'cos our group, like some people, like older girls that saw us, like with someone would be like, oh you slag or you slut because … just because they didn't know us, but just because they wanted to insult us … Cos we used to really care about it, and then we just got a bit like oh I don't care anymore … we just got used to it, and then … I don't really know what happened but it was just a random thing of where we were just like … 'she's my whore and I'm her slut. Whatever. Get over it!'. And then she'd say the same.
JR:	Okay. And how do you think other girls perceive that in your group? What do they think?
Denise:	I don't know. I haven't had anybody say anything, like girls being bitchy about it to me.
JR:	I remember you said, you know, other, older guys contact you and stuff, how do you think that might affect how people see you, like wider than your school community?
Denise:	I suppose that probably entices them a bit. But … but like if they do say anything to me I just literally tell them to fuck off!
JR:	Yeah?

Denise:	Because … I'll look at their Bebo and if they're like over 17 I'm just like, well you look like a bit of a perv to me, can you leave me alone, or something.

(Source: Ringrose and Barajas, 2011, pp. 128–9)

The first thing to say about Reading 1.3 is that it illustrates the way in which qualitative interviewers encourage their interviewees to talk freely and at length about some aspects of the social world they inhabit. Ringrose's questions attempt to elicit from Denise her own sense of what her use of social network sites is like from the inside. Ringrose is not following a set of pre-written questions. Rather, she is picking up on things Denise herself has raised. Sometimes she asks for clarification ('What do you mean by that?'); sometimes she asks Denise to expand on a theme ('How do you think that might affect how people see you?'); and sometimes she simply encourages Denise to carry on talking ('Yeah?').

As already suggested, what the interview seems to have been effective at is providing an insight into the reasons why Denise and her friends use the terms 'slut' and 'whore' in their social network profiles. Denise talks vividly about this and conveys a rich sense of the specific meanings she and her friends attach to them. In particular, what emerges is a strong sense that these terms mean something specific to these girls in their social context. That is what qualitative interviewing seeks to get at. Denise appears to be aware that an outsider, reading her description of herself as a 'slut' or 'whore', might see this as encouragement to pursue her sexually. However, her use of the terms does not seem to be intended to encourage attention of that kind, particularly from 'older guys' ('I just literally tell them to fuck off!'). Rather, in applying the terms to themselves, Denise and her friends' main intention seems to be to blunt the words' effectiveness as insults ('we used to really care about it, and then we just got a bit like oh I don't care anymore … "she's my whore and I'm her slut. Whatever. Get over it!"').

As well as providing an insight into this group's own self-understanding, however, the interview also complicates understandings of sexualisation, by allowing the meanings that Denise and her friends attach to the terms 'slut' and 'whore' to be made clear. If you had read Denise's social network profile without having read her interview transcript you might have imagined that a climate of sexualisation – one in which teenage girls can easily download 'slut/whore' digital backgrounds, for example – had led her to adopt an online persona that was inappropriately sexual for her age and that potentially placed her at risk. Even after reading the transcript, you might still disapprove of this kind of usage. But you might also notice that, in fact, Denise seems to be aware of that possibility herself ('like if you read it you'd be thinking, "Oh my god!"').

Figure 1.5 Digital media raise new concerns about childhood innocence

Allowed to speak for herself in the interview, it becomes clear that something more nuanced is going on. Denise appears less a straightforward victim of sexualisation and more what we might term a 'resourceful interpreter' of her social environment, actively negotiating the difficulties with which that environment confronts her and appropriating that to her own ends. It is made clear in the interview that 'slut' and 'whore' appear to be common terms of insult in the girls' culture, and it is not difficult to imagine they would have preferred not to have been subject to such abuse. But what the example shows us is that these girls are not simply passive recipients of various effects, subjects of a culture of sexualisation; rather, they are negotiating this culture as best they can, sometimes quite creatively and knowingly. What

Ringrose's research illustrates is the use of the qualitative interview to make visible ordinary people's processes of situated interpretation and negotiation in order to challenge images of them as passive victims or simple 'receivers' of media and popular culture.

3.3 Interpreting qualitative interview evidence

Section 3.2 suggested that qualitative interviews are good at capturing nuances of social context, meaning and process – nuances that are not easily revealed by standardised survey or questionnaire techniques which seek to identify aggregate patterns, relationships and trends. However, you should not think that qualitative research presumes that the nuances are easy to identify. One of the things qualitative social science emphasises is the role of interpretation in analysis – it is not assumed that the significance of an interview is transparent, or just lying around in the open waiting for the qualitative interviewer to spot. An important point is that the interpretation of qualitative descriptions will depend on the use to which the research is likely to be put – for example, the argument that the researcher is hoping to engage with, or perhaps the policy debate they hope to inform.

By their very nature, qualitative interviews often generate lots of loose and unstructured talk. Researchers have to decide which parts of interviews to make use of, depending on what questions they are seeking to answer. To illustrate this process of analysis, let's look again at Reading 1.2, used in the introduction to this chapter. This is an extract from the report *Sexualised Goods Aimed at Children*, written for the Scottish Parliament Equal Opportunities Committee by David Buckingham and his colleagues (Buckingham et al., 2010, p. 50). In the extract, you will recall that one of the mothers who participated in the research talks about the use of the Playboy bunny logo on children's merchandise. Here is the passage again:

> 'You don't want to force them to think about things that they're innocently thinking [is] a nice pink bunny. … Just allow them to be children for that bit longer. You don't always want to be the one that's coming in spoiling it and making them think of the bigger issues. There are times they … don't need to worry about who they're offending on their T-shirt. They don't need to maybe

> think about the moral issues of absolutely everything that they do, like what clothes to put on in the morning' (Mother, FG4).
>
> (Buckingham et al., 2010, p. 50)

This quote is taken from a longer stream of talk generated in the original focus group interview. Let's look at that quotation as it appeared in the context of the original interview transcript. In this transcript, reproduced here as Reading 1.4, the mother quoted above is identified as A. Other mothers participating in the interview are identified as L, S and V; the interviewer is identified as R. In focus group interviews people are interviewed together as a group, in order to gain insight into how they make sense of phenomena through the collective give-and-take of shared and disputed meanings. So, as you study Reading 1.4, you might want to look for the parts of the conversation where the participants (both the interviewees and the interviewer) seem to develop their sense of the meaning of the Playboy logo in dialogue with each other, by agreeing and picking up on previous remarks.

Reading 1.4

Transcript of interview, FG4, Lochend

R: Should the schools do anything? What's the role of schools and teachers in this?

A: I think that they have these personal social development things, PSATA, and maybe they do something like that but I think it would be worth while taking products in and asking the children this sort of thing and having a discussion during that time that they've got just to maybe highlight, to make them stop and think about the messages that they're getting from products that they might want to buy.

V: The Playboy, although a lot of them just see it as a nice bunny, some of them maybe don't realise what it's actually …

A: Hugh Hefner …

R: We've not come across a child yet who couldn't give us a full explanation of what this was about. It has a double value.

L: My daughters must know, I've just never asked them.

A: I don't know whether my daughter that liked that really really knew, sometimes you don't want to burst their bubble, you don't want to force them to think about things that they're innocently thinking that something's a nice pink bunny.

R: What could make it difficult is sort of introducing kids to products and debating maybe, if you wanted to preserve ...Why do you not want to ... ?

A: Just allow them to be children for that bit longer. You don't always want to be the one that's coming in spoiling it and making them think of the bigger issues. There are times they just don't need to think about. They don't need to worry about who they're offending on their T-shirt. They don't need to maybe think about the moral issues of absolutely everything that they do, like what clothes to put on in the morning is really what I mean, not that it's right to kill somebody.

R: No but at some point there's consequences the kids have told us and that's kind of ... there's a line where actually you need to realise the consequences of wearing these things. For them it was if you're in school it's one thing, if you're going shopping with your mates that's one thing but going out to the nightclub or going out to a party that's when you kind of have to.

A: But I think it's important for them to learn some of these lessons themselves. Not to have necessarily the government say you can't do this you can't do that. Then of course you've got that added attraction of something that you suddenly can't do is taboo so we want it.

S: I think everything you've said is valid and I agree with you but unfortunately not all parents are responsible.

A: I know. Sometimes I'm not that responsible myself.

(Source: unpublished material originally gathered for Buckingham et al., 2010. Reproduced by kind permission of the researchers)

As you have already seen, a quote from this interview was used in the report to the Scottish Parliament Equal Opportunities Committee (Buckingham et al., 2010). But you can now see that this quote was actually part of a wider discussion about how schools and parents should respond to potentially sexualised products and merchandise targeted at children and young people. You might want to stop for a moment and think about whether the quote on its own, as it first appeared as Reading 1.2 in the introduction to this chapter, seems to mean something different from when you read the same remarks in Reading 1.4 in the context of the original focus group.

On its own, the comment made by the mother in Reading 1.2 about the Playboy bunny could be read as an indication that she thinks it is better to let children enjoy what, for the children themselves, is nothing more than a 'pink bunny' than it is to 'burst their bubble'. Seen in the fuller context of the interview in Reading 1.4, a more nuanced picture of the quotation appears. For instance, A starts off by saying that she thinks schools should explore with children 'the messages that they're getting from products that they might want to buy', something that *would* imply bursting their bubbles. Similarly, one of the other mothers (identified as S) appears to indicate that she believes schools and/or the government have a role to play in relation to children's consumption practices ('unfortunately not all parents are responsible'). As that suggests, the mothers' views of the messages that children get from the products they want to buy are quite complicated – sometimes even contradictory.

In making use of this quote in their report, Buckingham et al. (2010, p. 50) took the view that the opinion expressed by A in Reading 1.4 – that children do not always understand the meanings of sexualised products – is not 'representative', necessarily, but it is one of the perspectives available to people when they try to make sense of sexualisation debates. That is a quite specific use of social science evidence, distinct from the type of use one would expect in quantitative research. In the qualitative approach, the aim is to make visible processes and practices through which people make sense of their worlds, and, in that regard, complexity, contradiction and nuance are not necessarily a problem. Qualitative research does make certain sorts of generalisations. In this case, there is a claim about the variety of available perspectives that people might adopt in relation to the topic of sexualisation, and there is the stronger claim about people being 'resourceful interpreters' as well. But these are not generalisations about predictability, effects or percentages. Qualitative research has different uses, compared with quantitative research. As you saw in the last section on Denise's use of Bebo (Reading 1.3), the interpretations that social scientists make of qualitative interview material frequently capture aspects of social life that would otherwise be missed or misunderstood. While experimental approaches of the sort discussed in Section 2 have the virtue of producing clear results by measuring the relationships between independent and dependent variables, qualitative interviews are meant to produce descriptions full of nuance, complexity and contradiction. This focus on depth and insight can be seen as one of the strengths of qualitative research.

4 Conclusion: researching childhood innocence and desire

In this chapter you have been introduced to two types of social science description generated by the quantitative experiment and the qualitative interview. It has been shown that both can be applied to research problems in which relatively intimate decision making has become a public issue. Both forms of description have centred on addressing the same issue: whether and how children are at risk from the media environments they inhabit.

The chapter has shown how different social science approaches generate distinctive descriptions of the relationships between television and behaviour (Section 2), and between commercial popular culture and identity (Section 3). Early research on television, using experimental approaches, generated descriptions that made visible a range of possible effects that television might have; subsequent research in this same vein tended to generate descriptions that supported particular understandings of these effects in terms of predictable cause-and-effect relationships.

Qualitative approaches make possible the description of other aspects of these sorts of relationships – they are particularly good at showing how people negotiate their own way around complex media environments. But these approaches do not only add a different layer of description. They also support a different sort of *understanding* of the social world, an understanding that focuses on human meanings and social context more than on effects and behaviour (concepts which we will return to in later chapters).

These differences between quantitative and qualitative approaches in social science are a crucial aspect of how social science is used in a variety of contexts. And this inevitably means that social science is used in different ways to inform and shape debates and controversies about public issues. In Section 3, we saw how contemporary debates about sexualisation have been informed by a range of social scientific interventions, offering an array of competing descriptions of the various phenomena that are identified with processes of sexualisation. Government-commissioned and other reviews, such as those identified in Section 3.1, have drawn on social science and other evidence to paint a picture of a hyper-sexualised culture, in which children and young people, they would argue, are not being allowed to develop 'naturally'. But in the same debates, social science using qualitative approaches has been used to argue that children and young people are considerably more active and resourceful in interpreting sexualised messages than is frequently assumed.

These two types of approach, supporting distinct descriptions and understandings, might lend themselves to different sorts of action. Clear-cut cause-and-effect accounts seem, on the face of it at least, to be quite good at identifying what should be done to address a specific issue. But things are rarely easy. Even in the case of the example discussed in Section 2 – the 9 o'clock watershed on British television – this policy was originally informed by detailed, quantified experimental research, which identified certain descriptive features about when people watched television, but raised as many questions as it provided answers about the effects of these patterns. The growth of qualitative research has tended to support differing styles of policy recommendations, which seek to support interventions by schools, parents and young people's own actions rather than to ban or restrict media.

Overall, this chapter has shown that social science uses different methods to generate distinct sorts of descriptions of social phenomena. These descriptions will, in turn, be closely related to different understandings of the dynamics of those phenomena. And the chapter has touched on the ways in which social science also informs and shapes – helps to enact – social phenomena as well. Another key focus of the chapter has been on quantitative and qualitative approaches. You will learn more about both of these approaches, and their uses in social science, in later chapters.

4.1 Chapter summary

In this chapter you have learned:

- how social scientific descriptions have contributed to public debates about children and media, using the examples of television viewing and commercially driven sexualisation of branded goods and merchandise
- how experiments are useful for describing and understanding the social world, as well as some of their difficulties and limitations
- how qualitative interviews are useful for describing and understanding the social world, as well as some of their difficulties and limitations

- that the relationship between quantitative and qualitative approaches is central to the uses of social science
- how social scientific descriptions and understandings can enact change, through informing policy decisions (Section 2) or shaping public debates (Section 3).

References

American Psychological Association (2007) *Report on the APA Task Force on the Sexualization of Girls*, Washington, DC, APA.

Bailey, R. (2011) *Letting Children be Children: Report of an Independent Review of the Commercialisation and Sexualisation of Childhood*, Cmnd 8078, London, HMSO.

Bandura, A., Ross, D. and Ross, S. (1963) 'Imitation of Film-mediated aggressive models', *Journal of Abnormal and Social Psychology*, vol. 66, no. 1, pp. 3–11.

Beckford, M. (2009) 'Playboy bunny T-shirts and pop music videos to blame for sexualisation of children, expert warns', *Daily Telegraph*, 12 August.

Buckingham, D. (1996) *Moving Images: Understanding Children's Emotional Responses to Television*, Manchester, Manchester University Press.

Buckingham, D., Willett, R., Bragg, S. and Russell, R. (2010) *Sexualised Goods Aimed at Children: A Report to the Scottish Parliament Equal Opportunities Committee*, Edinburgh, Scottish Parliament Equal Opportunities Committee.

Duschinsky, R. and Barker, M. (forthcoming 2012) 'Doing the Mobius Strip: the politics of the Bailey Review', *Sexualities*.

Flood, M. and Hamilton, C. (2003) 'Youth and pornography in Australia: evidence on the extent of exposure and likely effects', Discussion Paper no. 52, Canberra, Australia Institute.

Himmelweit, H.T., Oppenheim, A.N. and Vince, P. (1958) *Television and the Child: An Empirical Study of the Effect of Television on the Young*, London, Oxford University Press.

Livingstone, S. (1998) *Making Sense of Television: The Psychology of Audience Interpretation*, London, Routledge.

Maccoby, E.E. (1951) 'Television: its impact on school children', *Public Opinion Quarterly*, vol. 15, no. 3, pp. 421–44.

O'Conor, M. (1960) *Children and Television Programmes*, O'Conor Committee Report, London, BBC/ITA.

Ringrose, J. and Barajas, K.E. (2011) 'Gendered risks and opportunities? Exploring teen girls' digitized sexual identities in postfeminist media contexts', special issue: 'Postfeminism and the mediation of sex', *International Journal of Media and Cultural Politics*, vol. 7, no. 2, pp. 121–38.

Rush, E. and La Nauze, A. (2006) 'Corporate paedophilia: sexualisation of children in Australia', Discussion Paper no. 90, Canberra, Australia Institute.

Chapter 2
Quantifying intimate lives

Peter Redman

1 Introduction 57
1.1 Structure of the chapter 60
1.2 Aims of the chapter 61
2 Using surveys to describe intimacy 62
3 Doing survey research 65
3.1 Generating data 69
3.2 Sampling 72
4 The Kinsey survey 75
4.1 Kinsey's sampling technique 75
4.2 The Kinsey questionnaire 77
4.3 Assessing Kinsey's findings 79
5 The National Survey of Sexual Attitudes and Lifestyles 81
5.1 The Natsal I sample 82
5.2 Natsal I and the 'missing millions' 84
5.3 Assessing Natsal I 86
6 Doing surveys, making social worlds 89
7 Conclusion: surveys as descriptions of the social world 93
7.1 Chapter summary 95
References 96

1 Introduction

The previous chapter introduced two methods of social science description: the quantitative experiment and the qualitative interview. You saw that both can be used to describe intimate activities, to help make intimacy into a public issue. You also saw that researching intimacy is often a controversial enterprise. This chapter looks at ways in which social scientists have sought to describe some of the most intimate aspects of people's lives – their sexual acts and identities. It will do so by exploring the use of survey methods in social science, and it will show how the history of sex surveys can tell us some important things about the challenges of social science description in general.

The chapter looks at two episodes in the history of social scientific surveys of sexual intimacy. The first is an example from the United States in the late 1940s and early 1950s. This period saw the publication of two of the most famous and influential social science books ever written: Alfred Kinsey, Wardell Pomeroy and Clyde Martin's *Sexual Behavior in the Human Male* (1948) and *Sexual Behavior in the Human Female* (1953). Each over 800 pages long and densely populated with graphs and numerical tables, the books were unlikely best-sellers. Nevertheless, between them they sold some 500,000 copies and propelled Kinsey on to the front cover of *Time* magazine (Gathorne-Hardy, 2005).

Figure 2.1 Alfred Kinsey

The books created a fire storm of public controversy. Drawing on a survey that would eventually include over 18,000 men and women, they claimed to provide an authoritative description of the sex lives of the American population. Many Americans were shocked by what they found in the books, however. Among other things, Kinsey and his colleagues estimated that 37 per cent of American men had engaged in some form of homosexual activity to orgasm at least once during adolescence or adulthood and that, by the age of 45, 13 per cent of women had reached orgasm as a result of sexual contact with another woman. They also suggested that 69 per cent of men had had 'some experience with prostitutes'; that half of women had had sex before marriage; that some 50 per cent of married men and 26 per cent of married women had committed adultery; and that approximately 8 per cent of men had had 'sexual experience with animals', a figure that they said rose steeply in rural populations (Kinsey et al., 1948, pp. 585, 597, 623, 670–2; Kinsey et al., 1953, pp. 186, 416, 450–1).

For at least some Americans, such findings were too much to countenance. The *Boston Daily Record*, for instance, assured Kinsey that 'Adultery and kindred offenses involving sex are neither tolerated nor secretly practiced by most people in New England' (quoted in Igo, 2008, p. 252). Similarly, an irate correspondent from California complained that the '5,940 sex delinquents' whose responses had been collated in *Sexual Behavior in the Human Female* could not be considered **representative** of 'the hundreds of thousands of women and mothers ... who have never engaged in any pre-marital sex relationships' (quoted in Igo, 2008, p. 255).

A sample is said to be **representative** when there is a high degree of correspondence between the characteristics present in the sample and those present in the wider population from which the sample is drawn

The second example of a social science sex survey that the chapter looks at comes from the UK. Nearly forty years after the publication of *Sexual Behavior in the Human Female*, another large-scale survey, the first National Survey of Sexual Attitudes and Lifestyles (Natsal I), also sought to provide an authoritative picture of the sex life of a nation. Published for a general readership as *Sexual Behaviour in Britain* (Wellings et al., 1994), the National Survey did not provoke the same level of uproar as the Kinsey books had done. Nevertheless, it did become the focus of controversy and debate.

Carried out in 1990–1 as a direct response to the HIV and AIDS epidemic in the 1980s, the Natsal I survey aimed to generate data on sexual behaviour that would, among other things, help model the likely spread of HIV, the virus that causes AIDS. Given that HIV was disproportionately affecting men who have sex with men, it was vital – in order to protect their health – that Natsal I produce accurate data on men in that population group. However, the survey identified a far lower incidence of **same-gender sexual activity** than many people had expected. For instance, whereas Kinsey and his colleagues had estimated that, for at least three years of their late-adolescent and adult lives, 13 per cent of men and 7 per cent of women had had sex to orgasm 'predominantly' with a person of the same sex, the Natsal I estimates suggested that only 1.4 per cent of men and 0.6 per cent of women in the UK had had a sexual partner of the same sex in the last five years (Kinsey et al., 1948, pp. 650–1; Kinsey et al., 1953, pp. 450–1; Wellings et al., 1994, p. 187).

Same-gender sex is sexual activity between people of the same gender. Because not everyone who has same-gender sex identifies as, for example, gay, lesbian or bisexual, phrases such as 'same-gender sex' are often used in survey research in preference to identity-based terms.

The unexpectedly low incidence of same-gender sex uncovered by the National Survey led some critics to argue that its data were fundamentally flawed. Among the most trenchant of those critics was the sociologist Liz Stanley. Stanley (1995) argued that widespread hostility towards gay men and lesbian women meant that many people who engaged in same-gender sex would have refused to participate in the survey and that, consequently, the Natsal I figures should be considered 'a gross under-representation of gay male [and female] sexual behaviour' (p. 51). For its part, the Natsal I team stuck to its guns. Although it acknowledged that the figures should be seen as 'minimum estimates', it went on to point out that the survey's findings were 'remarkably consistent with … other, non-British surveys' conducted around the same time (Wellings et al., 1994, pp. 180, 188).

The Kinsey and Natsal I studies, together with the controversies they provoked, take us to the heart of the central question this chapter addresses: how do social scientists use surveys to generate *descriptions* of the social world and how accurate and useful are those descriptions? The chapter explores these questions through the example of sex surveys of intimate practices. However, as you discovered in the previous chapter, the descriptions of the social world that social science makes available do not simply measure or reflect what already exists. They also inform and influence the social world, and in the process of doing so help to remake it. So as you learn about the use of surveys to describe sexual intimacy, you will also see how social scientists' use of surveys helps to inform public debates and shape social phenomena – it helps to *enact* the social world as well.

1.1 Structure of the chapter

Section 2 of this chapter introduces some preliminary observations on the potential 'usefulness' of sex surveys. Section 3 provides a brief introduction to survey design and analysis. Following on from that, Section 4 considers the Kinsey survey itself: how it was carried out, what it found, and what some of its strengths and weaknesses were. Section 5 then reviews Natsal I and considers some of the criticisms levelled against it. Next, Section 6 explores how surveys can be said to enact social worlds as well as describing them. Finally, the conclusion provides an assessment of the extent to which sex surveys can be considered to generate accurate and useful descriptions of sexual behaviour and summarises the chapter's main teaching points.

1.2 Aims of the chapter

This chapter aims to:

- introduce survey research as an important means by which social scientists seek to *describe* intimate lives and the wider social world
- explore the extent to which survey research generates *accurate* and *useful* descriptions of sexual behaviour through a comparison of two prominent surveys of sexual behaviour – the Kinsey study and the first UK National Survey of Sexual Attitudes and Lifestyles
- consider the role played by survey research in *enacting* as well as describing social worlds and social selves.

2 Using surveys to describe intimacy

As with the forms of social scientific description that you read about in the previous chapter, sex surveys aim to generate descriptions of the social world that are useful for making publicly visible the private and individual dimensions of intimacy, so rendering them available for intervention and action. Both the Kinsey survey and Natsal I provide examples of that process. Kinsey viewed his survey as a source of scientific information on sexual behaviour that would be of value to the work of physicians, psychiatrists, educationalists and policy makers. Similarly, Natsal I was an explicit attempt to make visible previously hidden and unknown patterns of sexual behaviour in the UK population so that appropriate health initiatives could be mobilised in response. Indeed, the results of Natsal I were widely used by, among others, government agencies, health service planners and academic researchers.

It is important to recognise that the descriptions a survey generates will be useful only if they have some purchase on reality. This was the substance of Stanley's criticism of Natsal I. She suggested that the National Survey had insufficient purchase on the reality of same-gender sex to be of value. In Stanley's opinion, it was unlikely that people engaging in same-gender sex would have been willing to have participated in the survey in large enough numbers for it to have generated accurate, and therefore useful, information.

Stanley is not the only critic to have voiced doubts about the value of sex surveys. One of the most notable sceptics of this method is the evolutionary biologist Richard Lewontin. In an article in the *New York Review of Books* entitled 'Sex, lies and social science', Lewontin (1995) suggested that sex surveys are all but meaningless as a source of information on sexual activity because they record what people *say* about their sex lives rather than what they *do* in reality. For Lewontin, such is the likelihood that people will exaggerate, lie about or be unable to remember the details of their sexual behaviour that survey research on the topic is largely a waste of time.

But how reasonable are such criticisms? To address doubts about the accuracy of surveys as a tool of social scientific inquiry, the chapter uses the Kinsey and the Natsal I surveys as case studies, assessing each for the extent to which its descriptions of sexual behaviour can be considered authoritative. One of the reasons it is interesting to compare the two studies is that they adopted different approaches to **sampling** – to selecting who and how to elicit information from among a larger population in order to produce accurate descriptions of that population's sexual activities. Kinsey's research, although highly influential, was conducted before sampling techniques that are now considered standard had entered the mainstream of survey research. His study illustrates some interesting aspects of what happens in the absence of those techniques. In contrast, the sampling practices adopted in Natsal I are widely considered state of the art. As an exemplary piece of survey research, Natsal I provides a good case against which to assess the criticisms that have been levelled at survey methods.

A **sample** comprises individuals or cases drawn from a wider population in order to produce statistical estimates of the characteristics of that wider population.

If the Kinsey study and Natsal I are good examples through which to judge the accuracy of survey research on intimate lives, what might surveys tell us about 'enactment' – the ways in which social science informs and shapes the social world? You have already seen in Chapter 1 that quantitative methods have provided new ways in which to think about social worlds. Indeed, there is a long history of social science using quantification to bring new problems and issues into the public domain. Surveys are an important example of that process. For instance, the historian Sarah Igo has argued:

> In the concrete techniques of the questionnaire and the interview, in public debates over survey findings, and in encounters between researchers and the researched, a new mode of knowing 'ourselves' took shape … [M]odern survey methods helped to forge a mass public. They also shaped the selves who would inhabit it, influencing everything from beliefs about morality and individuality to visions of democracy and the nation. Social scientific representations underwrote entities as abstract as 'the typical American' and as intimate as an individual's self-understanding. Concepts as resonant as 'mainstream culture', 'public opinion', and 'normal sexuality' were brought into being, at least in part, by surveyors and their toolkit of empirical techniques.
>
> (Igo, 2008, p. 282)

Aggregation refers to the process of compiling data to produce a statement (usually numerical) about those data viewed as a whole.

In other words, as survey research developed from the 1920s and 1930s onwards, it did not simply describe pre-existing social phenomena. Rather, it made available new ways of seeing and thinking about them (for example, as 'mass' phenomena, as **aggregated** wholes), and new ways of relating to one's own self (as 'average', 'normal' or, perhaps, 'abnormal'). In short, survey research actively contributed to the making of the social world and social selves. One of Igo's prime examples of that process is Kinsey's sex survey. As you read through the chapter, and learn more about Kinsey's research, you should keep in mind an important aspect of Igo's argument: although social science may be undertaken with the explicit aim of supporting certain uses, sometimes the consequences of social scientific descriptions take an unexpected path. That was certainly true of Kinsey's work. As you will read in Section 6, the survey contributed to the emergence of, or helped enact, new sexual identities – the 'heterosexual', the 'gay man' and the 'lesbian woman'. What is perhaps surprising is that Kinsey himself was sceptical about the notion of fixed sexual identities and did not think his data supported their existence.

3 Doing survey research

One of the main aims of this chapter is to assess how survey research seeks to generate accurate and useful descriptions of sexual behaviour. In order to do that, it is important to be familiar with what survey research actually involves. There are four features of survey approaches that are particularly important to bear in mind when you read more about Kinsey and Natsal I:

- the ways in which questions are designed to elicit responses that are easily quantifiable and that can be used to identify general patterns and trends
- the use of sampling to generate representative descriptions
- the use of surveys to generate descriptions of average phenomena
- the use of surveys to provide descriptions of causal relationships.

Let's explore each of these four features in turn. At its simplest, survey research involves counting up the responses individuals give when questioned about their opinions, or about some aspect(s) of their lives or behaviour. You will recall from the previous chapter that qualitative interview approaches in social science tend to use open-ended, unstructured or semi-structured questioning techniques in order to elicit in-depth accounts of people's experiences and meanings. Survey research contrasts markedly with that approach, since it most often uses pre-determined, prescribed and **closed questions** in order to generate quantifiable data.

Closed questions restrict the answers a respondent is able to give. For example, the respondent may be asked to answer 'yes' or 'no' or to select an answer from a list that most closely matches his or her belief or experience.

Closed questions typically require interviewees to select an answer from a list of alternatives (for example, 'Have you ever had sex with someone of the same sex as yourself?' Answer: Yes/No); or position themselves on a scale (for instance, 'Is having shared interests important to a successful relationship?' Answer: 1 = very important, 2 = quite important, 3 = not very important, 4 = not important, 5 = don't know); or insert a number or value of some kind (in response to questions such as 'What age are you?').

Closed questions are important in survey research because they allow researchers to assign a numerical value to interviewees' answers and to aggregate them (see Figure 2.2). For example, the researcher would aggregate 'Yes' answers to the question, 'Have you ever had sex with someone of the same sex as yourself?' to arrive at the number of people questioned who'd had same-gender sex.

QUESTION 4

a) Have you ever had ANY kind of sexual experience or sexual contact with a **female**?
*Please tick 'yes' here, even if it was a long time ago or did **not** involve contact with the genital area/vagina*

Yes ☐ No ☐ → GO TO QUESTION 7

b) How old were you the first time that ever happened?

Write in age ....

c) Have you ever had sex with a woman involving genital area/vaginal contact?

Yes ☐ No ☐ → GO TO QUESTION 7

d) When was the last occasion? *(Tick one box)*

In the last 7 days ☐

Between 7 days and 4 weeks ago ☐

Between 4 weeks and 3 months ago ☐

Between 3 months and 6 months ago ☐

Between 6 months and 1 year ago ☐

Between 1 year and 5 years ago ☐

Longer than 5 years ago ☐

e) Was this the first occasion with that partner, or not? *(Tick one box)*

Yes, **first** occasion with that partner ☐

No, not first occasion ☐

f) What was her age (at that time)?

Write in age ....

NOW PLEASE ANSWER QUESTION 5

Figure 2.2 An example of closed questions: question 4 from the Natsal I women's questionnaire

Because survey questions are generally designed to be answered in tick-box fashion, responses to them can be added up or aggregated with relative ease and can then be searched for any patterns they may contain. At its most basic, that process involves extracting different strands of information from a survey's findings and matching them up in order to make broad statements about the characteristics of the population in question. For example, as you read earlier, Kinsey estimated that 50 per cent of married American men and 26 per cent of married American women had committed adultery. In other words, Kinsey extracted data on gender, marital status and adultery from his survey's findings and used them to estimate the percentage of the total male and female populations who'd had sex with someone other than their spouse while married.

Although surveys can be an efficient means of gathering large quantities of data, they rarely attempt to gather information on every single individual in a given population, particularly when those populations are very large. Most surveys, then, are not like nation-wide censuses, which do seek to survey the whole population. For example, it would have been beyond the resources available to Kinsey or the Natsal I team to have interviewed every adult in the USA or the UK about their sexual behaviour. Nevertheless, surveys frequently aspire to provide descriptions of the whole population. Indeed, the use that surveys might have to governments, companies, charities or other organisations lies in the survey method's ability to generate findings about a population at large. But if not everyone in a population is interviewed, how does a survey generate findings about that population? The answer is that it will take a sample of the population in question and then 'scale up' or **generalise** the findings from that sample to the wider population. Needless to say, in order to do so it has to ensure the sample mirrors the wider population as accurately as possible, a process that you will explore further in Section 3.2.

A finding is said to be **generalisable** when it can be shown to apply to a wider population or number of instances. Both survey research and experiments usually aim to produce generalisable descriptions of the social world.

As with all research techniques, surveys are used to produce particular types of description. Most obviously, surveys are commonly used to calculate *averages*. The Natsal I data, for instance, showed a decline in the median age at which first sexual intercourse occurred between men and women. (The median is the mid-point in a given set of data.) In other words, the Natsal data indicated that, on average, younger interviewees were likely to have started having heterosexual intercourse at an earlier age than was the case for older interviewees (see Table 2.1).

Table 2.1 Median age at the time of first heterosexual intercourse, by age group

Age of interviewees	**Median**	
	Men	**Women**
16–19	17	17
35–39	18	18
55–69	20	21

Source: adapted from Table 2.1 in Wellings et al., 1994, p. 38

Finally, in addition to being used to describe averages and general trends and patterns in populations, survey data can also be used to investigate possible *causal* relationships between variables. You have already seen in Chapter 1 how quantitative approaches are used to test the relationship between causes and effects. Whereas experimental approaches seek to identify potential causal relations by observing interactions between variables and then measuring them, survey approaches identify possible causal relationships by making connections between aggregate patterns in data. Survey data often contain patterns that indicate possible causal relationships of one kind or another, and such relationships are an important means by which social scientists generate understandings of the world – understandings that then inform policy, practice, or further research.

For example, the Natsal I team investigated if its data indicated a possible link between alcohol consumption and sexual behaviour. As Wellings et al. (1994) noted, 'An association between alcohol consumption and sexual behaviour might be expected on a number of grounds … [for example] the lessening of inhibition resulting from consumption might be associated with higher levels of sexual activity or multiple sexual partnership' (p. 283). In the event, analysis of their data led them to conclude: 'After controlling for age, social class and marital status, reporting of multiple sexual partnerships was significantly associated with … increasing levels of alcohol consumption' (p. 319). Note, they did not argue that alcohol consumption *causes* multiple sexual partnership (or vice versa), merely that there was a 'significant association' between the two variables. In other words, their analysis identified a potential causal relationship, one whose exact nature required further investigation.

So far, you have been introduced to some of the basic features of survey research – the use of closed questions, the use of samples, the generation of averages and the identification of causal relationships. Now you will explore some of survey research's more detailed aspects, in particular the design and administration of survey questionnaires and how a representative sample is constructed.

3.1 Generating data

A survey researcher's first task is to define *what* it is she wants to measure and *how* to measure it. That might sound relatively easy, but the example of sex surveys immediately shows it to be far from straightforward. For instance, the question of how to define and measure sex is something that has vexed many social scientists.

Kinsey's answer was to define sex in terms of practices designed to lead to erotic arousal, largely those involving the genitals. He then sought to measure those practices, using orgasm as a marker or 'indicator' for them. Although a practical solution to the problem, Kinsey's approach was not without difficulties. First, it is not clear that orgasm is an adequate indicator by which to measure sexual activity, since not all activities that people think of as sexual lead to orgasm. Second, it is not certain that sexual activity can be restricted to practices involving the genitals – kissing is an obvious example. More fundamentally, human sexual behaviour is laden with positive and negative meanings and emotions. Although those meanings and emotions form a significant part of most people's experience of sex, they do not feature in Kinsey's definition of sexual activity or in his way of measuring it.

The issue here is not that Kinsey's attempt to define and measure sex was poorly executed. Rather, the point is a more general one. Many features of the social world do not lend themselves to clear-cut definition, nor are there obvious markers that can be used as a basis by which to measure them. That does not mean that attempts to quantify and generalise are doomed to failure. But it does mean that survey researchers have to *translate* social phenomena into forms that can be clearly defined and easily measured. You saw an example of that process in the previous chapter's discussion of Eleanor Maccoby's study of children's television viewing, and the same process is at work in survey research. Translating opinions, beliefs and behaviours into clear-cut and quantifiable categories is often troublesome and frequently involves compromises.

You have already seen that survey research tends to make use of closed questions to make aggregation and analysis easier. But it is important to bear in mind that survey research, even though it is a quantitative approach, depends on engaging people quite actively – getting them to fill in forms and answer questions. The need actively to engage people raises a number of issues, in particular issues related to the ways in which a survey's questions, or the interviewer him or herself, can inadvertently shape the answers people give.

For instance, survey researchers think very carefully about how to word their questions in order to avoid influencing participants' responses. They will try not to use 'leading questions', for example, or ones that imply some kind of value judgement. Asked, 'Do you agree that adultery is always wrong?', for instance, an interviewee might well feel under moral pressure to answer 'Yes'. A better question would provide interviewees with a range of statements about adultery and ask them to pick the one that most closely matches their own opinion.

Prestige bias refers to the tendency of research participants to shape their answers or behaviour in order to gain the approval of the researcher or to avoid acknowledging something they do not want to acknowledge.

Similarly, in order to generate accurate descriptions, survey questions have to be designed with **prestige bias** in mind. The sociologist Alice Bloch defines this as follows:

> Prestige bias occurs when respondents distort their answers to impress the interviewer or fool themselves. Areas of activity that are often *over-reported* because of prestige bias include voting activity, reading books, contributing to charity and helping friends and family. Conversely some other areas are commonly *under-reported*, such as drinking alcohol and smoking.
>
> (Bloch, 2004, p. 172)

Prestige bias is a particular concern in research on sexual behaviour because of the sensitive nature of the issues involved. It is well established, for example, that men tend to over-report and women to under-report the number of sexual partners they have had (Ericksen with Steffen, 1999).

In survey research, **standardisation** is the term applied to the convention by which the questions used, and the order in which they are asked, remain constant each time a survey questionnaire is administered.

A further point about the generation of data in survey research relates to what is called **standardisation**. This refers to the way in which the questions' wording and the order in which they are asked are kept the same every time the questionnaire is used. Why is standardisation so significant? The answer is simple. How you ask a question and the order in which you ask it affect the answers people give.

For instance, the sociologist Julia Ericksen (1998) cites research indicating that, asked about masturbation, people gave very different responses according to the way in which the question was posed. In particular, people were more likely to acknowledge that they masturbated if the question was prefaced with a reassurance that the practice is commonplace. Equally, we can easily imagine that people's responses to a question about masturbation would be affected by where the query fell in the questionnaire. If the question was the first one asked, many respondents might refuse to continue with the interview; if it was posed later on, once participants had built up their confidence answering other questions, they might be more inclined to answer truthfully. As that suggests, if a survey were to vary the wording of its question about masturbation, or to change the point in the interview when that question was asked, it is possible those variations would influence the way in which the question was answered. In other words, the answers given might have more to do with the way in which the question was posed, or with the point at which it happened to fall in the interview, than with participants' actual behaviour.

If a questionnaire's design – particularly with regard to the phrasing and order of the questions asked – is important, so too is its administration. For example, participants' perceptions about interviewers – about, say, their age, class, gender, ethnicity and sexuality – can shape how they respond to questions (the so-called **interviewer effect**).

The term **interviewer effect** refers to the way in which the presence of the interviewer or participants' perceptions of the interviewer shape research participants' behaviour or responses. Survey research attempts to minimise that effect.

In order to minimise that problem, surveys are sometimes conducted over the telephone or through the internet. When they are conducted in person, interviewers generally adopt the role of the 'professional stranger'; that is, they 'remain neutral whatever the respondent discloses, maintain a social distance and never reappear in the respondent's life' (Ericksen, 1998, p. 136).

Importantly, survey interviews are also often conducted by people who are employed specifically for the task and who are not members of the research team. Because they are not members of the team and are not even told the research issues that the survey is designed to test, such interviewers are less likely inadvertently to encourage participants to give a preferred response (perhaps through a facial expression or other form of body language).

It is worth noting here that survey research is not unlike qualitative research in these respects. Both depend on social scientists going out in to the world, talking to people in their homes or workplaces or other locations, and trying to elicit useful information from them. And both approaches are also keenly aware of the ways in which the types of data generated from these encounters can be shaped in important respects by how social scientists design and undertake their research.

3.2 Sampling

Previously, you saw how social scientists take great care to design and administer surveys so as to ensure that the data generated are not unduly shaped by the research process. The aim is that the survey's findings should, as far as possible, represent participants' beliefs and behaviour as those exist in their everyday lives. Although a survey's design and administration are important, it was noted earlier that its usefulness will also depend on a further factor: the extent to which findings from the sample that is used can be generalised to a wider population. In short, the usefulness of surveys depends on the ways in which social scientists use sampling techniques to support their more general claims. For instance, Natsal I interviewed a sample of approximately 19,000 people as a basis for making estimates about sexual behaviour in the UK population as a whole. That is a large number of people, but still only a tiny fraction of the whole population. How did the Natsal I team seek to ensure that its sample was representative of the UK population at large?

Probability or random sampling is a technique in which participants are selected from a pre-identified sampling frame purely on the basis of random chance.

A **sampling frame** is a pre-identified list from which a sample is drawn.

You will see later in the chapter that the Natsal I team used what is known as a **probability or random sample**. Probability sampling is generally considered to be the method most likely to ensure that a sample is 'representative' of the wider population from which it is drawn. In a probability sample, participants are selected from a **sampling frame**: a list of all those within a population who can be sampled. As you can probably imagine, for the sample to be representative of the population at large the sampling frame must itself accurately reflect that population. There is a variety of different sampling frames available to researchers. Bloch explains:

> [Sampling frames for] the whole UK population include the electoral register ... and the Postcode Address File (PAF), though they [both] have limitations in their coverage. The electoral register, for example, may under-represent people who frequently move house, while those who do not register to vote will not be included. ... The PAF is more up to date and has greater coverage

> of the population than the electoral register and has the advantage of being available electronically. However, because the file used for sampling is the 'small user file', which lists addresses receiving less than 25 items of post each day, included in the file are businesses that receive few items of post while private households that receive large amounts of post are excluded. The PAF is therefore not a full and accurate list of the [UK] population, though it is more accurate than many alternatives.
>
> (Bloch, 2004, p. 173)

It is important to recognise that a random or probability sample is not one in which potential participants are approached erratically, for example by standing on a street corner and trying to catch the eye of anyone who happens to pass by. It is not 'random' in that sense. Instead, a fixed number of people are selected from the sampling frame strictly on the basis of random chance – for example, by drawing numbers from a hat or other form of lottery. Consequently, in a probability sample each person in the sampling frame has a known chance of being selected. For instance, if the sampling frame consists of 10,000 people from which a sample of 1000 people are to be drawn, then each person has the same, known chance of being selected: a 1 in 10 chance.

The randomness of a survey's sampling process is crucial to its capacity to generate accurate descriptions of the social world. Because the people who make up the sample have been selected on no basis other than strict random chance – 'the throw of a dice', as it were – the sample itself is likely to mirror the full range of characteristics present in the sampling frame. If people are selected in a non-random fashion, it is likely that particular characteristics present in a population will be over-selected, while others will be excluded. For example, if you were to select people by standing on a street corner and catching the eyes of passers-by, you would be likely to over-select people who use that particular street at that time of day, people who walk rather than drive and so on. As you will see in the following sections' discussion of the Kinsey and Natsal surveys, the extent to which a sample is representative will often become a major point of contention in debates over the accuracy of a survey's description of social phenomena.

One further issue should also be kept in mind in relation to probability sampling. In a probability sample, only those people selected are interviewed and, if they refuse to take part, their non-participation is recorded and the interviewer moves on to the next person identified by the random-selection process. In other words, the interviewer does not try to 'make up the numbers' by finding a replacement for the person who refused to participate, since that would disrupt the randomness of the selection process.

As that suggests, the findings of probability samples can be heavily skewed by non-responses. There are two common reasons for non-response. First, people may simply be unavailable at the time the researcher calls. Bloch (2004) notes that this problem can be reduced in various ways, for example by increasing the number of times individuals are contacted, or by varying the time of day or week when attempts to contact them are made, in order to increase the likelihood of finding them at home.

Stigmatisation is a social process in which individuals, groups, beliefs or behaviours are excluded from full social acceptance by the wider society.

The second reason for non-response is refusal to participate, something that can be a particular problem in research into sensitive or socially **stigmatised** behaviour. For obvious reasons, those practising a behaviour that is socially stigmatised (same-gender sex, for instance) may be reluctant to participate in a survey. The consequence of that, however, is that the group in question will be significantly under-represented in the probability sample that is generated. As noted earlier, non-response became a major point of debate in the criticisms made of Natsal I.

Section 3 has explored some of the issues involved in designing, administering and analysing survey research. In particular, you have been introduced to a number of critical issues that underpin a survey's capacity to make general claims or to 'scale-up' findings from its sample to the wider population. As you read on, you should keep in mind the extent to which the two sex surveys that are discussed – the Kinsey study and Natsal I – satisfy the rigorous requirements that, in principle at least, enable social scientists to generate accurate descriptions of average behaviours, causal relationships and emerging trends.

4 The Kinsey survey

The survey conducted by Kinsey and his colleagues was, by any standards, large in scale. As the introduction to the chapter noted, it encompassed in excess of 18000 interviews, although the data presented in the two Kinsey books drew on slightly less than two thirds of that total. It was also noted earlier that Kinsey presented the findings from his study as representative of the US population as a whole (Kinsey et al., 1948). With that in mind, we might expect that he would have used a probability sampling method of the kind outlined in the previous section. But he did not. In fact, Kinsey seems to have adapted his sampling method from his earlier work as a biologist.

4.1 Kinsey's sampling technique

Before turning to sex research in the late 1930s, Kinsey had made his reputation studying North American gall wasps, for which task he had observed vast numbers of individual insects in multiple locations from Mexico up to Canada (Gathorne-Hardy, 2005). When Kinsey began work on human sexuality, it seems he transferred this approach to his new field, setting out to collect as many sexual case histories from as wide an array of locales and social milieux as he could possibly find. Crucially, however, Kinsey's participants were not selected randomly from a sampling frame. They were volunteers – people whom Kinsey sought out or who sought him out.

By today's standards, Kinsey's sampling method appears surprising, although it was less so by the standards of his day. When he began his work in 1938, probability sampling was still in its infancy. Indeed, the statistical methods on which current probability sampling relies had been developed only in 1935 (Igo, 2008). Although Kinsey clearly knew of probability sampling, he appears to have had doubts about its practicality, particularly in the context of sex research. In Kinsey's view, people selected at random would be unlikely to participate in a survey on sexual behaviour, and the refusal rate would be such as to invalidate its findings (Ericksen with Steffen, 1999).

Even though Kinsey refused to use a probability sample, he was well aware of the risk of bias that his sampling method entailed and actively sought ways to mitigate it. In particular, he compared the findings from his general sample with those of a control group. This was a parallel sample made up from members of local branches of professional associations, clubs and societies. Since Kinsey interviewed each and every member of these '100 per cent groups', as they came to be called, and since those members could be assumed to include many people who would not otherwise have agreed to be interviewed, Kinsey reasoned that, if his main sample was biased, findings from the 100 per cent groups would reveal that imbalance. In all, some 25 per cent of Kinsey's overall sample came from 100 per cent groups and it seems he actively used the comparison they afforded to adjust, or 'weight', data from the main sample in order to make his findings more representative (Gathorne-Hardy, 2005, pp. 144–5, 362).

Although ingenious, Kinsey's use of 100 per cent groups did not make his sample as representative as he evidently believed it to be. In fact, the survey contained some notable absences and instances of over-sampling. Most obviously, and for reasons that are not entirely clear, Kinsey excluded black respondents from the data published in *Sexual Behavior in the Human Male* and *Sexual Behavior in the Human Female*. Whatever the reason for that decision, the absence of people of colour from the data analysed in the books invalidates their claim to provide a representative description of the US population as a whole. Equally, older people were under-represented in Kinsey's sample, while mid-westerners, college students, professionals and individuals recruited because they had a 'particular sexual interest' were over-represented (an example of the latter being supporters of homosexual rights organisations). The prison population and, in all probability, men who had sex with men were also over-represented in *Sexual Behavior in the Human Male*. Finally, working-class women were largely missing from *Sexual Behavior in the Human Female* (Ericksen, 1998; Igo, 2008).

4.2 The Kinsey questionnaire

Figure 2.3 Kinsey posing as if administering the survey's famous questionnaire

If, by today's standards, Kinsey's sampling strategy was problematic, what of the questions that were asked? Kinsey's interview schedule covered 350 questions, principally concerned with the methods by which the interviewee achieved orgasm and the frequency of those (although, to allow the interviewee to relax, questions about sex only appeared about twenty minutes into the interview). A further 171 supplementary questions were asked as necessary. The questions were memorised (a remarkable feat in itself) and answers were noted down by the interviewer on a single sheet of paper, using a code to preserve anonymity.

Kinsey was evidently well aware that people might lie or exaggerate when asked about their sexual practices, or might have difficulty recollecting facts. Consequently, as the historian Vern Bullough wrote:

> His interview technique included a number of checks for consistency, and if inconsistencies appeared, either from attempts

> to deceive or from faulty memory, the interviewer probed deeper until the apparent disagreement could be explained or eliminated. Kinsey strongly believed he could detect fraudulent answers, and certainly his ingenious coding system was designed to detect the most obvious ones.
>
> (Bullough, 1994, p. 173)

Kinsey was also alert to the fact that the wording of questions would shape respondents' answers. For example, he famously asked, 'When did you first masturbate?', rather than 'Have you ever masturbated?', thereby creating an implicit understanding that masturbation is normal and commonplace (Ericksen with Steffen, 1999, p. 57).

Similarly, Kinsey appears to have recognised that interviewees' responses would be subject to an 'interviewer effect', of the sort discussed in Section 3.1. To counteract that effect, interviews were conducted by Kinsey and a limited number of his colleagues, all married men, from similar social backgrounds (Bullough, 1994; Ericksen, 1998). Kinsey hoped that, by restricting the range of interviewers he used to a similar 'type' of person, he would limit the extent to which variation in his interviewees' responses could be attributed to their perceptions of the people who interviewed them.

As those precautions indicate, Kinsey clearly understood some of the problems that arise in survey interviewing. However, as Ericksen (1998) has argued, neither his questionnaire design nor his interviewing technique would be considered adequate today. For instance, interviewers were allowed to vary the wording of questions and the order in which questions were asked according to the perceived needs of the interview (Ericksen with Steffen, 1999). You saw in Section 3.1 that it is likely that, in consequence, interviewees will have responded differently to the same question.

Moreover, despite Kinsey's efforts to minimise the interviewer effect, his interviewing strategy probably amplified it. As Ericksen writes, 'Kinsey saw the interviewer's goal … as that of establishing a close rapport with the respondent' (1998, p. 136). It was only on that basis, so Kinsey believed, that people would feel able to reveal intimate details about their sexual lives. Although Kinsey's acknowledged success in establishing rapport with his participants probably meant that he elicited material he would not otherwise have obtained, it is likely that his approach shaped the responses his participants gave. Faced with a warm and sympathetic listener, interviewees may sometimes have given a response they imagined would please their interviewer, perhaps suppressing some details and enhancing others.

The interviewer effect may also have been amplified by the fact that the interviews were conducted by Kinsey and his colleagues. You read in Section 3.1 that today it is accepted practice in large surveys that questionnaires should be administered by paid fieldworkers rather than members of the actual research team. Unlike the research team, fieldworkers do not know the issues that the survey is attempting to address and cannot inadvertently influence respondents to tell them things that simply confirm the team's pre-existing assumptions. As Ericksen (1998) notes, Kinsey and his colleagues were sexual liberals and, in conducting their own interviews, it is possible they elicited data that confirmed their assumption that sexual behaviour was more varied than conventional morality allowed.

You can see, then, that in various respects Kinsey's research does not match up to the standards that contemporary social science might expect. In seeking to ensure as many people as possible spoke to him about potentially sensitive topics, Kinsey clearly contravened some of the 'rules' that shape current views of what makes for an accurate, representative survey.

4.3 Assessing Kinsey's findings

Given the range of criticisms that can be made of Kinsey's sampling method and interview technique from the perspective of contemporary social science, how useful should we consider the description of sexual behaviour that his survey generated? There is little doubt that Kinsey's data were far less representative than he believed. Consequently, his estimates for the incidence and frequency of specific behaviours should, to say the least, be treated with caution. We simply cannot tell on the basis of Kinsey's data whether or not 37 per cent of American men had engaged in some form of homosexual activity to orgasm, or if 26 per cent of married American women had committed adultery.

However, that does not render his findings meaningless. Just because it does not conform to the standards of our own day, Kinsey's work should not be dismissed out of hand. His methods have certainly been overtaken by subsequent developments in probability sampling and survey design. In fact, they were being overtaken even at the time Kinsey's study was in progress (Cochran et al., 1953). Nevertheless, his research stands as a serious attempt to describe a nation's sexual behaviour in social scientific terms. The size and ambition of his study, and the very fact that it was undertaken at all, illustrate one of the most basic uses of social science – the attempt to describe and thereby make visible aspects of the social world that were previously hidden. Moreover, although it is likely the survey over-stated the diversity of sexual behaviour commonly engaged in by the American public, it nevertheless revealed such behaviour to be more varied than was supposed at the time. In particular, Kinsey's work drew attention to same-gender sex, challenged the common idea that women frequently lacked sexual desires of their own, and suggested important class differences in men's sexual practices (Bullough, 1994).

Kinsey's research is an example of a survey conducted before current conventions of sampling and survey design had become firmly established. As you have seen, although large and extensive, it did not meet many of the criteria by which surveys are now evaluated. In the next section, you will investigate a survey whose design and sampling technique were widely regarded as state of the art: the first National Survey of Sexual Attitudes and Lifestyles. But despite its impeccable credentials, Natsal I's findings proved controversial. You will see below that its critics claimed the survey failed to generate accurate and, therefore, useful descriptions of at least some types of sexual behaviour. Those criticisms provide an opportunity to assess survey research as it is currently practised and, more importantly, its ability to describe intimate sexual lives accurately.

5 The National Survey of Sexual Attitudes and Lifestyles

As the chapter introduction noted, Natsal I was carried out in the UK in 1990–1 as a direct response to the HIV and AIDS epidemic. In the almost total absence of existing evidence, Natsal I aimed to provide data on a range of matters related to the sexual histories, practices, attitudes and identities of a representative sample of the UK population. In short, it sought to make visible a realm of social life that had previously been hidden.

Figure 2.4 Natsal I researchers Julia Field, Kaye Wellings, Anne Johnson and Jane Wadsworth

A large-scale survey of the sexual behaviour of a national population, Natsal I stood in a direct line of descent from Kinsey's earlier study. However, as you might expect from the previous section, there were numerous differences between it and Kinsey's work. One obvious difference was that the Natsal team opted for a fully standardised questionnaire, in which the questions' wording and order remained constant. In equally strong contrast to the Kinsey study, the questionnaires were not administered by the project team but by 488 trained interviewers, thus minimising the risk that the team's prior assumptions would in some way shape the data generated.

Perhaps the biggest difference between Natsal I and the Kinsey study, however, was the Natsal team's use of a probability sampling method. In Section 5.1 you will read a short extract from *Sexual Behaviour in Britain* (1994), in which Wellings and her co-authors discuss the sampling decisions they took and some of the consequences of those.

5.1 The Natsal I sample

You should now consider Reading 2.1, an extract from *Sexual Behaviour in Britain.* As you read the extract, ask yourself in what ways the Natsal I sample might have been more representative than Kinsey's, and what the possible limits of that representativeness might have been. To help you address those issues, you may want to refer back to the discussion in Section 3.

Reading 2.1

Sampling considerations in Natsal I

A [major] sampling consideration concerned the aims of the survey, one of which was to provide reliable estimates of the prevalence of relatively uncommon behaviours, such as paying for sex, injecting drugs, etc. … [That] pointed to a need for a general population sample, randomly selected from a reliable sampling frame, with a target of around 20,000 achieved interviews. The selection of personal interview as the data collection method narrowed the choice of sampling frame to a choice between the Electoral Register and the Post Office small-users Postcode Address File (PAF), each of which has advantages and disadvantages. The Electoral Register (ER) quickly becomes outdated. The coverage of addresses is incomplete and young people, members of ethnic minorities and the highly mobile are more likely to live at addresses not on the Register. The small-users Postcode Address File, a regularly updated computer-held file of largely residential addresses, is free from problems of failure to register or of mobility of residents; coverage of residential addresses is superior to that of ER and the few omissions are more likely to be random and not biased in any particular direction. The major disadvantage of the PAF is that it does not list the names of residents or how many there are. A sampling procedure [like that in Natsal I] that requires that only one person per household is interviewed means that those who live alone have a higher chance of selection than do individuals who live in large households. The PAF was chosen mainly on the grounds of its superior coverage of private residential addresses.

Interviewing began in May 1990 and was completed in November 1991. Interviewers approached listed addresses [randomly selected from the sampling frame] to establish whether the address was residential and occupied, and if so whether the household contained an eligible resident. One individual was randomly selected from households with more than one member using a standard technique for this purpose ... Interviewers were instructed to make at least four calls to each address, but in practice often made many more.

The response rate for any survey is important in assessing the representativeness of the sample and hence the extent to which the survey findings can be generalised to the population as a whole. [Of the] 29,802 potentially eligible addresses no contact was made at 1,027 (3.5%) and at 1,761 (5.9%) the person with whom contact was made refused to give information needed to allow the selection of a household member to take place. At 562 (1.9%) addresses the selected person was ill or away or unable to speak English, and at 7,517 (25.2%) the selected person refused to participate. Interviews were completed with 18,876 respondents, giving an overall response rate of 63.3%.

(Source: Wellings et al., 1994, pp. 22–6)

Looking back to the issues discussed in Section 3 and the limitations of the Kinsey surveys identified in Section 4, there seem to be good reasons to suppose that Natsal I's sample was far more representative of the UK population than Kinsey's had been of the US population of his day. In particular, in contrast to Kinsey's sample, the Natsal survey used a widely recognised sampling frame (the Postcode Address File, which was described in Section 3.2), adopted a random sampling method, and required its interviewers to make numerous calls back in order to minimise the non-response rate. Combined with Natsal I's adoption of a standardised interview schedule and its use of paid fieldworkers to administer its questionnaire, its sampling method suggests that the survey's findings should have been highly representative of the UK population as a whole.

Nevertheless, despite the fact that Natsal I adhered closely to the criteria by which survey research are currently judged, critical questions were raised about it. In particular, serious criticisms were made about the accuracy of Natsal I's description of same-gender sex.

5.2 Natsal I and the 'missing millions'

As was indicated in the introduction to this chapter, among the most contentious of the National Survey's findings were the lower than expected percentages of men and women reporting sexual experience with members of their own sex. In particular, you will recall that Natsal I estimated that only 1.4 per cent of men and 0.6 per cent of women had had a sexual partner of the same sex in the last five years. Lifetime figures were slightly higher: 3.6 per cent of men and 1.7 per cent of women were estimated to have had genital contact with someone of their own sex at some point in their lives, while a further 6.1 per cent of men and 3.4 per cent of women were estimated to have had a homosexual sexual experience of some kind (Wellings et al., 1994, p. 187). The Natsal team was careful to state that its figures should be read as 'minimum estimates' (Wellings et al., 1994, p. 180). Nevertheless, those estimates were significantly lower than many had believed they would be. You saw in the introduction to the chapter that for critics such as Stanley (1995), this suggested that aspects of the Natsal survey were flawed (see also Tatchell, 1993).

If the National Survey had gone wrong, where might it have done so? Critics argued that the design of some of the survey's questions may have influenced responses in an adverse way. For instance, it was argued that the question on same-gender sex could be read as implying that same-gender sexual practices were unusual or abnormal and thereby discouraged people from answering it honestly (Stanley, 1995). However, the main criticism levelled against Natsal I focused less on issues of design than on the usefulness of survey research as a means by which to generate accurate descriptions of same-gender sexual behaviour.

In particular, Natsal I's critics suggested that many people who engaged in same gender sex would have felt too vulnerable to participate in the Natsal study at all. For instance, Stanley (1995) noted that in a survey of 500 gay men carried out by an AIDS community organisation in advance of Natsal I's research, half the respondents indicated they would not participate if selected to do so. The reason for that is not difficult to find. In the 1980s, media reporting of HIV and AIDS had frequently blamed gay men for the epidemic and there was widespread intolerance of gay and lesbian relationships. For example, only two years before Natsal I, the Conservative government had passed legislation prohibiting the teaching in state schools of 'the acceptability of homosexuality as a pretended family relationship' (Sanders and Spraggs, 1989).

As Stanley (1995) argued, that climate of intolerance may well have been a factor in the Natsal survey's refusal rate. You will recall from Reading 2.1 that 25.2 per cent of individuals selected for interview declined to participate in the survey, and that in a further 5.9 per cent of households the interviewer was refused any information whatsoever about their residents (Wellings et al., 1994, p. 26). With that in mind, Stanley argued that the low rates of same-gender sexual behaviour that Natsal I found could be explained by men who had sex with men and women who had sex with women opting out of the survey completely. Equally, as Stanley also argued, where people who had same-gender sex did choose to be interviewed, it was possible that many would have decided not to reveal their sexuality. That possibility was again reinforced by the survey of 500 gay men conducted prior to the National Survey. This had found that 'a third [of respondents] said they would participate [in Natsal I] but hide the fact that they were gay' (Stanley, 1995, pp. 51–2).

The conclusion Stanley drew from her analysis of the National Survey was that, in the adverse moral climate of that time, survey research was simply not an effective tool with which to generate accurate and useful information on same-gender sexual behaviour. Indeed, for Stanley, the random selection of individuals for interview by a 'professional stranger' was singularly ill suited to that task. '[T]he National Survey', she contended, 'makes the assumption that a two-hour interview with a stranger will successfully enable self-disclosure', an assumption that involved 'an incredible failure to grasp the personal and political dynamics' at stake in disclosing sexual practices that are socially stigmatised (1995, p. 51). Perhaps surprisingly, Stanley went on to argue that, for all its faults, Kinsey's sampling technique was potentially more effective at generating data on same-gender sex than was Natsal I's probability sample. Kinsey's active efforts to recruit men and women who had same-gender sex, Stanley suggested, combined with his famously empathetic interviewing style, were more likely to have encouraged self-disclosure than was Natsal I's more 'rigorous' approach (Stanley, 1995).

5.3 Assessing Natsal I

Stanley's criticisms of Natsal I alert us to some of the potential limitations of survey research. As Natsal I's experience suggests, even when a survey is meticulously designed and conducted it will sometimes face problems eliciting accurate information, particularly information on behaviour that is socially stigmatised. People's understandable reluctance to report stigmatised behaviour, and the likelihood that they will refuse even to participate in a survey investigating stigmatised practices, mean that survey findings in this area should be treated with caution.

With that in mind, how should we assess Natsal I's estimates of the prevalence of same gender-sex? There is little doubt that the survey's estimates under-represented the actual level of same-gender sexual behaviour. But does that mean that the description of same-gender sex it generated was of no use whatsoever? Stanley's criticisms might seem to imply that was the case. However, there is a number of reasons why the Natsal I data can be considered to have been useful, despite their evident shortcomings.

First, although Natsal I almost certainly underestimated the prevalence of same-gender sex, that does not necessarily mean that its data were so awry as to be meaningless. Among the more recent estimates available at the time of writing, the Integrated Household Survey (IHS) for 2010 suggested that 1.5 per cent of the UK population is lesbian, gay or bisexual (Office for National Statistics, 2011); Natsal II, the second National Survey, conducted in 1999–2001, estimated that 2.6 per cent of both men and women had had a sexual partner of the same sex in the last five years (Erens et al., 2003, p. 54); and an actuarial exercise conducted by the Treasury in 2005 estimated that 6 per cent of the population is either lesbian or gay (Campbell, 2005). None of those estimates can be considered definitive and it is quite possible that even the highest figure under-represents the reality. Nonetheless, they give some sense of the possible range in which the actual level of same-gender sexual activity can reasonably be assumed to fall (the IHS estimate is almost certainly too low, so the likely range should probably be seen as running from 2.6 to 6+ per cent). Natsal I's estimates are below the bottom of that range but are not so distant from it as to render them worthless (recall that Natsal I estimated that 1.4 per cent of men and 0.6 per cent of women had had a sexual partner of the same sex in the last five years).

Second, as was noted earlier, the Natsal I team was well aware that its estimates for same-gender sex were likely to under-represent the reality. For instance, Wellings et al. wrote:

> [S]ince homosexual sex is stigmatized in Britain, it can be expected to be under- rather than over-reported. For the same reason it is possible that some people who had experienced homosexual sex would be less willing to participate in the survey. Because of possible reporting and response biases all prevalence figures relating to homosexual activity should be regarded as minimum estimates.
>
> (Wellings et al., 1994, p. 180)

Understood as providing minimum baselines rather than definitive statements of reality, Natsal I's prevalence figures were fed into such things as epidemiological models and health service planning processes. As such, there is little doubt that they were useful.

Finally, the data provide a benchmark against which subsequent trends in same-gender sexual behaviour have been tracked and measured. We have already seen that Natsal II's estimates of the prevalence of same-gender sex were higher than those identified in Natsal I. Given that Natsal II was conducted in a moral climate considerably more tolerant of same-gender sex, at least some of that rise will have been due to an increased willingness on the part of the survey's respondents to report same-gender sexual activity. However, the Natsal II team's analysis of its data concluded that the rise was attributable, in part, to an actual increase in same-gender sexual behaviour. In other words, the team concluded that more people were having same-gender sex in 2000 than in 1990, something they attributed to the more liberal social climate of the time (Johnson et al., 2001; Mercer et al., 2004). Natsal II was able to track that likely change in behaviour only because of the baseline established by Natsal I's estimates of the prevalence of same-gender sex. Without that baseline, Natsal II would have had no point of comparison against which to identify the trend.

So we can see that Natsal I's data on same-gender sex were perhaps more useful than their shortcomings might at first lead us to imagine. This returns us to a point first raised in Chapter 1. Social science research, including research that is quantitative, does not usually claim to provide absolute and infallible descriptions of reality. It is better thought of as an ongoing and always incomplete process whereby social scientists attempt to revise, adjust and develop more accurate descriptions and understandings.

6 Doing surveys, making social worlds

So far, the chapter has investigated the ability of survey research to generate accurate and useful descriptions of social phenomena, using examples of social science research into sexual behaviour. However, you will recall being reminded at the chapter's outset that the descriptions of the social world that social science makes available do not simply reflect what already exists. They also inform and influence the social world, in the process remaking it. You have seen how the Kinsey and the Natsal surveys both informed public debates about sexuality and intimate life. That was part of the intention of the researchers involved of course. However, survey research also illustrates a further aspect of the way in which social science can help to remake or shape the social worlds it seeks to describe. By making visible social phenomena at the scale of whole populations, survey research sometimes generates consequences largely unanticipated by social scientists. To illustrate this process, let's return to Kinsey's survey one final time.

Figure 2.5 Christopher Street became the centre of gay New York

Kinsey's findings on same-gender sex provide a telling illustration of the afterlife that survey data sometimes lead. One of the Kinsey study's most notable consequences was to make same-gender sex visible in a way that it had never been before. As Bullough puts it, the survey 'allowed American society to come to terms with the facts of life and to recognise the widespread existence of [homosexuality]' (1994, p. 177). As a consequence, people who engaged in same-gender sexual practices were able to recognise themselves as part of a much wider group than had previously been imagined, and to begin to identify themselves as members of a particular community or social constituency. Indeed, as Bullough goes on to argue, there is a good case to be made that 'the modern gay movement would … not have come into existence' without Kinsey, or 'at least [not] at the time it did' (1994, p. 177). As that observation suggests, Kinsey's survey was an important factor in the emergence of distinctive gay and lesbian identities in the second half of the twentieth century. In other words, his data did not just describe the social world. In important ways, they also provided a resource through which new social worlds were brought into being or enacted.

Kinsey, who died in 1956, would certainly have been pleased to know that his survey had added to a growing social tolerance of same-gender sexual relationships. However, it seems likely that he would have been bemused by the idea that its findings contributed to the emergence of distinctive lesbian, gay, or, for that matter, heterosexual 'identities' – ones that are understood to be largely exclusive and more or less fixed – and to people experiencing themselves in those terms. In fact, Kinsey was profoundly sceptical of the notion that there are 'homosexual' and 'heterosexual' personalities or types. He considered sexual preferences and behaviour to be learned rather than inborn and believed that his findings demonstrated sexual desire to be relatively fluid, often changing over the course of a person's life. As Kinsey and his colleagues put it:

> [T]he record … shows that there is a considerable portion of the population whose members have combined, within their individual histories, both homosexual and heterosexual experience and/or psychic responses … [People] who are involved in one type of relation at one period in their lives, may have only the other type of relation at some later period. There may be considerable fluctuation of patterns from time to time. … Males [and females] do not represent two discrete populations, heterosexual and homosexual. The world is not to be divided into sheep and goats. … The living world is a continuum in each and every one of its aspects. The sooner we learn this concerning human sexual

> behavior the sooner we shall reach a sound understanding of the realities of sex.
>
> (Kinsey et al., 1948, p. 639)

In other words, in Kinsey's view, not only do many people have same-gender as well as opposite-gender sexual desires, but those desires are also quite likely to change over time: sometimes tending to be predominantly homosexual, sometimes predominantly heterosexual, sometimes both.

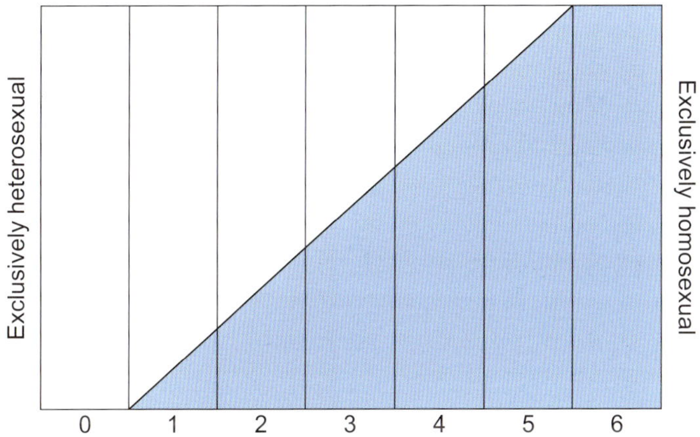

Figure 2.6 Kinsey's heterosexual–homosexual rating scale

Source: adapted from Kinsey et al., 1948, p. 638

Figure 2.6 shows Kinsey and colleagues' famous heterosexual–homosexual rating scale. As you can see, the scale runs from 0 ('Exclusively heterosexual') to 6 ('Exclusively homosexual'), with 3 at its mid-point (defined by Kinsey as 'Equally heterosexual and homosexual'). Given the extent to which Kinsey's work has entered popular consciousness, we might expect that the 'Kinsey scale' would have encouraged people to experience their sexual desires as being more or less fluid, subject to change over time, and as combining elements of attraction to both sexes. That was certainly what Kinsey hoped would happen. In the event, however, his findings contributed to the opposite notion, namely to the idea that there are distinctive gay, lesbian and heterosexual 'identities'. Rather than reading the scale in the manner Kinsey intended, people seemed to locate themselves at a fixed point along it (Bullough, 1994).

The impact of Kinsey's survey on popular consciousness provides a powerful example of the fact that social science not only describes and understands social worlds but sometimes enacts them as well, and in ways that are sometimes unexpected. Despite no longer being a model of a 'rigorous' survey method, Kinsey's study reminds us that the descriptions made available by sex surveys have been an important means by which people have come to imagine themselves and the social worlds in which they live.

7 Conclusion: surveys as descriptions of the social world

Now that you have reviewed the uses made of the Kinsey study and Natsal I, it is time to return to one of the principal questions raised at the start of the chapter: the extent to which social science generates accurate and useful descriptions of social phenomena.

You will recall from Section 2 that Lewontin (1995), from the perspective of a natural scientist, once dismissed sex surveys on the grounds that they report only what people say they do rather than what they do in reality. His point was that participants will inevitably exaggerate, lie about or be unable to remember the details of their sexual behaviour and that, as a consequence, sex survey data are all but meaningless. However, Lewontin's claim that the findings of sex surveys are all but meaningless is surely overblown. As is the case with qualitative interviewing, ordinary people seem willing to answer questions and talk to interviewers, even when the subject matter is highly sensitive. Although they must be interpreted with due care and caution, particularly when the behaviour concerned is socially stigmatised, the descriptions generated by large-scale probability surveys – such as Natsal I – seem able to produce useful descriptions. The fact that those descriptions cannot always be wholly accurate (as was the case with Natsal I's estimates of same-gender sex) does not mean that survey research on sexual behaviour is fundamentally flawed.

Having said that, survey research – like any other social scientific method – is not foolproof. If probability samples are likely to be more representative than was Kinsey's, they will only ever be as accurate as the sampling frame from which they are drawn. Furthermore, as you saw in relation to the controversy that surrounded Natsal I, low response rates leave even probability surveys open to the charge that particular social groups or practices are under-represented in their findings. Problems can also arise in survey research from the way in which questions are worded and the order in which they are asked. As you read in Section 3.1, when designing questions and selecting the order in which they will be asked, survey researchers must take particular note of prestige bias – the human tendency to answer questions in a way that presents us in the best light. A still more fundamental issue concerns the ways in which surveys translate reality into a form that is measurable. As Section 4 explained, Kinsey's difficulties in defining sexual behaviour and identifying a measure for it highlight the problems that social scientists often face when designing surveys. Indeed, Stanley (1995) has argued that a failure adequately to define sex means that much survey research did not register one of the twentieth century's most seismic shifts in sexual behaviour: women's rejection of a sexual role organised solely around men's desires and the expectation of motherhood. With few exceptions, post-war sex surveys simply did not ask the sort of questions that would have elicited data on women's changing expectations of sex.

However, none of those difficulties critically undermines the value of survey research as a tool for investigating social phenomena. As Natsal I and the National Surveys that followed it have shown, when properly designed and conducted, sex surveys generate important descriptions that lead to new understandings, in particular of broad patterns and trends of sexual behaviour present in large populations. The fall in the median age of first heterosexual sexual intercourse revealed by Natsal I provides one illustration of that point (see Section 3). Indeed, findings from the Natsal studies have proved invaluable to an array of high-profile activities and policy initiatives, ranging from government-sponsored projections of the HIV and AIDS epidemic to UK strategies on teenage sexual health (Overy et al., 2011). Without the findings of the Natsal studies, those initiatives would have been forced to rely on evidence that was at best partial and at worst fundamentally mistaken.

On the face of it, surveys may not seem well suited to the task of eliciting data on matters that are sensitive and personal. But, as this chapter has demonstrated, conducted properly and with an awareness of the limitations of survey design and implementation, they are capable of doing just that. If there are good reasons to be cautious about sex survey findings and to read any conclusions drawn from them with a critical eye, it remains the case that surveys are among the most powerful tools available to social scientific studies of intimate life. The aggregated, numerical descriptions which surveys generate have helped to transform understandings of sexual behaviour since the middle of the twentieth century. They have opened new avenues of research, and informed the design of health and social policy. And they have even helped to shape and transform the most intimate aspects of personal identities.

7.1 Chapter summary

In this chapter you have learned that:

- surveys are an important means by which social scientists seek to *describe* intimate lives and the wider social world
- survey research typically involves administrating a standardised questionnaire to a randomly selected sample drawn from a sampling frame
- probability, or random, samples allow findings to be generalised to a wider population with a high degree of confidence
- survey data can be aggregated to provide information on broad patterns of and trends in behaviour
- survey findings should always be interrogated critically; common problems that occur in survey research include prestige biases in response to questions asked, inadequate sampling frames, low response rates, and difficulties arriving at an appropriate definition and way of measuring the phenomenon under investigation
- survey findings not only describe the social world; they help to enact it by informing and shaping social processes and selves.

References

Bloch, A. (2004) 'Doing social surveys' in Seale, C. (ed.) *Researching Society and Culture* (2nd edn), London, Sage.

Bullough, V.L. (1994) *Science in the Bedroom: A History of Sex Research*, New York, Basic Books.

Campbell, D. (2005) '3.6 million people in Britain are gay – official', *The Observer*, 11 December, p. 13 [online], http://www.guardian.co.uk/uk/2005/dec/11/gayrights.immigrationpolicy (Accessed 25 March 2012).

Cochran, W.G., Mosteller, F. and Tukey, J.W. (1953) 'Some statistical problems of the Kinsey Report', *Journal of the American Statistical Association*, vol. 48, no. 264, pp. 673–716.

Erens, B., McManus, S., Prescott, P., Field, J. with Johnson, A.M., Wellings, K., Fenton, K.A., Mercer, C., Macdowell, W., Copas, A.J. and Nanchahal, K. (2003) *National Survey of Sexual Attitudes and Lifestyles II: Reference Tables and Summary Report*, London, National Centre for Social Research.

Ericksen, J.A. (1998) 'With enough cases, why do you need statistics? Revisiting Kinsey's methodology', *Journal of Sex Research*, vol. 35, no. 2, pp. 132–40.

Ericksen, J.A. with Steffen, S.A. (1999) *Kiss and Tell: Surveying Sex in the Twentieth Century*, Cambridge, MA, Harvard University Press.

Gathorne-Hardy, J. (2005) *Kinsey: A Biography*, London, Pimlico.

Igo, S.E. (2008) *The Averaged American: Surveys, Citizens, and the Making of a Mass Public*, Cambridge, MA, Harvard University Press.

Johnson, A.M., Mercer, C.H., Erens, B., Copas, A.J., McManus, S., Wellings, K., Fenton, K.A., Korovessis, C., Macdowall, W., Nanchahal, K., Purdon, S. and Field, J. (2001) 'Sexual behaviour in Britain: partnerships, practices, and HIV risk behaviours', *Lancet*, vol. 358, 1 December, pp. 1835–41.

Kinsey, A.C., Pomeroy, W.B. and Martin, C.E. (1948) *Sexual Behavior in the Human Male*, London, W.B. Saunders.

Kinsey, A.C., Pomeroy, W.B. and Martin, C.E. (1953) *Sexual Behavior in the Human Female*, London, W.B. Saunders.

Lewontin, R. (1995) 'Sex, lies and social science', *New York Review of Books*, 20 April, pp. 24–9.

Mercer, C.H., Fenton, K.A., Copas, A.J., Wellings, K., Erens, B., McManus, S., Nanchahal, K., Macdowall, W. and Johnson, A.M. (2004) 'Increasing prevalence of male homosexual partnerships and practices in Britain 1990–2000: evidence from national probability surveys', *AIDS*, vol. 18, no. 10, pp. 1453–8.

Office for National Statistics (2011) *Statistical Bulletin: Integrated Household Survey*, Newport, Office for National Statistics.

Overy, C., Reynolds, L.A. and Tansey, E.M. (eds) (2011) 'History of the National Survey of Sexual Attitudes and Lifestyles', *Wellcome Witnesses to Twentieth Century Medicine*, vol. 41, London, Queen Mary, University of London.

Sanders, S. and Spraggs, G. (1989) 'Section 28 and education' in Jones, C. and Mahony, P. (eds) *Learning Our Lines: Sexuality and Social Control in Education*, London, Women's Press.

Stanley, L. (1995) *Sex Surveyed 1949–1994: From Mass-Observation's 'Little Kinsey' to the National Survey and the Hite Reports*, London, Taylor & Francis.

Tatchell, P. (1993) 'Where are the missing millions?', *Gay Times*, January, pp. 14–15.

Wellings, K., Field, J., Johnson, A.M. and Wadsworth, J. (1994) *Sexual Behaviour in Britain: The National Survey of Sexual Attitudes and Lifestyles*, Harmondsworth, Penguin.

Chapter 3
Understanding shadow work

Gabe Mythen

1 Introduction 103
1.1 Structure of the chapter 106
1.2 Aims of the chapter 107
2 Establishing the facts about work 108
2.1 The Health and Safety Executive 110
3 Shadow work 115
3.1 Case study 1: Undocumented migrant labourers 117
3.2 Case study 2: Sex workers 124
4 Conclusion: bringing work out of the shadows 133
4.1 Chapter summary 135
References 136

1 Introduction

In this chapter, you will look at the different ways in which social scientists seek to describe and understand the social worlds of work. Work can take many forms. It is easy to slip into thinking that an activity counts as work only if someone is paid for doing it. However, that definition excludes all sorts of activities that might count as work but which are not done in exchange for money – for example, childcare, housework, or providing long-term care for family members.

Even if we use paid employment as the definition of work, however, things are far from straightforward, because paid work can take different forms. Paid work itself is usually taken to mean employment in the shape of a defined job, with a contract and regular agreed payments from which taxation is deducted. But not all paid work takes this form. Some kinds of paid work are much more casual, occasional and unpredictable. And some forms of paid work are deliberately hidden – perhaps from tax authorities, government departments and inspectors, or, more generally, from the public eye. In this chapter we direct our attention to *describing* and *understanding* those kinds of work which take place in these sometimes hidden, often shadowy zones.

This chapter focuses on 'shadow work', a term which will be used to describe the various forms of labour that go on outside of the **formal economy** of registered, waged and taxed employment. Shadow work may be undeclared and is largely unregulated by government offices and agencies. For this reason, it is often characterised by high levels of exploitation, risk and vulnerability. But as well as signifying something that is partly concealed, the term shadow work is also meant to indicate that the sorts of work involved may well mirror that performed in the formal labour market. In this chapter, I shall be inviting you to think about the ways in which social science engages with the experiences and problems faced by people involved in shadow work. I shall be asking you to think about how social scientists go about *describing* things that are hidden from public view, and also about how they analyse the evidence they gather to gain a better *understanding* of issues like shadow work. By looking at this relationship, by the end of the chapter you will have seen how social science understandings of data and evidence always involve an evaluation of what to study, how to undertake an investigation and how to interpret results. The example of social science investigations of shadow work illustrates the degree to which, we might say, 'facts don't speak for themselves'.

The **formal economy** represents all legitimate and officially recognised activities associated with the production, distribution, exchange and consumption of goods and services.

To introduce the topic, it is helpful to look at an example which illustrates some of the issues raised by considering the nature of shadow work. This is the case of twenty-three undeclared migrant workers from Fujian in China who died in 2004 while working as cockle-pickers in Morecambe Bay in the north-west of England. Reading 3.1 is an extract from a newspaper report on the aftermath of this tragedy.

Reading 3.1

Drowned cockle picker to be buried at home in China

A woman who was swept to sea with her husband in the Morecambe Bay cockle picker tragedy six years ago will be buried alongside her husband in China, a detective said today. An inquest ruled today that a human skull found on a beach in Silverdale, Lancashire, in July was that of 37-year-old Liu Qin Ying who went missing, presumed dead, on the night of February 5, 2004. The body of her husband, Xu Yu Hua, was recovered the following day after the alarm was raised in 2004. Police believe 23 Chinese men and women died but only 21 bodies were recovered after the disaster. All the victims, who were illegal immigrants, were caught in fast rising tides on Warton Sands, off Hest Bank. At least 26 children lost parents in the tragedy, including Xu Bin, now aged 19, the only son of the dead couple.

(Source: *The Independent*, 20 October 2010)

The Morecambe Bay disaster was one occasion when the nature of shadow work became a visible, public issue in the United Kingdom. The cockle-pickers were working without safety equipment at low tide in an area that became submerged in water. They were 'shadow workers', lacking documents authorising them to work legally in the UK, and dependent on gangmasters both to obtain work and to make temporary living arrangements for them. It later emerged that local people had been warning the authorities for some time about untrained cockle-pickers being put to work in dangerous conditions. Following the disaster, five people were charged with manslaughter, perverting the course of justice and assisting the contravention of immigration law. The gangmaster, Lin Liangren, was convicted of twenty-one counts of manslaughter and sentenced to fourteen years' imprisonment. The Morecambe Bay incident served to expose publicly the exploitation of migrant labourers, and highlighted the appalling conditions experienced by some of them.

Since the disaster, greater attention has been paid to the activities of gangmasters who organise casual migrant workers, with a Gangmasters Licensing Authority being established to monitor third-party labour providers. Despite the introduction of such forms of regulation and the severe penalties directed at people convicted of people-trafficking, a large number of undocumented migrants still work illegally in the UK. What is more, the conditions of neglect and mistreatment that characterised the Morecambe Bay disaster remain common problems for shadow workers, who are often involved in jobs that other people are reluctant to undertake in the formal economy. Many illegal labourers who work in construction, catering and farming, for example, exist on poverty wages and work long hours without adequate health and safety protection (Joseph Rowntree Foundation, 2006).

The Morecambe Bay tragedy highlights the close relationship between informal forms of shadow work and the experience of exploitation and vulnerability of those undertaking such work. There is a developing body of social science research that seeks to generate data and evidence about these activities, and to understand the effects of shadow work on those involved and on wider society. In this chapter, you will look at different examples of this type of social science research. One thing which will become clear is that research on this topic is unavoidably **evaluative** – that is, it involves interpretation, appraisal and judgement. There are two reasons for this. First, the topics covered in the chapter, such as the illegal employment of migrant labour, and sex work, are controversial public issues. Second, and related to this, the generation of data and the interpretation of the meaning of evidence about these topics are always shaped by particular purposes and intentions.

Evaluative signifies something that pertains to evaluation; that is, the assessment and judgement of value.

Figure 3.1 The Morecambe Bay cockle-pickers

1.1 Structure of the chapter

The **informal economy** represents all illegal, hidden and unofficial ('shadow') activities associated with the production, distribution, exchange and consumption of goods and services.

This chapter begins by looking in detail at the nature of shadow work in the **informal economy**, at the risks involved in such work, and at the ways that social scientists go about describing and developing understandings of shadow work. Section 2 discusses how social scientists use facts to generate descriptions and understandings of workplace risks, initially in the formal economy. Section 3 then examines in more detail the relationship between facts, concepts and theories, by focusing on two case studies of shadow work. In the first case study, the example of migrant workers working illegally in the UK is used to bring to the fore the ways in which social science addresses the dangers surrounding undocumented labour, the role of migrant workers in the wider economy and the regulatory position of the state. In the second case study, the ways in which social science investigates the experiences and practices of sex workers are examined.

1.2 Aims of the chapter

This chapter aims to:

- demonstrate the uses of social science research in *describing* and *understanding* hidden, informal areas of work (or shadow work)
- explain why, in the social sciences, 'facts don't speak for themselves'
- examine the relationship between facts and concepts in generating descriptions and understandings
- introduce the use of case study research in the social sciences.

2 Establishing the facts about work

In this section, you will look at how social scientists use facts, concepts and theories to generate descriptions and understandings of different forms of work. One of the classic social science accounts of work is provided by Karl Marx. Writing in the middle of the nineteenth century, Marx argued that in **capitalistism** societies most people have to work for a wage in order to support themselves. What he called the 'dull compulsion of economic relations' (1867, p. 737) means that people have no choice other than to sell their 'labour power' on the market. In Marx's view, this is the source of the sustained exploitation of the mass of workers by a privileged class of property owners. But Marx also emphasised how workers mobilise collectively in the effort to improve their working conditions – to increase their wages, certainly, but also to seek other improvements (for example, to reduce the length of their working day).

Capitalism is an economic and social system based on the related practices of privately owned business competing in a free market, producing and circulating commodititeis in the search of profits, where labour-power is sold as a commodity on the market like any other.

It is through the ongoing efforts of organised labour, making demands on employers and the state, that working conditions have been improved in what is now called the formal economy in much of the western world. For example, various forms of health and safety legislation have been introduced in order to try to outlaw inhumane working conditions. Exploitative child labour is illegal in countries such as the UK. And legislation such as the Equal Pay Act of 1970 has sought to narrow the gap between the wages of women and men in the UK. Moreover, systems of state-funded or state-provided welfare have evolved to support the changing nature of work and to provide support for people when they cannot work, because of unemployment, age or disability.

Nevertheless, across the world, including the western world, work very often remains a site of danger, exploitation and inequality for many people. The kinds of shadow work discussed in this chapter take place away from the gaze of regulation and are not subject to the rules and protocols of formal employment. The wages received for shadow work may be low, modes of payment may be uncertain, and the working environment may not be scrutinised by external regulators. Working to meet basic survival needs – such as food, clothing and shelter – still exposes some people to multiple risks.

Forms of work that are characterised by risks of some sort are a focus of a great deal of social science research. It is not only academic social scientists who generate data and evidence about the 'riskiness' of different forms of work. For instance, in the UK the Health and Safety Executive (HSE) is the public body that uses measures of fatality, injury and disease to compile databases and reports on safety in the workplace. This is an example of social science that uses quantitative data to generate descriptions of the risks associated with different sorts of work. According to the HSE (2011), based on formal data collected from employers, the four most dangerous jobs in the UK are those of:

- construction workers
- farm workers
- police officers
- refuse collectors.

In the UK, a range of legally binding employment rules and regulations exist to limit the risks that workers are exposed to. For instance, employers are duty-bound to undertake routine risk assessments in the workplace in order to ensure that equipment is in good condition and is properly deployed and maintained, and to ensure that appropriate and free protective equipment is provided (see HSE, 2011). At the same time, there has grown up a widespread popular debate about the idea that 'health and safety has gone mad'. Some politicians have helped perpetuate the idea that health and safety regulations have been over-extended, becoming ridiculous or a drag on employment and economic growth. Reflecting on the proliferation of risk regulation, the then Labour prime minister, Tony Blair, remarked, 'we are in danger of having a wholly disproportionate attitude to the risks we should expect to run as a normal part of life' (Blair, 2005). In a similar vein, the then soon-to-be Conservative prime minister, David Cameron, lambasted an 'over-the-top health and safety culture' which has 'become embedded in our national way of life' (Cameron, 2009).

Figure 3.2 Has 'health and safety gone mad'?

2.1 The Health and Safety Executive

How are we to evaluate these sorts of claims? Well, you might think that statistics could help here. In response to media tales of schoolchildren being banned from playing conkers in playgrounds unless they wear goggles, the HSE now routinely responds to populist claims about 'health and safety gone mad' by using its data to argue that, in practice, health and safety legislation and policy do have a role in reducing tangible harms in the workplace.

Consider the following example. In the construction industry in 2010/11, fifty fatal injuries were documented by the HSE (2011). This is a rate of 2.4 deaths per 100,000 workers in the sector. So the HSE helps to make visible the level of risk faced by workers in particular sectors of employment. Now, on its own, this figure does not necessarily tell us very much. Is this a high rate, or a relatively low rate?

To answer this question – to evaluate the data on the rate of deaths in one industry – requires some comparison with other sectors. Table 3.1 shows the HSE's data on the numbers of fatal injuries in various sectors. It places the figure for the construction industry alongside the figures for other sectors, and therefore enables you to evaluate whether this particular sector is more or less risky than others.

Table 3.1 Numbers of fatal injuries at work by main industry, 2010/11

Main industry SIC2007*	Agri-culture	Extractive; gas and electricity supply	Manufac-turing	Water supply; sewerage, waste and recycling	Construction	Services	All industries
Employees	13	3	25	10	32	37	120
Self-employed	21	–	2	–	18	10	51
Total	34	3	27	10	50	47	171

*SIC2007: Standard Industrial Classification 2007

Source: adapted from Health and Safety Executive, 2011

According to these statistics, a total of 171 workers were killed at work across all industries in 2010/11. In terms of industrial sectors, services and construction had the highest fatality rates, with forty-seven and fifty deaths occurring in these sectors, respectively. Thus, in *absolute* terms, construction looks to be the most dangerous of all the industrial sectors – since more people are killed in this sector than in any other.

But to assess whether in *relative* terms construction was the most dangerous sector, we'd have to obtain further data that compared the rate of deaths in construction with that of the rates in other industries. This information is shown in Table 3.2.

Table 3.2 Provisional rates of fatal injuries by main industry, 2010/11

Main industry (SIC 2007)	Agri-culture	Extractive; gas and electricity supply	Manufac-turing	Water supply; sewerage, waste and recycling	Construction	Services	All industries
Employees	5.6	#	1.1	6.8	2.6	0.2	0.5
Self-employed	10.8	#	1.1	–	2.1	0.3	1.2
Total	8.0	#	1.1	6.5	2.4	0.2	0.6

*SIC2007: Standard Industrial Classification 2007, # Rate not calculated

Source: adapted from Health and Safety Executive, 2011

This shows that the rate of deaths per 100,000 workers in agriculture, and the rate in water supply; sewerage, waste and recycling, are both higher than in construction, suggesting that these are actually – in relative terms – more dangerous forms of work.

To help put these facts into further context, we might want to note that fatalities at work tell only part of the story of the riskiness of contemporary employment practices. In 2009/10 the estimated number of *all* injuries at work which met the criteria to be reportable under HSE regulations was 233,000. In addition to fatalities and injuries at work, the HSE (2010) reports that 1.3 million people who worked during 2009/10 were suffering from an illness caused or exacerbated by their current or previous employment. Some 555,000 of these cases were classified as new conditions that had started during the previous year, including musculo-skeletal disorders, anxiety and depression. A further 800,000 ex-workers who had last worked over twelve months prior to 2009/10 were suffering from an illness which was caused or made worse by their former employment.

The example of the HSE data shows that, taken in isolation, a simple 'fact' – such as the number of deaths at work in a single sector of employment – does not necessarily tell us very much. In order to be useful, such information needs to be placed in a wider context – in this case, by comparing it with data from other sectors. That enables one fact to become the basis for an evaluation of the relative risks associated with working in, say, the agricultural sector compared with manufacturing. So, on their own, the facts about deaths in the construction industry don't speak for themselves.

If even at this most simple level facts don't speak for themselves, things become more complex when we look at the ways in which such statistics are actually generated. The figures above establish facts about *relative* rates of workplace deaths, by comparing them across sectors. But we might want to ask about the reliability of those figures in the first place. Some social scientists contest the accuracy of the HSE data, arguing that the actual incidence of injury and accidents at work is much higher than the HSE figures suggest.

This argument starts from the observation that the data collated by the HSE only involve fatalities, injuries and illnesses that are formally reported. For an accident to be counted by the HSE, it has to be reported by an employee and formally logged as an accident by the employer. Those accidents, long-term injuries and fatalities that employees and/or employers choose not to report slip through the counting net. Some employees may decide not to acknowledge a work-related health problem in order to protect loved ones from anxiety. Others may feel that their injuries were the result of personal negligence in working practices and may wish to conceal them. Some workers are so reliant on their working wage that they fear logging an accident will lead to dismissal. Furthermore, and particularly relevant to this chapter, HSE statistics represent those in formal employment, while those working undeclared in the informal economy remain uncounted. This is quite an omission, given that we know that much shadow work takes place in the most hazardous sectors, such as construction, services and agriculture.

There are also some more systematic problems with the data collection. Although the HSE (2009) is able to claim that the UK has one of the world's best records of health and safety at work, critical social scientists have argued that HSE statistics on injuries and fatalities at work underestimate the scale of the problem. The criminologists Steve Tombs' and David Whyte's research (2008), for instance, estimates that just a quarter of non-fatal injuries to employees are actually reported by employers. They go on to show that over 80 per cent of recorded work-related fatalities are filtered out in the HSE's headline figure and remain hidden in other categories of official data. For example, deaths caused in road traffic accidents in the course of working duties – which account for around 1000 deaths per annum – are excluded. Most European countries routinely include fatal road traffic accidents during working hours in their figures. The UK statistics also do not include work-related marine and air accident deaths, or individuals who die from occupation-related diseases.

The quality of the data is made questionable not only by problems of definition, but also by difficulties with recording procedures. Tombs and Whyte (2010) also observe that the number of HSE inspections, investigations and prosecutions fell dramatically in the ten years to 2008/09. Even very serious disabling injuries are not necessarily followed up by inspection. Set against this sobering information, the sentiment that 'health and safety has gone mad' looks as reckless as it is misplaced.

So when we look at the evidence in more detail, it turns out that the official data on health and safety risks at work might not tell the whole story. What such data present as 'the facts' depends in part on definitions, and in part on practices of reporting and regulation. The way in which the data are compiled, analysed and presented foregrounds some facts and may underestimate or conceal others. Nevertheless, these facts are circulated – as facts – and can inform, or shape, public understandings of the social world.

3 Shadow work

In Section 2, you saw how the risks associated with different forms of work are assessed through the generation and circulation of data on deaths and injuries in different sectors. And you saw that there are a number of difficulties involved in the collection of accurate and reliable data on these risks even in sectors that are part of the formal economy, not least because there is often something inherently 'troubling' about these issues for employers and employees, which may serve to constrain accurate data collection. So the facts about the risks associated with working in the formal economy are certainly far from straightforward. The issues associated with describing the nature of work in the informal economy are, you might suspect, even more complex. It is these issues that this section considers in more detail, by looking at two examples of how social scientists seek to make visible the experiences and perspectives of those involved in shadow work.

Most people in the UK who have paid employment can be classified according to 'recognised' occupational groups that are part of a hierarchical division of labour, paid according to carefully differentiated pay scales that reflect the negotiated rate for their skills, have their pay 'taxed at source', and are counted in various official statistics and so on. They work in the formal economy. But a lot of paid employment occurs outside the formal economy. The informal economy covers a very wide range of activities, not just unofficial, untaxed, unregistered work, but systems of exchange and barter that do not use money, forms of labour in which people are 'paid in kind' with accommodation, food or goods, and so on.

Some, but certainly not all, of this work is in risky occupations where the threat of harm is greater than in other forms of employment. Aside from the hazards that may result from working practices themselves, informal work is not protected by statutory health and safety standards and rights. And undocumented migrant workers who do not have permission to be employed in the UK usually lack insurance in the event of an accident, their employers have no statutory obligations to secure their health and safety commitments, and the workers invariably have no organised body to express their concerns.

Although it is difficult to know precisely the exact number of people who work 'undeclared' in this fashion, simply because they work outside the formal economy, it is estimated that the informal economy accounts

Gross domestic product (GDP) is a measure of the total value of goods and services produced by a country in any one year.

for up to 20 per cent of **gross domestic product** (**GDP**) across the European economic area (Joseph Rowntree Foundation, 2006, p. 2). In the UK informal working is thought to account for around 6.8 per cent of GDP, though this is recognised as a conservative estimate, with some assessments suggesting the figure could be as high as 30 per cent (Small Business Council, 2004). The scale of informal labour in the UK may come as a surprise to you. But it is worth bearing in mind that in much of the world, what is considered 'informal' in the west is much more like the norm. In countries such as India, Bolivia and Honduras the majority of work is undertaken in the informal rather than the formal economy (see International Labour Organisation, 2011, p. 3).

You have already seen in Section 2 some of the difficulties involved in describing the risks of various sorts of work. And you might well suppose these difficulties are only magnified when it comes to describing the risks involved in those activities this chapter focuses on: that is, various sorts of shadow work. But one of the most important uses of social science is to bring to attention the dangers, harms and hardships experienced by people who work in the informal economy and whose need to remain in the shadows is a major reason for the risks they face. In Section 2, you saw how quantitative evidence can be used to provide information about work practices, but also that this type of social science might have some limits when it comes to making shadow work visible. In this section, you will be introduced to an approach to social science research that is often used to try to better understand as well as describe the nature of social worlds – the use of case studies.

A **holistic** approach is comprehensive, complete and self-contained.

A case study is a detailed and intensive investigation that attempts to provide in-depth knowledge about a particular social phenomenon (Flyvbjerg, 2006). Case studies attempt to gain a close, thorough and situated understanding, and so often make use of research methods which are designed to generate rich and detailed qualitative data, such as observational, documentary and interview methods. To complement this material, case studies may often use contextual data, such as textual or documentary evidence; or employ quantitative techniques, such as surveys; or utilise existing statistical information or data. Whatever blend of methods is used, case studies always aim to look at activities like shadow work **holistically**: that is, they try to get a rounded picture of everything relevant that makes this kind of work available, as well as the particular conditions and experiences of the people who do it. This entails thinking about what is involved in these kinds of work. It involves asking questions such as:

- why is shadow work necessary?
- why are shadow workers' services required?
- what life circumstances lead people to undertake this work?
- what private troubles, if any, drive workers' choices and needs?

In the rest of this section, you will look at two examples of social science case studies on shadow work. Each of them shows how social science methods are used both to describe and understand hidden, shadowy activities. In particular, both examples illustrate the ways in which social science research can be used to bring into view aspects of shadow work that often remain unseen, and in so doing can help transform our understanding of the facts about shadow work. The first example is a case study of undocumented migrant labour; the second is a case study of sex work. These are, as you might know, both topics of public debate and often controversy, and one thing you should bear in mind as you read further is how social science research is used to support particular understandings of such issues.

3.1 Case study 1: Undocumented migrant labourers

As you saw in Section 2, one of the groups of workers not counted in HSE health and safety data is that involved in undocumented labour. Since the late 1980s and early 1990s, the mobility of people, goods and money around the world is often said to have increased greatly – as a result of what is often referred to as **globalisation**.

Globalisation is the process whereby places across the world become more connected through the movement of goods, services, people and ideas.

Figure 3.3 Migrant labourers strawberry picking in the UK

This has led to a net increase in migrant labour in many rich countries. There are tangible benefits for employers in having ready access to an international flexible workforce, such as being able to respond quickly to market demand, to increase and reduce outputs as necessary and to adjust prices. Successive UK governments have encouraged this flexibility to boost the UK economy, attract skilled workers and fill vacancies in unpopular jobs, while trying to maintain some control over inward migration. Many migrants work in finance, computing and engineering, for example, experiencing excellent conditions and commanding relatively high salaries. Documented migrant workers with permission to work in the UK are entitled to fundamental rights, welfare and protection. Employers must issue a pay slip, pay at least the national minimum wage and give due notice of the termination of a working contract. All legally registered workers are protected by various forms of employment and health and safety legislation: they cannot be forced to work more than forty-eight hours a week, and they have the right to breaks during the working day, specified days off and paid holidays. Their employers are bound by all the relevant employment and HSE regulations.

Yet a great deal of work undertaken by migrants tends to be in job categories that rank much lower in the occupational division of labour, typically in manual industries, in farming and in the service sector, often in hotels, bars and restaurants. A great deal of migrant work is clustered in sectors marked by poor pay, casual labour and relatively unregulated working conditions. While the majority of migrant workers in the UK have been granted permission by the Home Office to work, some – such as the Morecambe Bay cockle-pickers – have not, and they are effectively working illegally.

The difference between legal and illegal migrant work is critical in so far as safety, rights and protection are concerned. Illegal migrant workers come to work in the UK for a range of reasons: some have moved from countries in which paid employment is scarce; some wish to earn higher incomes and to send money back to their families; some may have fled their homelands after persecution; some may have come to join family already residing in the UK. Often migrant workers who have been forced to leave their countries of birth for fear of persecution but have had asylum claims rejected are effectively left 'stateless' – unable to return home and rendered illegitimate citizens in the country where they have sought asylum. This makes them vulnerable to exploitation, especially in undocumented work. In cases such as that of the cockle-pickers from Fujian, vulnerability can be exploited by unscrupulous employers or gangmasters looking to increase profits by employing cheap labour and providing no insurance. Understanding why migrant workers take the risk and put up with the difficulties involved in such work is one key area of social science research. You have already seen in Section 2 that collecting reliable quantitative data about the risks of work can be difficult. You will also recall from Chapter 1 that one way in which social scientists attempt to bring to light the perspectives of ordinary people is through qualitative work. But undertaking qualitative research on a topic such as shadow work is also a difficult task. Accessing the experiences and perspectives of migrant workers labouring without legal authority presents a number of challenges to social scientists. Living in a situation of anxiety about exposure, illegal workers are often wary of talking to strangers.

Nevertheless, social scientists do succeed in generating qualitative data about the lives of migrant workers, often through detailed case study research. For example, the criminologists Jon Burnett and David Whyte (2011) undertook a case study where they were able to reassure a group of asylum seekers whose claims had been refused that they could tell their stories in confidence, using pseudonyms. Most of the participants were not working at the time of the interviews, but all of them had worked illegally in the past and expected to do so in the future. Reading 3.2 presents part of Burnett and Whyte's findings.

As you read this extract, you might want to consider the following questions:

- How do the authors describe the conditions that make this kind of illegal work possible?
- How do they link their account of these conditions with the perspectives provided by their source interviews?
- How do they use this qualitative source material to propose a particular *understanding* of the relationships between migrant workers and employers in this sort of labour market?

Reading 3.2

The wages of fear: risk, safety and undocumented work

Working as an undocumented worker, as the interview respondents in this study all asserted, often means having no contract of employment, and no regular pattern of working hours and times. All fourteen respondents emphasised how their working lives have been marked by instability and insecurity. A job that provides work for more than 6 months is rare, and when work is secured, the hours worked each week can differ enormously. The reasons for this vary. But of central importance is the structural position that undocumented workers occupy in the labour market. Undocumented workers must show their willingness to work as and when required. Bekele, for example, worked for an employment agency where they assisted him in falsifying a national insurance number to secure employment. Ready to work, he was told to turn up at the agency early every morning to see what was available. As he explained: 'you just sit in the office till nine in the morning. You go at six in the morning, and sit there waiting for a job. They have employers who work with them continuously and somebody rings and says "I need people"'.

Undocumented working is therefore marked by insecurity and uncertainty. Hours worked may be curtailed when labour is no longer needed, and there may be periods when work is simply not available. In periods when work is available, undocumented workers are frequently required to work unusually long hours. Fabio explained this in detailed terms: 'you work twelve, thirteen hours (a day) because they know you haven't got permission … Basically they abuse everybody. But still, when you are working they act like they are God to you because they know you haven't got work permission'.

Whilst the EU Working Time Directive provides adult workers with entitlement to twenty minutes break every six hours worked … for many undocumented workers breaks and rests are denied. As Hamad explained, 'you are sometimes not even allowed to have a break for 10 minutes … [I]f it is eight hours, you have to do eight exactly'. Extreme levels of fatigue were commonly reported by respondents. Working without a break often means working without any chance to stop and eat. Respondents reported that working long hours is necessary to compensate for low wages. As Fabio reported, 'I am shattered but I have no choice'. It is to the issue of how this lack of choice – central to the exploitation, casualisation, and subordination that undocumented workers experience – is reinforced by the manipulation of wages that the report now turns.

Most respondents reported having worked for 'cash in hand' or 'off the books'. The highest wage that anyone reported receiving was minimum wage level or slightly above. The lowest was £1.50 per hour. Abdul recalled his first labouring job in the UK: 'I was working for somebody and they didn't give me any money at all … sometimes people are like that. For the first time I came to this country, in London, there were three of us and we came back and they didn't pay'.

With no access to welfare benefits there is no safety net for undocumented workers and it remains difficult for 'refused' asylum seekers to access medical treatment. For most of our respondents, being ill is not something that can be afforded. The destitution that often follows a claim for asylum being refused, quite literally forces people into work in order to survive. As Richard explained:

'I have a family and if I have a choice between working illegally or starving my family I will work illegal. Whether they catch me or not, I will never let my family starve. We apply hundreds of times to get work papers but they always say no. The reason? No reason, they just say no'.

The threat of destitution compounds the relative powerlessness of workers and disciplines them into compliance with degrading working conditions. The fact that employers have 'more workers waiting' is an integral part of the economy of undocumented labour. Indeed, it is this, combined with the stark reality of the situation that undocumented workers find themselves in that forces them to acquiesce to appalling conditions of work. Richard explained a job he had where: '[T]he shop owner was very badly treating us. He didn't pay good. … He was using us too much, for more than 14 hours a day. It was for £25 and if we were late for just half an hour he would take £5 from our wages'. Wage manipulation of this kind can have a devastating impact upon people who are paid well below the minimum wage, and exist far beyond the poverty line. Yet mechanisms of redress are virtually non-existent and employees are aware that complaining may risk dismissal. The consequences of a lack of organised representation are reinforced by the fact that there are many others in a similarly vulnerable position waiting to take the place of undocumented workers who leave their employment. Richard was bold enough to challenge his employer about the level of his wages and explained 'I complained every day but he didn't care. He said "if you want to go then just go. There are a thousand people out there wanting this job"'.

Predicaments such as the one that Richard found himself in are reinforced by policies which effectively criminalise undocumented workers for supporting themselves through work. In this context it is hardly surprising that respondents often used the word 'slavery' to describe a situation whereby their wages paid only provided for bare levels of subsistence.

Undocumented workers enter a market in which they have very little power relative to employers. Employers are empowered by the knowledge that they are more desperate for work than other groups of workers and that there is a ready supply of equally vulnerable labour.

(Source: Burnett and Whyte, 2011, pp. 16–21)

Let us return to the three questions you were asked to consider. First, consistent with a case study approach, Burnett and Whyte outline some of the background conditions that make illegal migrant labour markets possible. Of primary importance is an immigration system that creates a particular group of persons identified as 'refused', or sometimes 'failed', asylum seekers. Because of their status as illegal residents, these groups face significant restrictions that limit their workplace rights and entitlements. In labour market terms, this *supplies* a pool of workers who need to survive economically, but have limited opportunities to do so legally. The existence of illegal, undocumented work is also premised on increased *demand* for cheap labour from those employers who are unwilling to pay minimum wages or carry the costs and responsibilities of formal employment. The collusion of institutions such as employment agencies is also noted as another condition enabling illegal and undocumented work to flourish.

Second, the reading reveals how social scientists, using the qualitative testimonies of migrant workers themselves, can illustrate some of the **experiential** consequences of working in this shadow zone of informal, undocumented labour. The illegal migrant workers in the study reported experiencing a range of personal, physical, financial, legal and emotional risks. The researchers argue that by failing to adhere to basic health and safety regulations, culpable employers are routinely exposing workers to unnecessary harm. Serious deficiencies in this regard were raised by participants in the study, including a lack of training, guidance and supervision, and inappropriate or non-existent safety equipment. Poor wages, long hours and low status were also common. In their wider study, Burnett and Whyte also noted that nine of the fourteen interviewees had been seriously injured while engaged in undocumented labour. They also found that complaining to employers may result in instant dismissal, eviction from accommodation and ultimately deportation from the UK. This burden weighed heavily on many, and led to frequent moves from job to job so as to avoid detection by immigration enforcement authorities. Those who are refused asylum in the UK are not allowed to work, have no guaranteed housing provision and limited access to statutory support agencies.

Experiential signifies that which pertains to experience.

By giving 'voice' to these workers' concerns, Burnett and Whyte demonstrate that qualitative inquiry can generate descriptions of issues that are not available to quantitative approaches. They use qualitative methods to provide close, situated and in-depth descriptions, and connect these to the analysis of wider socio-economic contexts. Their case study provides a holistic picture of the problems and issues that surround illegal and undocumented work.

Third, this example demonstrates how social science description is closely related to social science understanding. By combining a description of the background conditions to illegal work with the perspectives of migrant workers themselves, Burnett and Whyte are able to give a strong sense of what it is like to work in this sort of labour market, and particularly the risks and vulnerabilities faced by people working illegally. But these descriptions are also used to throw new light on how such practices might be understood in *conceptual* terms. They use the words of their informants to analyse this world of shadow work in terms of the specific concepts of **power** and 'powerlessness'. In using the words and experiences of the migrant workers themselves, Burnett and Whyte are able to show how the risks involved in shadow work are related to workers' relative lack of power to shape their own lives. The relatively powerless position of undeclared workers exposes them to a palette of risks which they have little scope for controlling or limiting. Or, to put it another way, this understanding in terms of power suggests that migrant workers in this situation have relatively little choice in their working lives – they are pushed into particular parts of the informal economy, and find themselves exposed to various risks as a result. To express this in conceptual terms, they are able to exercise relatively little **agency** over the patterns and conditions of work they engage in. The concept of agency will be developed further in the next chapter.

Power, understood as the capacity to act, can be understood in two related but distinct senses: as power 'over', something exercised by one actor at the expense of another; and as power 'to', the capacity to act, to make a difference or take control over one's own situation.

Agency is the capacity to act freely according to one's own choices, intentions and desires.

In this example of case study research in social science, you can see how the approach provides a way of describing the dangers of shadow work. In Section 2, you saw how quantitative data can be used for this sort of description too, but also how they might be limited in their capacity to throw light on various forms of hidden work. In this first case study, you can see how contextually sensitive qualitative methods can be used to provide in-depth accounts of the lives of undocumented workers by earning their trust and hearing their stories. In turn, you have seen how this sort of qualitative data can be used to provide a specific sort of *understanding* of the plights and traps of shadow work. In this example, the description was used to support an understanding of the relationships between workers and employers in terms of the concept of power.

3.2 Case study 2: Sex workers

The concept of power is also important in research on the second topic to be discussed in this section: the example of social science investigations of sex work. Like issues of migration and employment, this is a topic of public debate and controversy. And perhaps even more so than that topic, the issue of sex work involves social scientists becoming involved in generating descriptions and understandings that are inherently, unavoidably evaluative – not just in the narrow sense of evaluating data and evidence, but in a broader sense of expressing *values* about the topics of research, in terms of why they *matter*.

It might be helpful to start with a definition. In social science, sex work refers to any act of providing services of a sexual nature in return for payment. It may be virtual or physical; it may involve one or all of a very wide range of sexual interactions, including those acts monitored in the sex surveys discussed in Chapter 2. Sex work exists in many guises, including lap-dancing, escorting and performing sexual acts on camera. So long as one person pays another for it, it is sex work. Before we discuss our second case study involving sex workers employed 'indoors', we are going to focus on those who work 'outside' in street prostitution. This is a controversial topic, one which draws into view the relationship between social science research and contested values. In looking at this second example of case study research on shadow work, you will see that social science debates about sex work often do not simply focus on questions of the morality or otherwise of sex work, but revolve more specifically around different *understandings* of the power and powerlessness of those people involved in such work practices.

While both women and men are employed as sex workers, most social scientists have tended to focus on the working lives of women in the sex industry, often from a feminist theoretical perspective. But feminist researchers are far from united in their views about sex work. Some feminists are vehemently opposed to sex work and see it as a form of exploitation and as a manifestation of male power that is degrading to women, treats them as sex objects and permits sexual violence. In contrast, other feminists deny that selling sex is inherently exploitative, and argue that women make informed decisions in deciding to engage in prostitution. In this view, sex work is a legitimate choice that enables women to earn an income. These disputes, then, centre on different understandings of power as it is manifested in sex work.

Social structures are stable and enduring social institutions, organisations or arrangements that make up the social world, and that appear to exist independently of individuals and their agency. Social scientists think of class, gender, ethnicity and nationality as social structures.

These differences of opinion within feminist social science are not just based on different sets of empirical evidence. Rather, they are informed by different value positions that are reflected in different understandings of sex work. For those who view society as male-dominated and inherently unequal, sex work is likely to be seen as a reflection of **social structures** that constrain women's capacity to exercise power over their own lives. In contrast, other feminist social scientists tend to focus on the ways in which women who earn money from sex are not just passive victims, but can be understood to be exercising some degree of choice – or agency – in their decisions to engage in this type of work. Taken as a whole, feminist research shows us that women who work in the sex industry do so for a range of reasons. Some will be coerced into sex work by manipulative and abusive partners or others; some may have resolved to work in the industry for a set period to generate a lump sum of money; some may be working to pay off debts; others may be funding a drug addiction. Across this variety of rationales, however, it is agreed that sex work is a dangerous profession (Lowman, 2000, p. 987). Sex workers can be exposed to a range of harms, including abuse, violence, robbery and rape (O'Neill, 2001). On average sex workers are twelve times more likely to die from violence than women of a similar age not working in the sex industry (Ward et al., 1999). And it should also be emphasised that prostitution is big business. An estimated 80,000 women are involved in street, escort, sauna and brothel prostitution in the UK and the turnover from prostitution is estimated at more than £770 million a year (Bindel, 2008).

Figure 3.4 Street sex workers in a European city

To appreciate the risks involved in this sort of shadow work, consider the example of street prostitution. It involves publicly soliciting for 'punters'. Money is usually taken in advance of the sexual act concerned, which normally takes place in the client's car, in an alleyway, or in a dwelling close to the original encounter. Clearly, this kind of work can be dangerous for the women involved. Prostitutes may suffer violence at the hands of their pimps (employers/managers). Men who use sex workers may try to avoid paying them, and local residents may harass sex workers in an attempt to prevent them from working in the areas in which they live.

3.2.1 The facts about street prostitution?

Beyond the risks involved in working illegally and in public spaces, other harms associated with street sex work include health issues associated with the spread of sexually transmitted diseases and drug use. In the UK, government-sponsored campaigns have sought to highlight public awareness of the dangers and harms associated with street prostitution. For example, in 2008 the Home Office published online an account of 'the facts' about street prostitution. This was informed by its ongoing research, including a report it had recently produced entitled 'Tackling the Demand for Prostitution'. The 'facts' that the Home Office published are reproduced here as Reading 3.3.

As you read this account, consider how this understanding of street prostitution presents the relative power of women who sell sex, criminals who traffic women, and men who pay for sex.

Reading 3.3

The facts

Most women involved in street-based prostitution are not there through choice. They are among the most vulnerable people in our society. Nearly all prostitutes are addicted to drugs or alcohol.

Many of them have been trafficked into the country by criminals, and are held against their will. Many were abused as children, and many are homeless.

> Kerb crawlers, on the other hand, have a choice. Men who pay for sex are indirectly supporting drug dealers and organized crime groups, and funding violence and abuse.
>
> (Source: Home Office, 2008)

One thing that should be clear from the reading is that this is not actually a straightforward presentation of 'the facts'. It is not that the claims made in the extract are necessarily false or unreliable. But you should notice that they are presented in the form of an argument – against the view that street prostitution is about women's choice, while asserting that choice, and by extension responsibility, lies with men who pay for sex. In this example of the official use of social science-based evidence, then, the facts about prostitution are being used to support a particular understanding of this phenomenon. In the reading, 'the facts' are being presented in a way that emphasises the general powerlessness of women who sell sex, and the different forms of power exercised over them by other people.

So, this is an example of social science evidence being used for a particular purpose, and it illustrates the point that 'facts don't speak for themselves'. In this example, 'the facts' are being used to support a broader policy focus on regulating street sex workers and kerb crawlers, a policy focus that also emphasises the risks for women involved in sex work as kidnap, trafficking, violence, and substance and alcohol abuse. These are very real risks. Social science research has estimated that well over 100 sex workers were murdered in Britain in the first decade of the 2000s, and that street sex workers are at greater risk than indoor sex workers (Levy, 2011).

Nevertheless, in light of the first example of case study research on migrant work that we discussed in Section 3.1, you might still want to know a little bit more about the views and perspectives of sex workers themselves – this is one thing that you should expect social science to be able to describe. You will notice that 'the facts' presented by the Home Office tell us about the women who are involved in street prostitution, but not about what they think and feel about their work. In Section 3.2.2, our focus turns to this very issue, but with a different set of sex workers – those who work 'indoors' rather than 'outdoors' on the street.

3.2. *Sex Work: A Risky Business*

Teela Sanders is a sociologist whose book *Sex Work: A Risky Business* (2005) is based on embedded case study research with a group of indoor sex workers, conducted over a ten-month period. She used a range of qualitative methods, including situating herself in the premises where participants worked, observing the environment, monitoring working routines and talking with sex workers. Having amassed over a thousand hours of observation, Sanders interviewed fifty-five women working in saunas and brothels and as escorts, conducted follow-up visits and engaged in outreach work to build up a rich picture of the working lives of indoor sex workers.

On the basis of this sort of holistic approach, Sanders provides a different kind of description of the lives of women sex workers, a description that is closely related to a specific type of understanding of the power that these women are able to exercise and the sorts of power to which they are subjected.

The first important finding of Sanders' study challenged the widespread idea that women sex workers (whether working indoors or outdoors) are always passive victims who are rendered vulnerable by their work. While the undocumented migrant workers considered in our first case study had relatively little autonomy and scant opportunity to reduce their exposure to risks at work, Sanders' shadow workers had developed fairly extensive risk management strategies. These included the following:

- the *screening* of clients, through which judgements were made about the suitability and safety of potential customers
- taking *precautions*, including taking payment in advance, deliberately keeping certain items of clothing on in case the need to escape should arise, and not wearing items of jewellery that could be used to choke them
- using *deterrents* to regulate unruly clients, such as inventing imaginary pimps and mentioning doormen in the course of conversation
- putting *remedial protections* in place to manage attacks should they arise – high heels served as ad hoc weapons, and knives and CS sprays were kept handy.

Further, in contrast to the Home Office's description of an endemic drug problem among street prostitutes (Reading 3.3), just four of the fifty-five indoor sex workers Sanders interviewed said that they used Class A drugs. Two thirds said that they had never been attacked or robbed in the course of their work. Sanders was able to demonstrate, therefore, that indoor sex workers had some power over their working conditions and were less exposed to certain risks than street prostitutes.

Yet she also was able to expose other kinds of risk for indoor sex workers. For street prostitutes, the risks highlighted in Reading 3.3 were of a medical and physical nature. The participants in Sanders' study, in contrast, discussed the psychological and emotional risks that they ran. Among those who had kept their work a secret, the risk of their occupation being revealed to families and friends was a constant concern. To avoid shame and stigma, various lies and alibis were constructed, and many of the women worked far from their homes, often under pseudonyms. They created various stories about the jobs that they did in order to mislead partners and loved ones. One of the participants who made the pretence of being a cleaner routinely sprayed herself with furniture polish at the end of the working day in order to maintain the facade.

Figure 3.5 Sex workers' rights march in Brussels

Sanders' study therefore throws a different perspective on to the lives of women sex workers compared with that offered by the Home Office. Not only does she study different kinds of sex workers (those working 'indoors' rather than 'outdoors'), in different establishments and environments, she is able to differentiate the types of risk that workers might be exposed to. Her distinctive contribution is to show the varied nature of sex work and the different and diverse experiences of women who undertake it.

There are two important issues to take from this in terms of social science understanding. The first issue to note is the distinctiveness of Sanders' approach to establishing the 'facts' in hand. Her use of qualitative interviews and observations, in an integrated case study approach, offers a complex and nuanced account of sex workers' lives. Even though she uses some numerical evidence, her study was not designed to be the kind of statistically representative study you encountered in Chapter 2 – case study research has a different purpose, seeking to provide in-depth analysis and interpretation of lived experiences, rather than general 'facts' or aggregate patterns and trends. What Sanders' study does, then, is to show not only how sex work is varied, and that there are varied relations of power, risk and dangers associated with it, but also that getting at these facts might require some detailed observing, talking and listening to women sex workers themselves.

The second important feature of Sanders' study relates to the conceptual understanding it provides of sex work. Her book describes the working lives of these women on the basis of extensive observations, which enables her to record the range of risk management strategies sex workers adopt. But Sanders then interprets and explains these activities in terms of the particular concept of **rational risk actors**. According to this idea, these women were making conscious choices about their occupation, and utilising various elaborate strategies (such as those listed above) to reduce risks to themselves and their co-workers. Sanders further argues that the women themselves operated with a 'hierarchy of harms' (2005, p. 44) through which risks were routinely and tacitly assessed, classified and ranked. This hierarchy explains the way in which indoor sex workers organised and prioritised dangers according to their perceived consequences and the amount of control they had in limiting their occurrence.

Rational risk actors are people who have the capacity to recognise and manage their own exposure to personal risks.

Sanders' argument that the participants in her study can be understood to be rationally assessing and ranking risks – to be rational risk actors – clearly acknowledges that women sex workers do have some power – and therefore some agency – to shape their own working lives. In this understanding, this power is presented in terms of the choices available to these women but within a broader structure of constraint – defined by their background, personal histories, position in the labour market and so on. The dynamic relationships between choice and constraint will be elaborated in the next chapter, which focuses on different social science understandings of the concepts of agency and structure.

In light of the issues discussed in Chapter 2, you might be wondering what authority Sanders' findings actually carry and how far her findings can be generalised. As already noted, this was not designed as a representative sample. So what use is this sort of case study?

There are two answers to this question. First, as you have already seen, qualitative research of the sort Sanders prioritised in her case study is particularly useful in providing insights into what social activities mean to those people involved in them – whether it is watching television (as in Chapter 1), or working illegally in risky occupations (as in Burnett and Whyte's research, quoted in Reading 3.2), or working as an indoor sex worker (in the case of Sanders' study). Second, Sanders' research is a particularly good example of the use of case study research, in that it uses a wide range of evidence to provide holistic and detailed descriptions that invite interpretation and evaluation through the application of concepts and theoretical frameworks. Sanders went about her research by accumulating data through observing the women at work. This enabled her to describe the complex tactics used to minimise and manage risk. She in turn presented this description in support of an *understanding* of sex work that emphasised a particular set of concepts related to the operation and exercise of rational action, choice and constraint, which informed a theory of power relations and their operation in a particular (sex) work context. What case study research is particularly valuable for – one of its most important uses in social science – is precisely the sort of ambition that Sanders' argument about 'rational risk actors' illustrates. Unlike surveys, the findings of case studies are not meant to be thought of as results that can be generalised. Rather, by providing holistic, in-depth analysis, often led by qualitative methods, they are meant to generate new conceptual understandings of situations and processes. These new understandings might be tentative, speculative and ambitious, and all the better for that – because then they can provoke further research, both quantitative and qualitative, by opening up new avenues of enquiry. What is more, case studies are an important part of the process of theory building in social science, a topic about which you will learn more in Chapter 4.

4 Conclusion: bringing work out of the shadows

This chapter has revealed very different kinds of risks and potential harms encountered by people in the course of making a living. The main focus of this chapter has been on the idea that 'facts don't speak for themselves'. One thing you have seen in this chapter is that facts tend to be used for particular purposes – in the examples discussed here, they are used to make visible the risks, harms and vulnerabilities associated with various forms of shadow work. Quantitative and qualitative data can be used for this purpose, but the facts about shadow work end up looking a little different depending on which approach is adopted. Statistics can be used to identify broad patterns and make large comparisons; in-depth case study research can be used to reveal the experiences, motivations and rationales of people engaged in shadow work.

You have seen in this chapter that describing people's social worlds, and the private troubles they navigate, is by no means straightforward. Social science has particular methods and standards for constructing credible descriptions. But facts, however generated, never just speak for themselves – they require interpretation and evaluation. Official statistics of the sort produced by the HSE, for example, don't just speak for themselves. To make them tell us something about the relative and absolute risks involved in different occupations, they need to be assembled into meaningful clusters, then compared and analysed. Sometimes they may fail to provide the most accurate or complete picture.

Not only did you discover that the facts about workplace risk might not speak for themselves, you also saw that in the case of shadow work they might not be obtainable in the first place. The chapter then looked in particular at the ways in which qualitative case study research can be used to throw light on forms of hidden activity, on shadowy forms of work. In the two case studies that were discussed in Section 3, you saw different types of methods and analysis being used by social scientists to generate and then give conceptual meaning to facts, to turn descriptions into the basis for understandings. Here, it was by giving space to the voices and interpretations of shadow workers themselves that you saw social scientists developing understandings, in particular, understandings that drew out the relationships of *power* that shape the experience of migrant workers or sex workers. In Burnett and Whyte's study (2011), attention was drawn to the relative powerlessness of migrant workers in risky occupations, while Sanders (2005) offered what is perhaps a counter-intuitive account of the opportunities for indoor sex workers to exercise control, or agency, over their working lives. Sanders' understanding of power, you will recall, contrasted with the understanding of power that informed Home Office understandings (2008) of the lives of street prostitutes, which presented women as victims without much capacity for choice making, or agency. Sanders presented a different set of facts about sex work, facts that were based not just on delineating the objectively different risks between street and indoor sex work, but on women's own understandings of their capacity to exert agency in these, and possibly other, risky work environments.

In showing you that 'facts don't speak for themselves', this chapter has begun to open up the role that concepts play in making sense of social science research findings – in making them useful by enabling social scientists (and others) to present facts in support of particular understandings of why certain things happen and what to do about them. And you saw in the discussion of case studies that concepts, such as understandings of power used to make sense of shadow work, can be used to generate theoretical claims that require further investigation. So it's not just that concepts are added to facts once the description is complete; if case studies can be used to provoke new research, then this suggests that concepts, and the broader theoretical frameworks that they belong to, also shape the generation of data and evidence right from the very start. In other words, this is an example of how conceptual and theoretical understandings can inform or provoke new descriptions. Chapter 4 develops this idea further.

One final thing about social science research on shadow work is worth emphasising. As with social science research on the effects of television on children's development, or social science surveys on people's intimate sexual lives, social science research on shadow work is inevitably entangled with public controversies – debates about immigration, about health and safety culture, about violence against women, about standards of decency, and so on and so on. If 'facts don't speak for themselves', then it seems that this is partly because they are inevitably tied up with values – and so can be used to present particular understandings of the causes and consequences of different private troubles or public issues. Facts are, in turn, always likely to be *contested*, and so are the understandings they are used to support – and not only on 'technical' grounds of the sort you have already come across, because of issues of sampling, or experimental design, or the generalisability of qualitative findings. Social science descriptions and understandings are contested because the topics that social science engages with are topics that people often disagree about quite fundamentally. The contested nature of social science is also developed in Chapter 4, and further elaborated in later chapters.

4.1 Chapter summary

In this chapter you have learned that:

- social science can be used to describe and understand different forms of informal, hidden or 'shadow work'
- establishing the facts about the risks of both formal and informal work is fraught with difficulty
- 'facts don't speak for themselves' – since not only are they sometimes partial and incomplete, they also always have to be analysed and interpreted in order to produce meaning
- case studies offer a useful way of obtaining facts about social phenomena that can overcome some of the difficulties of understanding shadow work
- moving from description to understanding requires the application of concepts, in the context of theoretical frameworks.

References

Bindel, J. (2008) 'Penalizing the punters', *Guardian*, 21 November.

Blair, T. (2005) 'Future challenges: living with risk', speech delivered to Institute for Public Policy Research, London, 26 May [online], http://www.ippr.org/events/archiv, 2e.asp?id=1497&fID=44 (Accessed 25 October 2011).

Burnett, J. and Whyte, D. (2011) *The Wages of Fear: Risk, Safety and Undocumented Work*, Leeds and Liverpool, Positive Action for Refugees and Asylum Seekers (PAFRAS) University of Leeds and the University of Liverpool.

Cameron, D. (2009) 'Reducing the burden and impact of health and safety', speech delivered to Policy Exchange, London , 1 December [online], http://www.conservatives.com/News/Speeches/2009/12/David_Cameron_Reducing_the_burden_and_impact_of_health_and_safety.aspx (Accessed 25 October 2011).

Flyvbjerg, B. (2006) 'Five misunderstandings about case-study research', *Qualitative Inquiry*, vol. 12, no. 2, pp. 219–45.

Health and Safety Executive (HSE) (2009) *A Guide to Health and Safety Regulation in Great Britain*, London, Office of Public Sector Information.

Health and Safety Executive (HSE) (2010) *Health and Safety Statistics 2009/2010*, London, National Statistics.

Health and Safety Executive (HSE) (2011) 'Fatal injury statistics', [online], http://www.hse.gov.uk/statistics/fatals.htm (Accessed 25 October 2011).

Home Office (2008) 'The facts' [online], http://www.homeoffice.gov.uk/crime-victims/reducing-crime/prostitution/ (Accessed 14 October 2011).

The Independent (2010) 'Drowned cockle picker to be buried at home in China', 20 October.

International Labour Organisation (2011) 'Statistical update on employment in the informal economy', 13 June [online], http://www.ilo.org/global/statistics-and-databases/WCMS_157467/lang–en/index.htm (Accessed 11 April 2012).

Joseph Rowntree Foundation (2006) *People in Low-paid Informal Work: Need Not Greed*, York, Joseph Rowntree Foundation.

Levy, A. (2011) 'Crossbow cannibal: he killed because it was easy', *Guardian*, 5 March.

Lowman, J. (2000) 'Violence and the outlaw status of street prostitution in Canada', *Violence against Women*, vol. 6, no. 9, pp. 987–1011.

Marx, K. (1970 [1867]) *Capital: Volume One*, London, Lawrence & Wishart.

O'Neill, M. (2001) *Prostitution and Feminism: Towards a Politics of Feeling*, Cambridge, Polity Press.

Sanders, T. (2005) *Sex Work: A Risky Business*, Cullompton (Devon), Willan.

Small Business Council (2004) 'Small businesses in the informal economy: making the transition to the formal economy', London, Stationery Office.

Tombs, S. and Whyte, D. (2008) *A Crisis of Enforcement: The Decriminalisation of Death and Injury at Work*, London, Kings College London, Centre for Crime and Justice Studies.

Tombs, S. and Whyte, D. (2010) 'The state we're in', *Hazards*, no. 109, January–March [online], http://hazards.org/deadlybusiness/thestate.htm (Accessed 11 April 2012).

Ward, H., Day, S. and Weber, J. (1999) 'Risky business: health and safety in the sex industry over a 9 week period', *Sexually Transmitted Infections*, vol. 75, no. 5, pp. 340–3.

Chapter 4
Theorising the value of leisure

Mark Banks

1 Introduction 143

1.1 Structure of the chapter 147

1.2 Aims of the chapter 147

2 Free leisure? Understanding agency 148

2.1 Defining agency 148

2.2 Leisure as escape 149

2.3 Leisure as investment 151

2.4 Theories of agency 157

3 Constrained and patterned leisure? Understanding social structures 162

3.1 Defining social structure 162

3.2 Class and leisure: material and moral inequalities 163

3.3 Gender and leisure: opportunities and constraints 169

4 Conclusion: comparing and contrasting agency and structure 177

4.1 Chapter summary 180

References 181

1 Introduction

In the last chapter, you saw how social science research on shadow work illustrates the idea that 'facts don't speak for themselves'. This chapter develops two of the issues that emerged from the previous chapter. The first is the idea that social science descriptions and understandings are informed by concepts and shaped by theoretical frameworks. The second is the idea that social science descriptions and understandings, because they are entangled in controversial and contested issues, are shaped by *values*.

This chapter focuses on two particular social science concepts. You will recall that Chapter 3 looked at social worlds in which people seem to be forced to undertake forms of work that are risky and potentially dangerous, because of the need to make ends meet. But it also showed the ways in which people do, in certain ways, shape their own lives even in circumstances which seem at first to be all about constraint and **necessity**. They are able, in social science terms, to exercise some agency over their lives. This chapter looks in detail at the ways in which social scientists use theoretical frameworks to generate descriptions and understandings of agency, and how they understand the relationships between agency and the wider social structures in which people's actions take place.

Necessity refers to those activities that are seen as fundamental for allowing human survival – such as earning money, working, or caring for others.

The chapter explores the concepts of agency and structure through the topic of *leisure*. As you will see, leisure is a topic studied widely in social science, but its definition and meaning can vary. At the simplest level, leisure is most often defined as the 'opposite' of work. You will discover that this is actually a contested definition, and that definitions of leisure are always wrapped up with debates about the value of work and other activities. Writing in 1967, the French sociologist Joffre Dumazedier proposed a clear definition of leisure.

> Leisure is activity – apart from the obligations of work, family and society – to which the individual turns at will, for either relaxation, diversion, or broadening his knowledge and his spontaneous social participation, the free exercise of his creative capacity.
>
> (Dumazedier, 1967, p. 17)

Being **autonomous** means being able to choose for one's self, freely and independently of constraints.

There are three things to note about Dumazedier's definition. First, he defines leisure as an **autonomous** activity, a realm of freedom separated from the 'obligations' of work, family and society. The second interesting thing about this definition also relates to the value of freedom: leisure is activity undertaken to exercise freely our creative capacities for social participation, pleasure or self-betterment. Third, you might have also noted that the description is gendered: it presumes that it is a 'he' who undertakes leisure in this way. This is worth bearing in mind as you read further, because it raises some interesting questions about the conditions for exercising the sort of agency associated with leisure that will be returned to later in the chapter.

You can see that this particular social science *description* is premised on a distinctive *understanding* of the relationships between individual and society. It places the value of freedom, exercised by an individual *agent*, at the heart of the description of leisure.

Pause for a moment to think about your own leisure activities. Do you feel as if you are the kind of 'free' agent of leisure Dumazedier describes? Or are the leisure choices available to you restricted or constrained in any way? In fact, do you even *have* any leisure?

Perhaps you do feel that you are largely free to undertake leisure 'at will' – how, when and where you choose. But maybe you can also think of factors which inhibit or constrain your access to leisure – perhaps you don't have the time, or money, or perhaps access to leisure opportunities is limited by where you live.

Thinking about your own leisure activities probably brings to mind the ways in which the choices you make about the things you would like to do are constrained or shaped by factors beyond your control; in other words, how your ability to exercise your own agency is shaped by wider social structures. To give you a sense of how leisure activities are formed through this relationship between agency and structure, read the following account of one person's weekly leisure routine.

> A couple of times a week I go to a gym near where I live. I work mostly from home and so (usually) have the flexibility to go whenever I want. The gym is part of a well-known commercial 'chain'. It is often quite busy, and so appears to be widely used

> and accessible to all. The car park is always full, anyway. But looking more closely, I can see that there are some discernible patterns of use. If I go in the daytime ('off-peak') slot, the gym tends mostly to be occupied by older people and women, with the busiest period being around the lunch hour or in the afternoon before 3 o'clock – the place starts to get a little empty around this time. After 4 o'clock, when the more expensive 'peak' membership begins, the place will fill up again, but with different types of user; a lot more men come in, and the machines are quickly taken up by people who appear to be very active – they're all in good shape, wear professional-looking kit and appear to be serious enthusiasts. They do spend a lot of time on their mobile phones while running, which seems a bit strange. The town where I live is a traditional English market town in a relatively affluent part of Cheshire – and it is noticeable that not many black, Asian or non-white people use the gym.
>
> Once a week I play football at another gym in south Manchester, in an area considerably less affluent and much more ethnically diverse. This gym is run by a government services company on behalf of Manchester City Council. I can't help noticing that the building is crumbling and the facilities are in a pretty poor state; many of the showers don't work and the place is often closed for repairs. There is talk that it might be closed down for good.

This is actually an account of my own weekly leisure activities, mainly going to the gym and playing football. My account reflects a few themes: how access to leisure is partly shaped by my other activities, including my work, and how this determines when I'm able to go to the gym; but also how leisure is shaped in part by access to facilities, and how engaging in leisure is rarely a solitary activity, but involves entering into various social worlds. Reflecting on your own leisure time, you could probably write a similar account, although you might enjoy doing different things, or experience different constraints or opportunities.

The two points you should take away from reflecting on your leisure time (and having a glimpse into mine) are, first, that patterns of leisure activity are shaped by social structures and are not just the outcome of free choice; and, second, that agency is both constrained *and* enabled by these structures. It is important to bear this dual sense of structure in mind as you read this chapter.

In social science the concept of social structure is used to describe the relatively stable and enduring arrangements, institutions and organisations which make up the social world. Social structures are often theorised as imposing constraints on individual choices and behaviours, or even as 'determining' them in some way. But, just as important, the concept of social structure is also used in social science to identify patterns of difference between people – difference based on age, class, ethnicity, gender or sexuality, for example. Depending on one's position within these sorts of social structures, the degree and type of agency one might be able to exercise might vary considerably. This second sense of social structure is worth bearing in mind as you read on, because it suggests that structures are not just constraining factors – rather, they might also be thought of as providing different resources or opportunities to differently placed, differently identified people.

You have already seen that moving from social science description to understanding involves reviewing and interpreting evidence, evaluating facts, and suggesting concepts that aid explanation. In Chapter 3, the concepts that social scientists were shown to be using in order to understand shadow work tended to focus on questions of power and (a related point) on what we have so far in this chapter called 'agency'. The degree to which migrant workers or sex workers are subject to the power of others, or are able to exert some choice and control over their own actions, was an important dimension of the social science case studies discussed there. You may have noted, implicitly, that the previous chapter conveyed the sense that it is actually more desirable for shadow workers to possess agency than to be controlled by others. In moving from description to understanding, then, the use of concepts is closely associated with the endorsement of particular *values*. As we have seen already in the definition of leisure, 'agency' is not just a concept; it is associated with positive values of freedom, choice, autonomy, and is offset against negative-sounding values of constraint, necessity and obligation. This chapter is going to look in more detail at this relationship between the concepts that social scientists use and the values associated with social science research, and will demonstrate the ways in which particular theoretical frameworks or traditions combine and interpret values and concepts in distinctive ways.

1.1 Structure of the chapter

Section 2 of this chapter examines the extent to which leisure can be judged as a form of free choice exercised by autonomous individuals. It looks at two theories of agency in social science – theories of **rational choice** and of **individualisation** – and identifies the values that underpin them. Section 3 looks at how social science theorises the role of social structures in shaping people's agency when they undertake leisure activities, in particular examining the influence of structures of class and gender inequality. Looking at the ways in which social science has theorised leisure in terms of concepts such as agency and structure, the chapter will show how social science descriptions and understandings are inevitably shaped by values associated with these particular concepts.

Rational choice theory emphasises that individuals are able to act autonomously in order to rationally calculate and assess the costs and benefits of any particular course of action.

Individualisation theory suggests people are becoming more separated or estranged from traditional social structures and arrangements, to the extent that they have to actively choose or 'create' their own lives and careers, outside of these structures.

1.2 Aims of the chapter

This chapter aims to:

- explore the social science concepts of agency and structure and show how they have been applied to different theories of leisure
- demonstrate how social science concepts are associated with particular values
- compare and contrast different theoretical approaches to understanding leisure, including differences both between and within agency-led and structure-led approaches
- show how all social science understandings rely on the combination of concepts and values in theoretical frameworks, and how these theoretical frameworks help to shape the generation and interpretation of descriptions, data and evidence.

2 Free leisure? Understanding agency

In this section we look at the concept of agency, and how it relates to leisure. First, we examine how leisure might be theorised as an area of life where people exert their free choice in order to 'escape' from social constraints and necessities. Second, we examine how an alternative concept of agency can be used to describe people using their leisure for **instrumental** purposes, as a way of accruing certain advantages in realms of social life, including worlds of work.

Instrumental means being used for a specific purpose or means. In social science, the word is often related to efficiency and cost-effectiveness in terms of satisfying particular ends, as well as ideas of self-interest and seeking individual benefits.

2.1 Defining agency

As you will by now have gathered, agency is a significant concept in social science. It is widely used to refer to the capacity of people to act on the basis of their own intentions, interests, or preferences in order to bring about observable outcomes in the world. It is a concept that is often associated with the values of individuality, choice and freedom. Debates about the degree to which individuals are able to act as they choose, free from external influences or pressures, and the degree to which their actions are constrained or determined by 'structural' factors, are central to a range of theoretical traditions in the social sciences, and across all disciplines.

Implicit within social science debates about agency is the idea that human beings have the capacity to reflect on and influence their social world independently of external constraints. This idea is associated with the notion that the outcome of any action is not determined in advance, but is shaped in important ways by the capacities and concerns of individuals acting on their own or in association with others. But as we have already seen, this notion of agency is not just a neutral or purely objective concept. It is associated with a set of evaluations of the desirable and beneficial capacities of being able to act intentionally, autonomously, free from outside pressures and so on. For example, when the sociologist Nick Crossley, in his ethnographic study of people's use of health clubs and gyms, describes how exercise can intrinsically 'restore an agent's sense of self' (2006, p. 47), he is not only describing a particular aspect of leisure, he is also affirming this range of leisure activities as valuable because it provides the opportunity for people to demonstrate their capacities to act autonomously and to reflect on and evaluate those actions. Agent-centred approaches are found across the interdisciplinary range of the social sciences, and they are useful for foregrounding the creative potential of people to comprehend the social worlds they find themselves in and, just as importantly, to act to change those social worlds as well.

2.2 Leisure as escape

Figure 4.1 Sir Roger Bannister: striving for freedom?

As you have already seen, leisure is strongly associated with agency because it is often regarded as one area of life, perhaps more than any other, where we are in control: leisure represents our personal time to do with what we will. As well as free choice, agency in the area of leisure is additionally associated with the idea of individual escape or the transcendence of ordinary obligations. For example, here is the former UK athlete Sir Roger Bannister, famous for being the first person to run a mile in less than four minutes, describing his motivations for participating in one very popular form of leisure:

> We run, not because we think it is doing us good, but because we enjoy it and cannot help ourselves … The more restricted our society and work become, the more necessary it will be to find

> some outlet for this craving for freedom. No one can say, 'you must not run faster than this, or jump higher than that.' The human spirit is indomitable.
>
> (Bannister, 1994, p. 249)

Bannister rather nicely captures the affinity between leisure, choice and freedom that was noted in Section 1. Leisure is linked here to freedom in terms of an escape from the restrictions of society and work.

The idea that we are freely choosing sport and exercise, and reaping their benefits, away from work and the various other 'traps' of life, is further developed by the sociologist Neil Lewis. In his study of rock climbing, he describes the sense of freedom enjoyed by climbers. He presents climbing as:

> an act of intentionality that thwarts the desensitizing and pacifying proclivity of the body under modernity, providing a moment of remembrance, a time of reaffirmation, to that which modernity ultimately seeks to replace: human embodied agency. In the perceptual world of the senses, the real world of the adventure climber is mapped via tactile navigation, via a body moving through an environment. Consequently, freedom becomes a form of embodied awareness: a choosing to sense, and, more specifically, a choosing to *feel* and *touch* an environment.
>
> (Lewis, 2000, p. 58)

For Lewis, modern life is 'desensitizing' and 'pacifying' and displaces authentic human feelings. These are to be attained only through sensitive, physical engagements with the world; in this case, in the form of mountains and nature. For him, such encounters offer the best opportunities to develop what he terms 'human embodied agency'. You don't have to be a rock climber to recognise this idea. People often talk about leisure and exercise 'energising' their bodies or 'making them feel alive', or say they feel 'fulfilled' only when, for example, they are playing a guitar, dancing, or riding a bike. The idea that leisure is one area where people can exercise their own agency, and so escape from restraints and obligations, is quite common.

In Lewis's account of leisure as a site for realising agency, two assumptions are at work. The first is the idea that leisure involves free choice. The second is the idea that leisure is a separate and quite distinct activity from other socially necessary activities and obligations, such as paid work or caring for others. This is perhaps the most popular, common-sense understanding of leisure, one shared by athletes such as Bannister and theorists such as Dumazedier. In the next section, I bring this separation into question by presenting a different understanding of how and why agency is exercised through leisure activities, one that suggests that it is possible to exercise agency – to express one's free choices – through leisure activities that lie not outside but within the contexts of work, and, by extension, in close relationship to forces of obligation and pressures of necessity.

2.3 Leisure as investment

While many people choose leisure activities because they are enjoyable or pleasing, or offer a form of relaxation or escape, it is also possible to think of leisure as a kind of deliberate and conscious investment – as a way of building up one's resources in the competitive hustle of the social world. In this understanding, agency can be identified in leisure activities not in so far as they represent an attempt to escape from work, but in so far as they are undertaken for instrumental purposes closely related to work. We might even say that leisure itself can sometimes be seen as a *kind* of work.

Individuals can use their leisure instrumentally to better themselves, to improve their social position. This is an idea proposed by the sociologist Pierre Bourdieu, who suggests that members of professional classes in particular invest heavily in certain kinds of leisure activities because of the 'material or symbolic profit they can reasonably expect from it' (1984, p. 202). For Bourdieu, leisure is undertaken because doing so is perceived to confer certain economic and social advantages. In a similar vein, you might be able to think of ways in which people use leisure to improve their prospects at work – for example by joining a golf club in order to develop some 'contacts'; or by going for a night out with work colleagues, or even with the boss, to try to 'fit in' with the office culture. In these cases, agency is exercised through leisure not as an escape from work, but as a kind of complement to the worlds of work that people find themselves in.

And if leisure is something that can be undertaken alongside work activities in this way, then it might also be possible to think of leisure as a kind of work in itself. For example, nowadays in western societies people are increasingly and consciously using their leisure time to 'work' on the self; that is, to physically train and manipulate their bodies and personal appearance in order to 'get on' in life. Some social scientists have suggested that in the competition for enhanced social and occupational status, building up what might be termed bodily or physical **capital** has become important among certain groups and populations. This is evidenced in the recent explosion of interest in working out; going to the gym; developing slender, toned and muscular bodies – in fact, in the whole culture of 'looking good and feeling great'. Indeed, the leisure, health and beauty industries have become quite tightly entwined with the worlds of work and employment, as choosing to 'work on the self', *outside* of work, comes to be seen as a way of securing advantages *in* work.

Capital refers to money or other forms of assets that confer wealth or other advantages on their owner.

Figure 4.2 The fit body: a form of 'physical capital'?

In order to better grasp this sense of agency being exercised through leisure activity as a part of strategies to sustain and enhance position and status in the world of work, you should turn to Reading 4.1, which is an extract from a research paper by Amanda Waring, an expert in leisure studies. Waring's work uses qualitative interviews and observational methods to explore the use of 'premier' leisure clubs by professional financial workers in the City of London. As you read, you should pay attention to the way in which Waring interweaves her own analysis with the words of her research subjects.

Reading 4.1

The symbolic value of working out

[T]here is a perceived association within and across the city workplace between 'healthy body and healthy mind' underpinned by a utilitarian emphasis on 'good health'. This is extremely interesting as it suggests that by working on their health and participating in body work during their 'non-work' activities, individuals will enhance their physical capital within a work context.

Within the city workplace the healthy body is more than just a resource which enables individual employees to perform their work effectively; it is a resource that can be drawn on to make a statement about, and for the self. Many interviewees reflected on the importance of body 'image' or 'style' among professional city-workers.

The research found that within the context of the city workplace the body is perceived as a visual representation of personal characteristics, in line with the old adage 'first impressions count'. As Jane put it:

> … working in the city, we are all presenting all the time and going out meeting clients[,] and it is important to present the right image [,] and appearance is always a major part of that …(Jane, lawyer)

In this way, there is a positive value attached to 'presentability' in the city workplace that encourages and reinforces the cultural and tacit importance of engaging in health and fitness practices. Specifically it supports an individual's quest to 'create the right impression'. Interestingly, the research suggests that the ability to 'make the right impression' is only possible because of the extent to which the value of health and fitness, and in turn presentability, prevails within the city workplace. In this respect, kudos can only be achieved if the activities are recognised by others …

The thing about working out is it takes a lot of hard work. People recognise this and if you look good it is kind of evident that you are working hard at working out. …(Jane, lawyer)

The pertinent point in relation to the competitive nature of health and fitness pursuits is that where there is competition, there is the potential for individuals to 'win'. As individuals internalise an awareness of the tacit value of health, engaging in health and fitness practices becomes a way for them to develop a competitive edge. Furthermore, colleagues are in competition with each other as they strive to be regarded as 'better' employees through a demonstration of motivation and dedication towards health and fitness …

Working out and getting yourself fit is obviously good for you but it also screams 'hey look at me, I am fit and able'. …(Danny, accountant)

The act of working out within the premier club environment therefore serves to reinforce the characteristics of a professional city-worker. In this respect, simply going to the gym, demonstrates and reinforces the virtues of competition, success and professionalism as individuals are seen to be conforming to the corporate ethos of health and fitness.

(Source: Waring, 2008, pp. 304–6)

Waring uses the words of professionals who work in the city to provide a sense of their reasons, motivations and intentions in undertaking particular sorts of leisure activity. In this way she provides a description of them as autonomous and rational agents, engaging in leisure activities that are motivated by the competitive desire to obtain advantages in the workplace, such as earning more money and status. While employers may well encourage this kind of leisure behaviour, it is the workers themselves who consider that they are doing the choosing. They are making a 'presentable' statement about their worthiness and value, by working hard in the leisure environment. Waring identifies an affinity between the kinds of leisure undertaken – focused and targeted gym work, attaining fitness goals – and the virtues in the corporate workplace of being 'fit' and competitive in business. In this example, then, we can see that people are exercising agency, but they are doing so within a context that rewards and encourages certain sorts of leisure activities depending on the degree to which they support particular cultures of work.

The freely chosen and instrumental aspects of surrendering one's leisure to the interests of work are further explored in research into what is called 'the creative class'. This term was coined by the economist Richard Florida (2002) to describe the growing numbers of professional workers in the arts, media, high-technology and other design-intensive 'creative' industries. In my own research on the creative class, I have observed that workers in such industries tend to speak enthusiastically of the 'necessity' of using leisure time spent in the 'great outdoors' to develop the physical and mental attributes that will help them in the workplace. In 'creative' professions that tend to favour radical thinking, individualism and personal risk-taking and innovation, working on the body, in your 'free' time, is one means of ensuring success in the workplace. Here is how I summarised this finding:

> [T]he creative class appear to view the natural world not as a retreat and escape from the wearying constraints of base commerce but, rather, as a resource for the cultivation of a more focused and effective economic body. Rock climbing, cycling, trail running, kayaking, adventure sports in general are valued for their creative 'freelance' qualities, for their capacity to reinforce what Florida calls the 'I'm doing it' factor, for their abilities to set 'you against nature [and] your own physical and mental limits' ([2002,] p. 181). Nature, in providing the opportunity for continuous bodily engagement, mental stimulation, and a catalogue of individualized tests and attainments, offers an ideal proving ground for appraising the effectiveness of the enterprising new-economy 'creative'.
>
> (Banks, 2009, p. 674)

In my research, I argued that sports and leisure that involve personal, individualised 'tests' offer the chance to cultivate virtues associated with 'getting on' in the creative and knowledge industry workplace – such as autonomy, self-reliance and independence. And it is important to recognise that participants in the research undertaken by Waring, Florida and myself on these topics tend to regard this kind of work-focused, instrumental leisure as their own personal choice, not as an imposition determined by bosses or by wider social structures. Florida goes so far as to positively assert that, as a member of this alleged class himself, using leisure as a source of energies for future work 'is part of what we need to do as creative people' (2002, p. 169). Florida tells us that he spends time in long or intensive road biking – not for fun or escape – but in order to 'recharge' for work (2002, p. 169).

Figure 4.3 Road biking: pleasurable escape or training for work?

It is interesting to compare Lewis's earlier account of rock climbing with this account of leisure as a kind of investment in work-related activities. While both accounts emphasise agency, in terms of the human capacity for 'freedom of choice', the purpose and the ends of choice are very different in each case. The former sees leisure as an escape from work and necessity, while the latter sees leisure as a means of accruing advantage *within* the realm of work and necessity. Both accounts draw heavily from the self-understandings of participants themselves, using the kinds of qualitative approaches you have already come across. But they seem to support quite distinctive understandings of the concept, and the value, of agency.

Ask yourself whether your leisure activities display aspects of either of these accounts. Could any of your leisure activities be seen as a means of accruing personal benefits or social advantages? Or are they better described as a means of 'escape'?

2.4 Theories of agency

One thing that this chapter seeks to do is show how particular theoretical frameworks or traditions combine and interpret concepts and values in distinctive ways. Both accounts of leisure and agency that you have just read about in Sections 2.2 and 2.3 make use of the concept of agency, and affirm agency as an important value as well. But, in doing so, they tell different stories about the relationships between work and leisure. So how might social scientists make use of theory to place these descriptions of participants in leisure activities into wider understandings?

As already indicated, there are a number of theories of agency in the social sciences. Here we shall touch on just two of them. The first is an approach called rational choice theory, often associated with economics but also used in other social sciences, such as sociology or political science. It is a theory that suggests that social processes arise from the aggregation of the freely chosen actions of individuals. The agency of individuals is understood in a quite distinctive way in this theoretical tradition. Individuals are rational in so far as they assess and calculate their 'optimal' choice from among available options. They are assumed to be seeking to 'maximise their **utility**'; that is, to decide on the best course of action in order to achieve their desired ends or goals. Just how these ends or goals – called 'preferences' – arise, or even whether they are justifiable, is not a primary concern of this tradition. It has little to say about *how* or *why* people have arrived at the preferences they choose to pursue. We shall return to this point below, when we move on to consider questions of structure as well as agency. Individual action is 'rational' from this perspective in so far as the chosen means to pursue a given end is the most likely to maximise the chances of that end being attained.

Utility means something that is perceived to be beneficial or provides satisfaction. To 'maximise one's utility' is to attempt to obtain the greatest possible satisfaction from any particular action or activity.

This perspective might, then, throw light on the idea, discussed in Section 2.3, that people 'invest' in leisure as a means of optimising their career goals at work. The choices of Florida's creative workers, Waring's leisure subjects, or Bourdieu's professionals appear to confirm this ability of people to optimise strategically in order to maximise the utility of leisure in their work careers. Waring's research seems to show people who are involved in conscious, strategic calculation of what is in their own best interests. No one is coercing them into going to the executive health club; they do so because it maximises opportunity for personal advancement in the competitive job market. Florida goes further, quite consciously and happily endorsing the idea that leisure is a means to develop vital capacities and capabilities that can be applied to work.

None of these writers is associated with rational choice theory directly. But, actually, the idea of 'rational action' in rational choice theory is just a highly refined version of a notion that is much more widespread in social science, and which is particularly important in establishing the value associated with the concept of agency. And we can see in these examples that a notion of rational, calculative and strategic intention exercised over leisure choices is being used to affirm the value of agency as a concept with which to understand social practices.

Another approach that might be relevant to understanding the practices of leisure agents discussed so far in this chapter is the theory of individualisation associated with the sociologist Ulrich Beck (1992).

The risk society hypothesis suggests that modern societies are characterised by more pervasive 'risks' than previous periods. These include both personal risks that arise as a consequence of individualisation, and broader societal risks such as global environmental threats and dangers.

Self-reflexive means being able to assess and monitor one's own actions in a deliberate and self-conscious way, and to change one's future actions in response to these deliberations.

As part of his broader interest in what he calls **risk society**, Beck emphasises that individuals have become more exposed to many of the personal risks of the workplace, but also that people have become more **self-reflexive** and individually responsible with respect to securing advantages and rewards in the workplace. This, he argues, has been caused by a number of factors, including:

- the decline of standardised employment contracts and collective wage bargaining associated with traditional jobs in industrial societies
- the widespread promotion by governments and commercial institutions of 'free market' ideas of choice, self-responsibility and independence in work
- the decline of traditional social structures (such as class, gender, the nuclear family, neighbourhood and community) that tended to impose a common experience and instil a desire to conform to prevailing social norms.

Consequently, Beck argues that individuals are now more inclined to present and promote themselves as autonomous and singular beings in control of their own lives. Through what Beck calls the imposed 'necessity of choice', people have been forced to take control of their own work and leisure fates. We can see evidence of what Beck would recognise as 'individualisation' in the accounts of leisure discussed in Section 2.3: people taking on the mantle of promoting and expressing themselves as capable, free-thinking and autonomous agents, with no choice but to do so. The city and creative industry professionals using their leisure time to 'work on the self' could be seen as prime examples of a new kind of individualised and self-determining employee, eager to positively stamp their personalities on the workplace and make their personal mark.

While rational choice approaches tend to emphasise individual calculative acts and the conscious maximising of utility within the context of existing constraints, in contrast to this Beck provides a narrative of systemic social transformation in which established structures of constraint have *declined*, so requiring people to become more responsible for their own lives – whether they like it or not. For Beck, social structures such as class, gender, ethnicity, family, neighbourhood and community appear to have receded and so become much less effective in shaping individual choices than they once were, shifting the burden of responsibility to the 'individualised' agent. In this theory, the decline of established structures has both negative and positive consequences. It leads to an increase in personal risk and insecurity, as people are required to fend for themselves, but it also increases levels of independence from traditional social ties and constraints, and so enhances an agent's capacities for personal choice. In this theory, 'agency' has become more important as the result of a shift in the way in which social worlds are organised.

Both rational choice approaches and the theory of individualisation seem to throw some light on the ways in which people make use of their leisure time. Both focus on the exercise of agency by people able to effectively pursue their own goals. In rational choice approaches, the primary emphasis is on the calculated and conscious decision making of individuals, who express preferences in seeking to maximise their utility. In this perspective, social structures are acknowledged to exist but only as 'background' constraints that provide a pattern of available options for people to choose rationally between. Beck's theory of individualisation emphasises the increasing importance of individual agency as a result of the historical *decline* of social structures that previously determined people's life chances.

Both of these approaches, though different in important ways, emphasise the exercise of human agency in their understandings of social processes. In each case, structural understandings seem less important, either because of analytical assumptions about their relative unimportance compared with individual action (in rational choice approaches), or because of claims about changing historical processes (in theories of individualisation).

It might be useful at this point to remind ourselves of the type of people who are the focus of the social science accounts of leisure discussed so far in Section 2. They all belong to a particular section of contemporary society, marked out by professional and educational qualifications, well-paid and rewarding jobs, who have possibly inherited social status, wealth and ideas as members of a relatively affluent class. Is it likely that through having or acquiring this status, and occupying a particular position in the class *structure*, the members of this section of society have greater opportunity to exercise 'agency' relative to other, poorer or more marginalised social groups?

This question – of the differential capacity of people to exercise agency depending on their location within social structures – is not something that either rational choice approaches or the theory of individualisation is well placed to provide an understanding of. To examine the issue, we might return to the ideas of Bourdieu, who posited that strategic investments in one's body and leisure are not autonomous choices, but are patterned according to social structures. Bourdieu (1984) argues that people's leisure activities are actually quite closely correlated to the position they hold in social structures determined by class background, education, occupation, income and related factors. He has amassed a large amount of descriptive statistical data to support his argument. In this view, those city and creative professionals we saw claiming to be singularly and independently choosing their leisure activities might turn out to share certain collective characteristics in terms of interests or tastes that perhaps belie their claims to individuality. From Bourdieu's perspective, the fact that professionals are able to exercise choice is not because of an innate human capacity to rationally optimise their utility or because of a general societal shift towards individualisation. Rather, it is because as a group they share certain social, cultural and economic resources that allow them to do so. And the implication of this argument is that other people, with fewer resources, might have less opportunity to exercise 'agency'.

It seems, then, that any consideration of the concept of human agency as a means of understanding social processes such as leisure activity ends up leading us to ask certain questions:

- To what extent is the capacity to exercise choice, to act rationally in pursuit of one's goals, or to meaningfully express 'individualised' interests and desires shaped by factors beyond one's immediate control?
- How might choice be differentiated by patterns of privilege and inequality, wealth and poverty, power and powerlessness?

In short, any consideration leads us back to the concept of social structure.

3 Constrained and patterned leisure? Understanding social structures

This section considers the role of *social structures* in shaping leisure activity. The concept of structure points you towards forces and processes that constrain, enable and shape individual agency.

3.1 Defining social structure

As outlined in Section 1, social structure is a concept used to describe and understand the relatively stable and enduring patterns of social organisation that make up the social world. 'Thinking structurally' helps us grasp what connects individuals, or what common or shared forces or institutions shape people's lives – regardless of their individual desires or intentions. Social structures are often regarded as pervasive, systemic and geographically dispersed, and as having the capacity to exert some determining influence on individual action. In this sense, structure appears as something that stands outside agency, as a *constraint*. Importantly, however, as already indicated in the introduction to this chapter, the concept of social structure is also used in a second sense.

In this second sense, structure is used to identify *patterns* of difference between people – based on age, class, ethnicity, gender or sexuality, for example. Depending on our position within these sorts of social structures, the degree and type of agency we might be able to exercise will vary considerably. This second sense of social structure suggests that structures are not just constraining factors. They can also be thought of as providing different resources or opportunities to differently placed, differently identified people to exercise agency. In this second sense, structure and agency are closely entwined, and related in terms of the differentiation and patterning of opportunities and access.

These two senses of structure are closely related, and in this section we shall explore further the way in which the concept of social structure is used in social science by looking at how social relations of class and gender can be thought of as 'structuring' leisure activities in important ways. We shall look at how Marxist and feminist theories make use of concepts of structure, and, as you do this, you will see how the use of the concept of structure in social science is also closely related to the endorsement of particular values.

3.2 Class and leisure: material and moral inequalities

Class has a variety of meanings in social science. It is a concept most often used as a way of distinguishing groups according to their common material circumstances and interests, and social scientists tend to think of class in economic terms. It is measured through the use of criteria such as wealth, income, education and occupation.

In social science, the concept of class is associated in particular with Marxist theory. As you saw in Chapter 3, for Karl Marx, modern industrial societies were characterised by class division: between capitalists, who were the owners of property; and the working class, who were obliged to sell their own labour power on the market in order to survive. This is of course a rather simple picture of class structure. There are all sorts of fine distinctions within these two broad categories, but from a Marxist perspective this is the fundamental division that drives social processes.

In the new factory systems that emerged in western Europe and North America in the nineteenth century, most industrial workers laboured six days and often up to seventy or eighty hours a week. They did not have much time for what we would now recognise as leisure. Industrial workers' limited opportunities for leisure were further compounded by low wages, poor housing, ill health and early death. Job insecurity and unemployment were constant fears, and the lack of any significant system of welfare further increased the risk of falling into poverty.

From a Marxist perspective, the historical emergence of a distinct category of activity called 'leisure' can be traced to the struggle between these two broad social classes over these conditions of work. On the one hand, leisure time was the tightly prescribed and regulated surplus time that capitalists afforded their workers as a 'reward' for work, and as rest time sufficient to ensure their return to the factory refreshed for the next working day. On the other, shorter working days and paid holidays have long been a focus of the demands of organised labour movements such as trade unions. In such an analysis, through the dynamic between these two sets of interests, leisure became defined as a distinctive sphere of life: one that was the antithesis to paid work.

Leisure time was expanded slowly – for example, in the first part of the twentieth century a primary demand of organised labour movements in the United States was for a five-day week, leading to the emergence of 'the weekend' as a time of rest and relaxation. Nevertheless, leisure time was subjected to the same sorts of discipline that characterised modern systems of industrial production. In the industrial division of labour, workers were subjected to 'factory discipline' and clock time, which maximised the value to be had from the work of every employee, and prioritised work as a distinctive and necessary sphere of life to which all other activities must be subordinated. While leisure time was provided for and gradually expanded, it became the object of attempts to impose *moral* discipline to ensure that workers spent it in 'suitable' activities that would not compromise their abilities to exercise their labour power. Thus drunkenness, idle behaviour and 'immoral' activities became frowned on and workers were encouraged to take up suitably 'useful' or 'edifying' pursuits outside of work, such as physical exercise and study, to ensure that their newly established and demarcated 'free' time was appropriately spent. Social scientists John Clarke and Chas Critcher (1985, pp. 58–9) argue that the provision and close regulation of the leisure of the working class was nothing less than an attempt at 'the taming of a workforce', an imposition of 'proper' values in the interests of supporting and maintaining capitalist interests. Moral panics about the unruly behaviour of labouring classes fuelled movements that sought to discipline the slowly expanding area of modern leisure, such as the temperance movement, which attempted to regulate alcohol consumption and improve the morals of the working classes (see Figure 4.4).

So, from a Marxist perspective, modern leisure activities – as a set of practices of relaxation and rest, and a set of times and places where leisure is undertaken – emerged through the give and take, push and pull of different class interests. These include both the demands of workers for shorter working days, better facilities and better pay; and the attempts to discipline leisure time to ensure that it was spent productively, in line with the overall interests of profit and social order. In the terms already used in this chapter, we can see this process as an attempt by working people to exercise greater agency over the terms of both their working and non-working days; but also as an attempt shaped by the structural constraints, both material and moral, within which they were placed.

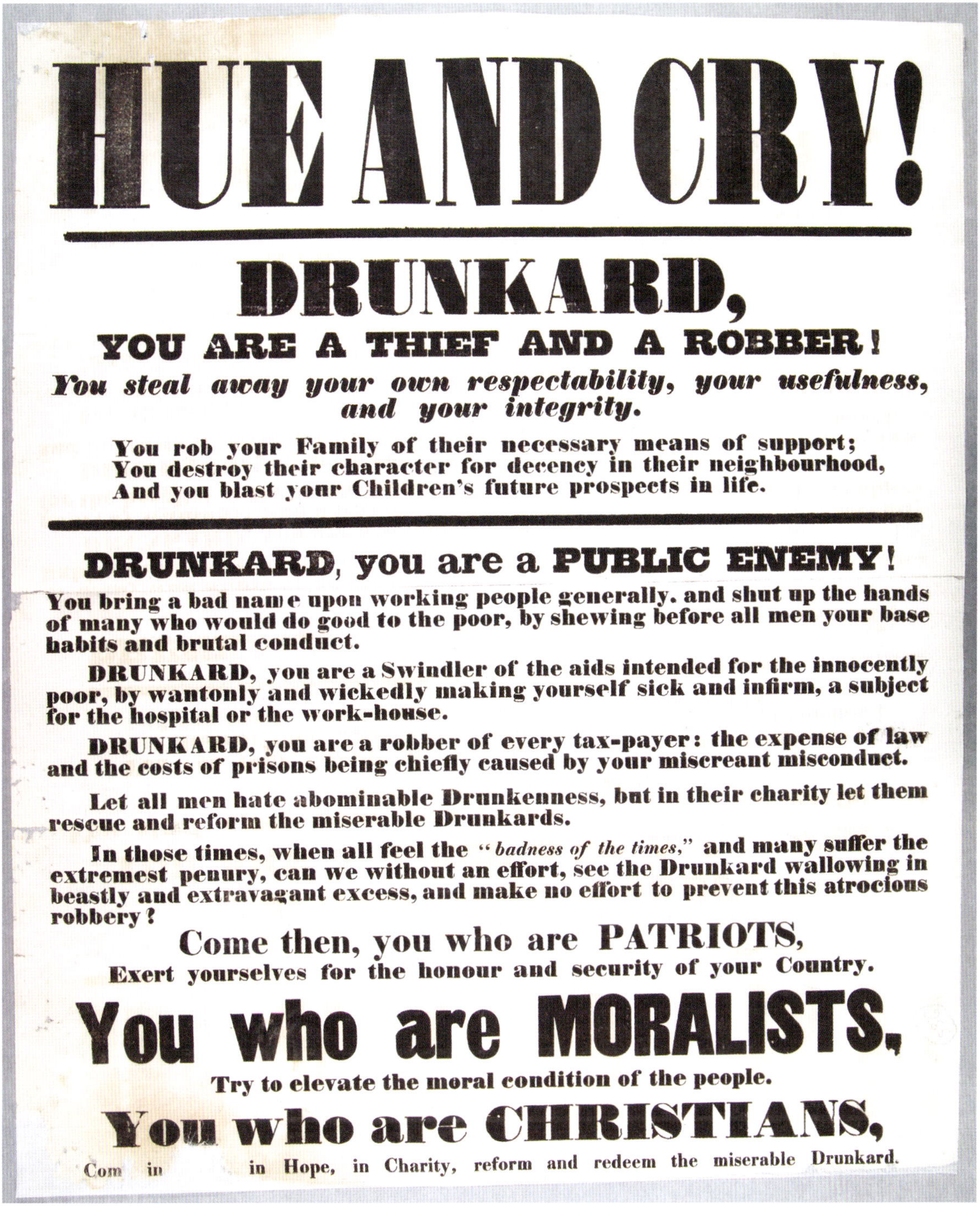

HUE AND CRY!

DRUNKARD,

YOU ARE A THIEF AND A ROBBER!

You steal away your own respectability, your usefulness, and your integrity.

You rob your Family of their necessary means of support;
You destroy their character for decency in their neighbourhood,
And you blast your Children's future prospects in life.

DRUNKARD, you are a PUBLIC ENEMY!

You bring a bad name upon working people generally. and shut up the hands of many who would do good to the poor, by shewing before all men your base habits and brutal conduct.

DRUNKARD, you are a Swindler of the aids intended for the innocently poor, by wantonly and wickedly making yourself sick and infirm, a subject for the hospital or the work-house.

DRUNKARD, you are a robber of every tax-payer: the expense of law and the costs of prisons being chiefly caused by your miscreant misconduct.

Let all men hate abominable Drunkenness, but in their charity let them rescue and reform the miserable Drunkards.

In those times, when all feel the "*badness of the times,*" and many suffer the extremest penury, can we without an effort, see the Drunkard wallowing in beastly and extravagant excess, and make no effort to prevent this atrocious robbery?

Come then, you who are PATRIOTS,
Exert yourselves for the honour and security of your Country.

You who are MORALISTS,
Try to elevate the moral condition of the people.

You who are CHRISTIANS,
Com in in Hope, in Charity, reform and redeem the miserable Drunkard.

Figure 4.4 Victorian temperance pamphlet: regulating leisure?

Today, we might imagine that such struggles have disappeared. But we saw in Chapter 3 that contemporary work remains dangerous, arduous and potentially highly exploitative for those at the bottom of the labour hierarchy, working in the shadows. This should lead us to suspect that the same sorts of issues – of inequality and difference – might still be at work in contemporary leisure activities as well. Contrary to Beck's position, from a Marxist perspective structures of class remain significant, and in fact they are observable not least in terms of social divisions in access to leisure. For example, significant inequalities in income mean that the poorest members of society are unable to access certain forms of leisure, and the public provision of leisure facilities in the most deprived neighbourhoods is insufficient to offer the kinds of high-quality, affordable and accessible leisure enjoyed by wealthier populations. As already suggested, the sorts of agency involved in leisure described in Section 2 might well be the preserve of particularly privileged segments of a class-divided society.

In order to grasp the relevance of the concept of structure in understanding the constraints and patterning of leisure activity, you should now study Reading 4.2. This is an extract from a newspaper report about levels of child poverty in the UK.

As you read it, consider how the leisure choices of Courtney's family might be shaped by social structures – and what these structures might be. You should also ask yourself whether Courtney is describing her situation in the same terms of agency that you saw in Section 2.

Reading 4.2

Children in poverty

Courtney lives in a bare-walled terrace house on the Canterbury estate in Bradford, West Yorkshire, one of the most deprived parts of Britain. She's been hearing a lot about money, she says. It is the only thing on anyone's mind as the summer holiday approaches, a time when having nothing makes the days drag by longer.

The eight-year-old has a list of what they won't be doing: swimming. Ice-cream. Seaside. 'About this credit crunchy thing,' Courtney says. 'It's stopped all the money and we've got no food.'

A quick check of the fridge reveals two small bottles of medicine and a two-litre jug of milk. 'We had to have tea at, like, almost 12 o'clock at night … and we've got no cereal, nowt, and I could go, like, another week with no food, but I'll at least have to have a biscuit or something.'

Payday is Friday in Courtney's house, where her mother Fran, a single parent with three young daughters and a son, is struggling to juggle childcare, benefits and finding a job. 'My mum says … she's gonna try and fill the cupboard up as much as she can, and that she's gonna put some money away,' Courtney says, but everything comes down to cash. 'We even have this box, and we have to put a pound in it every time the TV runs out. I just think that's crap.' She remembers the time last winter when Fran forgot to charge the other meters, and the gas and electricity ran out. They stayed huddled in bed as no one could bring themselves to go down the icy road to Fran's mum. 'I feel cross,' Courtney says, returning to their empty cupboard. 'I feel like I could just stamp my feet and click my fingers and it'll all be back to normal.'

Courtney is one of 1.6 million British children living in extreme poverty, defined as surviving on less than 50 percent of the average UK household income. This means getting by on less than £134 a week for a single parent with a child, or less than £240 a week for a couple with two children. Then there's straightforward poverty – a family surviving on less than 60 per cent of the average household income – which takes the number of children living hand-to-mouth to 3.8 million. That's one in three under-16s in the UK.

Four out of five children on Courtney's estate are from low-income families. A lone horse chews in the meadow, nosing between bags of trash. 'We're a poor family,' Courtney says. 'We're different. People with money, they have more stuff to play with in the garden. They have things in the house.'

(Source: Scott-Clark and Levy, 2011)

Courtney's story suggests that even the simplest leisure choices, such as whether to watch television, swim, or go on holiday, are constrained by access to resources, and patterned by inequalities linked to poverty and social class. People living in poverty, dependent on dwindling levels of benefit, unemployed, or in low-paid jobs – all of these groups are likely to have fewer leisure options, and of diminished quality, than other groups. Multiple material deprivations linked to income, occupational status, housing, neighbourhood, educational attainments and access to health and welfare services act as structural constraints, which can curtail and restrict individual agency.

But this does not mean that poor people have no agency. While structural factors inhibit choice, they do not entirely remove it. Let us think about the two theories of agency we encountered in Section 2, and the sorts of understanding of Courtney's story they might propose.

First, Courtney and her family might be regarded as acting 'rationally', choosing to spend their meagre resources on food rather than leisure: this might be the 'optimising' decision that it is better not to starve than to have fun. Remember that rational choice approaches suggest people make choices based on assessments of their own needs and interests. In rational choice approaches these needs and interests are not, in themselves, the focus of attention. These approaches have little to say about the content of those preferences, or the differential distribution of resources that shapes the set of choices available to different people. In an abstract sense, everyone has the capacity to exercise agency by making rational decisions, but this tells us little about how and why the range and quality of choices available to some people seem to be far wider and deeper than those available to others.

Second, we might reflect on the extent to which the experience of Courtney's family reveals agents who have been progressively 'individualised' by being freed from traditional social structures. In Reading 4.2 there is some evidence of agency and self-determination, certainly of persistence and perseverance, shaped by the necessity of choosing between limited options. But it is hard to identify the kind of free-choosing, individualised agents implied in Beck's theory: those making their own decisions and living creative and fulfilled lives. On the contrary, residents on the Canterbury estate seem to be living in the dark side of Beck's 'risk society' – they are trapped by poverty, unemployment and lack of opportunity, a situation only exacerbated by the decline of established forms of formal and informal support associated with strong welfare systems and robust labour movements. In this case, it seems that the decline of established social structures leaves some people with diminished opportunities for individual agency, lacking access to the resources that enable 'individualised' choices of the sort discussed in Section 2.

In summary, social science informed by the 'structural' imagination inherited from the Marxist tradition of class analysis sees systemic social structures of class as determining patterns of choice in leisure. Material inequalities shape leisure choices, affording greater opportunities to some people and imposing greater constraints on others, depending on their positions within various structures, such as the division of labour, educational level, housing markets and so on.

This perspective contrasts markedly with the idea of leisure as a realm of unrestricted agency, since it is claimed that opportunities for exercising agency in and through leisure are actually differentially distributed. While, as a tradition of thought, Marxism values a notion of 'the good life' quite similar to Dumazedier's ideals of leisure free from the imperatives of work (discussed in Section 1), it tends to see this ideal as inhibited by modern forms of economic organisation, rather than being ushered in by them. In the next section, we turn to look at another tradition of social science which looks on the worlds of leisure in terms of structural constraint and patterns of inequality.

3.3 Gender and leisure: opportunities and constraints

Feminist social science has particular contributions to make to understandings of processes of work and leisure. The principal focus here is on social relations of gender, and in particular on inequalities and differences between men and women in different spheres of social activity. Feminist scholars, from a variety of interdisciplinary backgrounds and perspectives, have shown how the capacity for agency is shaped by structures of gender inequality in the realms of paid work, domestic labour and leisure. In particular, it is a routine finding of social science research that men have more leisure time than women. Furthermore, from a feminist perspective that emphasises social relations of gender, this relative advantage is acquired at the expense of women's leisure time.

The reasons for gender inequality in leisure are many, including the traditional, historical dominance of men in the public sphere (especially in paid employment and job seniority) and the relative restriction of women to the private sphere of the home. Historically, in modern capitalist societies, as the 'breadwinners', men took for granted their entitlement to free leisure time outside of work. The traditional role of women as 'home-makers' or 'housewives' ensured that they carried the burden of domestic labour and childcare, and were often denied leisure time either in the home (as a place of unrecognised, unpaid work), or outside of it. These patterns may have altered to some extent, not least with the increasing entry of women into the labour market, but patterns of inequality in leisure and domestic labour remain stubbornly gendered and unequal.

These historically resonant patterns of gendered inequality also have conceptual significance. You will recall from Section 1 that it is common for social scientists to define leisure time as the opposite of paid employment in the public world of work. However, feminist social scientists have pointed out that this definition is insufficient because it has rendered women's experience of both work and leisure invisible. In Reading 4.3 the social historian Claire Langhamer suggests why this might be so.

Reading 4.3

The problems of defining women's work and leisure

[Feminist scholars] have argued that a conceptualisation of leisure as fundamentally distinct from work is unhelpful to the study of women's leisure, and, indeed, actually invalidates the experiences of women. Unwaged domestic labour is excluded from the category 'work' in this conception; consequently, the leisure experiences of those who work in the home are ignored … Feminists also argue that a conceptualisation of leisure as separate and opposite to paid work distorts the experience of women. Many women – notably those with family responsibilities – do not necessarily experience a sharp distinction between work and leisure, and for many the two interact, often occurring simultaneously. For example a 'work' activity such as ironing may be accompanied by the 'leisure' of listening to the radio. Other activities may be work and leisure at different times (an example would be cooking) and in other circumstances, work and leisure can be different dimensions of the same thing, the self-catering holiday being one such case.

(Source: Langhamer, 2000, pp. 16–17)

Feminist scholarship therefore reveals that the conventional way of conceptualising work and leisure as distinct or opposing realms of activity – one as a realm of necessity and the other as a realm of agency – creates problems in terms of properly describing women's work and leisure. In particular, it tends to hide from view the work that is involved in making possible leisure activities, not least the ordinary tasks of everyday life still disproportionately undertaken by women.

Figure 4.5 A view of gendered work and leisure

The image of the majority of women as housewives, labouring in the home and denied employment and leisure choices, might seem outdated. But while the traditional gender division of labour has been challenged, particularly since the latter part of the twentieth century when women began to enter the labour market in increasing numbers, differences in the leisure time enjoyed by women and men remain significant. For a start, in the UK women are still, on average, paid less than men: in 2010, forty years after the Equal Pay Act, men earned 10.2 per cent more than women in hourly full-time pay and 19.9 per cent more in median annual salary (Office for National Statistics, 2010). This represents a significant gender inequality in the ability to pay for leisure services. Women are also more likely to have multiple jobs, often juggling part-time, casual and informal work in lower-status job roles that permit less flexibility and freedom over terms and conditions of work, which further compromises opportunities for leisure time. And it is still the case that women on average undertake the bulk of unpaid caring and domestic labour outside of the formal workplace, especially in the home. These differences are illustrated in Table 4.1, which shows the daily 'time use' of men and women.

Table 4.1 Gendered uses of time in the UK, 2005

	Average hours and minutes per day	
	Males	Females
Sleep	8.04	8.18
Resting	0.43	0.48
Personal care	0.40	0.48
Eating and drinking	1.25	1.19
Leisure	5.25	4.53
Employment and study	3.45	2.26
Housework	1.41	3.00
Childcare	0.15	0.32
Voluntary work and meetings	0.15	0.20
Travel	1.32	1.22
Other	0.15	0.15

Note: All figures are for people aged 16 and over

Source: Adapted from Lader et al. (2006)

This table is worth reading carefully, because it suggests that patterns of work and leisure are gendered in interesting ways. In terms of overall leisure time, these figures confirm the fact that men have greater access to leisure time than women. You might pause for a moment and reflect, not only on these differences between men and women, but also on how the differences might be *related* – on how far the greater leisure time of men is dependent on the lower figure for women. It is this sort of relationship that a structural understanding is very good at pointing out, as we saw in the case of class above. For example, men, according to these figures, undertake about half as much housework and childcare as women do, on average. From a feminist perspective, the higher leisure time figure for men is enabled by the higher figure for housework and childcare undertaken by women.

As we saw in the discussion of class and leisure, the ability to exercise agency in leisure is shaped not only by access to material resources like income or time. Women's agency in leisure is also shaped by values about the 'proper' role of women in society, which influence their patterns of leisure participation. Just as there is a history of moral concern over the leisure pursuits of working people, so too there is a history of moral concern over the uses that women, and in particular young women, make of their leisure time. Reading 4.4, an extract from Langhamer's research on newspaper reporting of the rise of the 'flapper' and 'mill girl' in 1920s Manchester, illustrates this pattern.

As you read it, ask yourself whether this account of gendered moral concern has any contemporary resonances.

Reading 4.4

The rise of the 'flapper'

Throughout the interwar period, the leisure activities of young women provoked a contradictory mixture of concern and approval among readers of and contributors to the *Manchester Evening News*. For example, leisure behaviour was used to both identify, and to condemn the flapper: a woman to whom the pursuit of personal pleasure was deemed more appealing than marriage and – crucially, at a time of birth-rate concern – child-bearing. In 1920, one article recorded the words of Dr R. Murray-Leslie under the title 'Too Many Women. Is it the cause of social unrest?', and condemning the 'frivolous, scantily-clad, jazzing flapper, irresponsible and undisciplined, to whom a new hat, a dance, or a man with a car are of more importance than the fate of the nation'. … Similar concern at the leisure behaviour of the flapper was expressed by the male reader, later in the same decade, who claimed:

'a great number of flappers do swear and smoke. Two cafés, not a stone's throw from where I live, are every Sunday evening simply packed with this type of girl, joking and sipping coffee in the company of boys …'

'The flapper' constituted one archetype of the interwar period – popularly, although not entirely accurately, perceived to be an unmarried middle-class girl with time and money to spare. Within Manchester 'the mill girl' represented another image of young womanhood, identified as much by her leisure behaviour as by her employment. For example, an *Evening News* article at the start of the period expressed surprise, and an ill-disguised disapproval, of the leisure opportunities apparently enjoyed by this young worker. Under the somewhat sensational headline 'Dressy Mill Girls. Saturday Afternoon House Parties. Money to Burn. Chocolates, Cinema and the Hesitation Waltz', a Special Correspondent recorded the consequences of increased pay for the adolescent worker: 'A new type of factory girl has arisen since 1914. She can afford to entertain friends generously and she dances the hesitation waltz'. Thus an underlying fear of the economically independent working-class woman was articulated with reference to her leisure behaviour.

(Source: Langhamer, 2000, p. 53)

In the reading, Langhamer reveals how women's leisure in the early and middle parts of the twentieth century, across all social classes, was subject to the disapproving scrutiny of respectable male society, particularly when it appeared that women were emulating the activities of men.

This sort of moral concern about the leisure activities of young women has not disappeared. You can still find it at work, for example, in contemporary discussions of women's 'bad habits', not least in debates in the UK about female 'ladettes' and 'binge drinkers'. Reading 4.5 is an extract from a newspaper article which draws on a social science report about aggressive behaviour in teenage girls.

As you read it, you might try to identify similarities between it and the previous reading.

Reading 4.5

Young women drinkers – out of control?

The number of teenage girls who are physically aggressive and lash out at school and at home has risen at an alarming rate, experts claimed yesterday

More and more girls are binge drinking and – tired of being regarded as the passive sex – are emulating male behaviour.

The disturbing trend has been noted by the British Association of Anger Management, which is dealing with increasing numbers of 'out-of-control' and aggressive young women.

The association's findings echo statistics which found the 'ladette' yob culture was on the rise, with 200 women convicted of violent crime every week.

The number of women found guilty of murder, vicious assault or other attacks has risen by 81 per cent since 1998.

Leading anger management psychotherapist Mike Fisher said there was a strong link between the rise in binge drinking among young girls and their physical aggression.

(Source: Eccles, 2010)

Langhamer's account in Reading 4.4 reveals something of the double standard that operates in popular discourse on men's and women's leisure. Historically, men have enjoyed the fruits of economic independence and leisure more freely than women, with women often being condemned when they attempt to indulge in pleasures deemed to be the preserve of men. Reading 4.5 is another example of a popular media representation that focuses on the habits of young women, rather than young men, who – as in the 1920s – still exhibit more of this kind of 'out-of-control' leisure behaviour. As in Reading 4.4, the concern of the newspaper article is couched in terms of how such behaviour represents a danger or threat to what are commonly perceived as 'civilised' values and so-called 'natural' notions of femininity. As they were for the flapper and the mill girl, the apparently hedonistic leisure pursuits of the modern woman are stigmatised as an affront to what is considered to be normal female behaviour. The relevance of this example is that this sort of moral discourse around women's leisure activities is intimately related to changes in gendered divisions of work in the home and in the labour market – just as with the history of class and leisure, the gendering of leisure is a site for contested understandings of what leisure is good for, how this time should be spent and to what ends.

To summarise: in analysing patterns of leisure, feminist scholars draw on concepts of gender, understood as the structural social relations that shape men's and women's lives. Ongoing gender inequality ensures that women have less leisure time than men, and that they are more likely to come under disapproving moral scrutiny when they exercise their agency in leisure activities. The structural imagination of feminist social science focuses on how these patterns of inequality and difference in terms of agency are the outcome of the relationships between men's leisure and women's work, paid and unpaid. As you saw in Chapter 3, feminist social science often seeks to affirm the agency of women even in the most marginalised of social situations; but what we have seen here is that in feminist social science the value of agency is closely related to the critique of inequality – the structural imagination of this tradition emphasises the degree to which capacities for agency are unevenly and unequally distributed according to people's position in gendered social structures.

In Section 3, you have seen how two traditions of social science make use of a structural imagination to put into perspective social science understandings of the value of agency. Structural concepts of class or gender emphasise the constraints and conditions on exercising agency in leisure activities; and they also bring into view different patterns of leisure between different groups of people. These structural perspectives (those of Marxism and feminist social science, for example) do not deny the importance of human agency. Far from it, since agency remains an important concept in both traditions, which emphasises the capacity of working people and women, respectively, to act and organise to address the structural conditions they find themselves living with. But both traditions have a less optimistic and unfettered view of agency than those theoretical approaches discussed in Section 2. Where rational choice approaches and theories of individualisation see agency as the primary force shaping social life, these more structural approaches see agency as a rarer thing, constrained, shaped and patterned by social inequalities. In this respect, the primary value of these two latter approaches discussed in Section 3 is not agency per se, but a strong sense of equality, which shapes the aspiration that opportunities for agency, in work and leisure, may one day become more egalitarian.

4 Conclusion: comparing and contrasting agency and structure

In this chapter, you have been introduced to different theoretical approaches which use concepts of agency and structure to generate understandings of social worlds of leisure. You have seen that some theories adopt an agency-led approach, as discussed in Section 2. In these approaches, a concept of agency is made central to social science understanding, although different approaches endorse particular understandings of the *value* of human agency. In Section 3, theoretical approaches which adopt structure-led views were discussed. These approaches do not reject the explanatory importance of agency, but they do place agency in the context of constraints and patterns of inequality. Nor do they reject the value of agency – far from it: it remains an important **normative** reference point in theories which strive for greater equality and fairness. They do, however, adopt a less optimistic and more qualified understanding of agency, emphasising it as a shared, but differentially distributed, capacity to engage in social worlds.

Normative means something that is concerned with ideas about desirable standards and values, and what *ought* to be considered normal and accepted – even if this is currently not the case.

The use of the concept of human agency in social science is, then, closely related to the affirmation of a particular set of values. There is a distinctive moral concern animating rational choice theorists' insistence on respecting the subjective preference of individuals, and in the desirability of individuals to be able to express their own sense of self that animates theories of individualisation. They both chime with broadly shared ideas that people should be in control of their own fate and destiny, able to choose their path through life. Structural approaches also attach importance to the value of agency, but they see this as a value still largely unrealised rather than one easily exercised or obtained. A concern with matters of social structure is often dismissed as implying that this sort of perspective sees people as wholly manipulated or as passive dupes of forces beyond their control. There is a grain of truth in this criticism, but it confuses the descriptive focus of structural accounts like Marxism or feminism with their normative orientation. It is, after all, sometimes useful to be reminded that people are not always free to do as they choose, and that they are often subjected to forces beyond their control. This is true for some people more than others. Structural approaches attach the values associated with agency more strongly to the values of equality and fairness, and in turn they understand inequality, injustice and exploitation not just as moral judgements but as animating forces – as descriptive facts about social worlds – which help shape social processes and practices.

This chapter has worked through these issues of agency and structure, concepts and values, in relation to different theories of leisure. Table 4.2 provides an outline of the main features of agency-led and structure-led approaches, in relation to leisure. The categories at the top of each column – primary concept, theoretical approach, principal assumptions, object of study, values – are categories you can apply to other topics, in this book and beyond, as a way of helping you make sense of the differences and similarities between different social science understandings.

Table 4.2 Comparing and contrasting agency- and structure-led understandings

Primary concept	**Theoretical approach (e.g.)**	**Principal assumptions**	**Object of study**	**Values**
Agency	Rational choice	Leisure is the outcome of free choices made by conscious and calculating rational actors in the context of 'background' social structures	Individuals who act as 'utility maximisers'	Rationality, freedom, validity of individual preferences
	Individualisation	Leisure is the outcome of free choices made by actors progressively 'released' from traditional and declining social structures	Individual 'self-reflexive' social actors	The progressive realisation of human agency as a capacity for self-making, best expressed in non-work activities of creativity and self-expression
Structure	Marxist	Leisure is defined by class relations and differentiated by enduring social patterns of inequality	Individuals acting in concert with others on the basis of shared class interests; patterns of class division and inequality	Patterns of exploitation should be superseded by social arrangements that equalise work and leisure opportunities
	Feminist	Leisure is defined by gender relations and differentiated by enduring patterns of gender inequality	Individuals acting in concert with others on the basis of shared gender identities; patterns of gender differentiation and inequality	Opportunities for agency should be equally and fairly distributed

Perhaps we should end this chapter by thinking a little bit more about the topic of values in social science. One issue that this chapter has focused on, building on Chapter 3, is the idea that social science concepts are intimately related to the endorsement of particular values. It is quite common to think of values as being merely subjective or normative matters, that are offset against the properly objective matter of generating 'positive' (in the sense of 'factual' or 'truthful') social science descriptions:

> Positive statements are about what is, was or will be; they assert alleged facts about the universe in which we live. Normative statements are about what ought to be. They depend on judgments about what is good and bad, and are thus inextricably bound up with our philosophical, cultural and religious positions.
>
> (Lipsky, quoted in May, 1997, p. 43)

In this view, facts and values are clearly distinct and should be kept far apart. You should already have a sense that this is not as easy as it sounds, nor necessarily a good idea either. In this book we presume that facts and values are actually inextricably linked together, that values are an aspect of all parts of social science inquiry. You might worry that this means that social science isn't really 'science' at all, but just a matter of personal, subjective preference or even bias.

But consider for a moment the issues that you have come across so far – social science addresses issues of considerable public significance, whether it is engaged in gathering evidence about sexual practices to inform public health policy, or trying to make sense of the risks and dangers faced by people in different sorts of employment. Social science research is undertaken for particular purposes, to inform debate and shape policy, to enhance awareness and improve understanding. It is for this reason that values are inextricably part of social science investigation: because the topics that social scientists investigate matter – to people, to governments, to corporations and business and to charities.

And the sorts of issues that social science addresses, as you have also already seen, are rarely matters of consensus and agreement – they are controversial, sensitive, contested issues. So it is because social science is inevitably involved in enacting social worlds, as well as in describing and understanding them, that values are part and parcel of social science investigation. Values guide and shape the questions that social scientists ask and the topics they think are important. If this wasn't the case, social science wouldn't be terribly interesting, or important, or, in the final analysis, very useful.

4.1 Chapter summary

In this chapter you have learned that:

- the facts about leisure do not 'speak for themselves' but only through the application of concepts and values as part of theoretical frameworks
- leisure has been an important topic around which social science understandings of agency and structure, freedom and necessity have been developed
- agency is a foundational concept in social science and is used to inform different theories; it is also an important value affirmed by social science investigation
- structure is a foundational concept in social science and is used to inform different theories; it is used to bring into view the relationships between action and its conditions, constraints and consequences
- social science theories are both 'positive' and 'normative': they combine factual descriptions and understandings with values, because the topics of social science investigation are matters of importance and are contested and controversial.

References

Banks, M. (2009) 'Fit and working again? The instrumental leisure of the creative class', *Environment and Planning A*, vol. 41, no. 3, pp. 668–81.

Bannister, R. (1994) *The Four Minute Mile*, New York, Lyons and Burford.

Beck, U. (1992) *Risk Society*, London, Sage.

Bourdieu, P. (1984) *Distinction: A Social Critique of the Judgment of Taste*, London, Routledge.

Clarke, J. and Critcher, C. (1985) *The Devil Makes Work: Leisure in Capitalist Britain*, Basingstoke, Macmillan.

Crossley, N. (2006) 'In the gym: motives, meanings and moral careers', *Body and Society*, vol. 12, no. 3, pp. 23–50.

Dumazedier, J. (1967) *Towards a Society of Leisure*, New York, Free Press.

Eccles, L. (2010) 'Angry young girls: binge-drinking culture "creating a generation of aggressive and out-of-control women"', *Daily Mail*, 29 November.

Florida, R. (2002) *The Rise of the Creative Class*, New York, Basic Books.

Lader, D., Short, S. and Gershuny, J. (2006) *The Time Use Survey, 2005: How We Spend Our Time*, London, Office for National Statistics.

Langhamer, C. (2000) *Women's Leisure in England 1920–60*, Manchester, Manchester University Press.

Lewis, N. (2000) 'The climbing body, nature and the experience of modernity', *Body and Society*, vol. 6, nos. 3–4, pp. 58–80.

May, T. (1997) *Social Research* (2nd edn), Buckingham, Open University Press.

Office of National Statistics (2010) *Annual Survey of Hours and Earnings (ASHE)* [online], http://www.ons.gov.uk/ons/rel/ashe/annual-survey-of-hours-and-earnings/2010-results/index.html (Accessed 7 July 2012).

Scott-Clark, C. and Levy, A. (2011) '"Some people bully you because your house is not all fancy"', *Guardian*, 4 June.

Waring, A. (2008) 'Health club use and lifestyle: exploring the boundaries between work and leisure', *Leisure Studies*, vol. 27, no. 3, pp. 295–309.

Chapter 5
Forecasting the future of transport

George Revill

1 Introduction 187
1.1 Structure of the chapter 191
1.2 Aims of the chapter 193
2 Social science and contested public issues 194
2.1 Contesting 'predict and provide' 196
2.2 Using social science to contest public issues 202
3 Contested understandings of causality 205
3.1 Does building more roads reduce congestion? 205
3.2 Car use: poison or cure? 212
4 Conclusion: contested understandings of the future 221
4.1 Chapter summary 222
References 224

1 Introduction

Chapters 3 and 4 looked at the ways in which social science understandings are arrived at through the application of concepts and values within theoretical frameworks. This chapter moves beyond looking at *contrasting* understandings, and introduces the idea that they are often *contested*: that is, the idea that they come into conflict with each other, because they have very different implications in terms of how to think about and act on public issues. The chapter focuses on the role of social science in forecasting, modelling and planning for future patterns of mobility. It looks in particular at the ways in which social science is involved in contested understandings of the future development of different modes of transport in the UK, such as the car and railways. And you will see that social science understandings of mobility are contested not least because they can play an important part in enacting policy and public debates around transport issues.

Understandings of the car as a mode of transport are central to the ways in which social science has been involved in shaping patterns of mobility in the UK since the middle of the twentieth century. The car is an interesting case study for exploring contested understandings because it draws together some basic issues in social science. One of these is the relationship between individual choices and aggregate outcomes, and in particular the problem of what is sometimes called **unintended consequences**.

Unintended consequences are the unexpected, unanticipated and unplanned outcomes of actions, decisions and processes.

This idea is often associated with the work of American sociologist Robert Merton (1936), who first used the phrase 'unanticipated consequences' to conceptualise the problem of how purposeful actions might not achieve their desired aim because of the complexity of social systems. It is an idea, however, that is a basic theme of social science going back much further, at least to the late eighteenth century and Adam Smith's discussion of the 'invisible hand' of the market – the claim that the aggregate effect of lots of individually self-interested actions would be to the benefit of everyone. This is an example of a positive unintended consequence. But you can have negative unintended consequences too – the environmental costs of increased car use would be one example, where everyone ends up being negatively affected by the impacts generated by lots of individual actions. The idea of unintended consequences reminds us that seeking to control the development of social processes is rife with difficulties and dangers. In this chapter, you will see how social science understandings are used to try both to maximise positive unintended consequences and to minimise negative unintended consequences.

The problem of unintended consequences that the growth of car use illustrates can be understood with reference to the concepts of structure and agency discussed in previous chapters. On the one hand, the car has often been understood as a vehicle, literally, for the expression of personal freedom, as the very embodiment of uninhibited individual agency. The sociologist Richard Sennett, writing in the 1970s, captures this view of the car:

> Today, we experience an ease of motion unknown to any prior urban civilisation … we take unrestricted motion of the individual to be an absolute right. The private motorcar is the logical instrument for exercising that right, and the effect on public space, especially the space of the urban street, is that the space becomes meaningless or even maddening unless it can be subordinated to free movement.
>
> (Sennett, 1977, p. 14)

Sennett sees the car, and its association with the value of unrestricted mobility, as defining the meaning of modern life. Car travel provides the opportunity to move quickly, over long distances, and in pursuit of one's own interests or values: to commute from a home in one place to work somewhere else, to drive to the supermarket, to go on holiday and so on.

Figure 5.1 M6 Toll motorway under construction, August 2001

Of course, Sennett also intimates that this value of unrestricted mobility comes at a cost, in particular to the rhythms and interactions of street life. This is the dark side of the agency afforded by car transport. Chapter 4 discussed two related senses of the concept of structure, and both apply to this case. First, the pattern of car use is unevenly and unequally distributed across different social groups: not everyone has access to car use; and, as we shall see later in this chapter, the increase in car use by some people might negatively impact on the mobility of non-car users if it affects the viability of other types of transport. And the costs as well as the benefits of car use might also be worth remembering. Personal car transport depends on an infrastructure of roads, car parks, shopping malls, industrial parks, oil fields and refineries that generates gridlock, accidents, pollution and environmental degradation.

This brings us to the second sense of structure, understood in terms of a constraining or even determining factor that shapes the degree to which people can exercise agency, if they can at all. For example, the kinds of negative consequences which Sennett points to might also mean that car use becomes as much an obligation as a right – if you cannot walk to local shops anymore, driving to a supermarket might be the only option available to you. The anthropologist Daniel Miller (2001) captures this sense that car culture might be a structuring feature of modern life in the following vignette. Miller uses an imaginative narrative to transform our understanding of the facts and values associated with car use:

> When I used to accompany my daughter to her school bus I often made up stories to amuse her as we walked. One was a description of the earth and its inhabitants as told by an alien examining us from a space ship above London. This alien had observed that the earth is inhabited by strange creatures called cars mainly with four wheels although some are great beasts with twelve wheels and some little creatures with only two. These creatures are served by a host of slaves who walk on legs and spend their whole lives serving them. The slaves constantly ensure that the cars are fed their liquid foods whenever they are thirsty and are cured if they have accidents: but the slaves also help in the reproduction and disposal of cars. The slaves are deposited in boxes set up almost everywhere a car wants to go and are always ready to be taken away as soon as the car makes up its mind to go somewhere else. Cars were never seen to go anywhere without at least one slave. The slaves build and maintain long and complex networks of clear space so that cars have little trouble travelling from place to place. Indeed the earth's creatures seem constantly pampered by their fawning army of slaves.
>
> (Miller, 2001, p. 1)

Here Miller reverses the sense in which cars are understood as vehicles of personal freedom, drawing out the degree to which social patterns are dependent on car use to such a degree that it might be impossible to imagine a social world without cars. The patterns of social life that have grown up around car use have become inescapable in Miller's vision. Far from enabling us to take control over our lives as we wish, car use ends up controlling what we can and cannot do in ways perhaps never anticipated.

Both these senses of the structural factors shaping car use illustrate why debates about travel, transport and mobility can become highly contested. The personal freedoms afforded by car use can generate unintended consequences that become public issues, in terms of unwanted environmental impacts for example. And attempts to shape individual mobility in certain directions – to favour more road building over investment in other modes of public transport, for instance (see Figure 5.1) – will inevitably have unequal impacts on the degree of agency different people can exercise over their own mobility patterns.

Social science becomes involved in these disputes because it is used by governments, corporations and non-governmental organisations to try to shape future developments in transport patterns. These disputes around mobility arise, as we have seen, because transport issues always involve trade-offs between freedom and constraint, and because intended actions can generate unintended consequences. But it is also because debates around mobility are debates about contested visions of *future* social arrangements: transport issues are all about planning for potential outcomes, and social science is an important instrument used to *measure*, *predict* and *model* future trends and possible patterns that could follow from particular decisions. Debates about mobility, and in particular planning and designing for future mobility patterns, are hotly contested because different interests and values are at stake according to how they are resolved. As you will see, social science is sometimes used as a way of *supporting* particular understandings of future possibilities, but it can also be used to *challenge* understandings of mobility and provide alternative perspectives.

The overall aim of the chapter is to show how the facts, concepts and values which enable social science to generate understandings of public issues are always implicated in wider contexts of public debate, competition and conflict. The chapter deals with two related senses of contested understandings: first, the idea that public issues themselves are deeply contested, with different interests interpreting issues in competing ways; and, second, the idea that social science understandings themselves are contested, not least because of their involvement in contested issues of the first sort. Around any one issue, it is never likely to be the case that social science provides one single understanding, pointing towards one single preferred path of action: social science understandings are contested because different approaches combine facts, values and concepts in different ways, supporting potentially different and competing recommendations about what to do, about how to shape the future.

1.1 Structure of the chapter

This chapter looks at how social science is used in attempts to forecast future transport demand and travel patterns. And it looks at how, as a result of this, social science becomes implicated in public debates and controversies about future mobilities. At the core of this use of social science in contested public issues are different ways of understanding the relationships between transport provision and travel patterns, and between transport practices and a wider range of social activities and processes.

Predict and provide is a form of transport modelling that uses statistical techniques to measure existing travel patterns and estimate future trends. It assumes that current trends can tell us a lot about future use.

Section 2 of the chapter begins by considering why prediction of travel behaviour is so difficult in a complex and often unpredictable social world. It introduces an approach to forecasting known as **predict and provide**, which was highly influential in shaping transport policies in the UK in the second half of the twentieth century. It then discusses the dispute around the future of the Settle–Carlisle railway line in the 1980s, using this case study to illustrate how social science was used to contest the policy recommendations that followed from the 'predict and provide' approach. The section shows that social science is used in contested public debates to broaden out and to complicate understandings of causal relationships between proposed policies and likely outcomes.

Counter-factual analysis is a mode of imaginative reasoning that tries to compare what actually happened with what would have happened under different circumstances.

Section 3 examines in more detail two aspects of this use of social science in contesting understandings of future mobility patterns. It considers how social science develops counter-intuitive understandings of the likely effects of increasing road capacity – showing that, far from reducing congestion and increasing efficiency, road building tends to generate more traffic rather than relieve pressure on road systems. It then discusses the use of **counter-factual analysis** in social science, to show how this style of reasoning can be used to question received understandings of cause-and-effect relationships, and open up new questions about the degree to which patterns of mobility are shaped by transport systems or by broader social processes.

1.2 Aims of the chapter

This chapter aims to:

- show how attempts to forecast future patterns of mobility inevitably generate contested public issues, using the example of the car in UK transport policy
- examine the role played by social science descriptions and understandings in these contested public debates about mobility
- consider how contested understandings have implications for both the prediction of future mobility and the enactment of travel patterns
- show how social science is used to support and challenge understandings of the likely causes and effects of changes in transport systems.

2 Social science and contested public issues

In this section, we look at the ways in which social science has been involved in contested debates about the future of mobility in the UK since the end of the Second World War. Social science has been used to support particular policies, but also to challenge policies and suggest alternatives. Central to this use of social science have been different understandings of how to forecast future patterns of mobility on the basis of current patterns, as well as different values about how to respond to changing patterns of mobility.

The 1950s and 1960s were a period when considerable faith was invested in the idea that the future of transport in the UK lay in the growth of car use. Economic growth was associated with a steady rise in individual car ownership, and the role of transport planning was seen as ensuring that road capacity increased to match this. This approach became known as 'predict and provide': it was a method that used statistical techniques to measure existing travel patterns and estimate future trends. The *prediction* of future demand for transport was, in turn, associated with a presumption that the key task of government was to ensure that the appropriate transport network should be *provided.*

As a basis for transport policy, 'predict and provide' gathered data about current transport use, and examined trends in the growth or decline of particular modes of transport. In the context of post-war economic growth and urban development, 'predict and provide' became associated with policies that seemed almost automatically to favour more and more road building: car use was growing and seemed the inevitable trend of the future, as other modes of transport declined in comparison. 'Predict and provide' is an example of the use of statistical techniques to enact particular outcomes: because transport infrastructures are often expensive and complex and take a long time to construct, governments and private sector organisations make use of the evidence base provided by this approach to make decisions about long-term investment and planning.

While 'predict and provide' approaches can produce some evidence about future trends, it should be noted that forecasting future transport levels and travel patterns can be an unpredictable business, one fraught with difficulties. Simply taking current trends and projecting them into the future requires that we have confidence in the assumptions we make about how people act and how social life will develop in years to come. As you will see in this chapter, the assumptions made about the relationship between current behaviour and future trends are central to the contested nature of social science understandings in the field of transport policy. There are a number of factors that make forecasting future patterns of mobility difficult:

- Social and cultural changes are often hard to forecast. Who, for instance, would have predicted that cycling would become popular among affluent, middle-aged and professional men, or that so-called sports utility vehicles (SUVs) would often be preferred to more fuel-efficient vehicles as family cars?
- Changes that sometimes appear unrelated to transport itself can have important implications for the number and pattern of journeys made. For example, the rising number of one-person households has implications for the number of cars in use and car journeys made, and the amount of parking required in residential areas. Or, to take another example, the increase in the active retired population has implications both for public transport provision and for private vehicle use.
- Unpredictable events, including economic or political crises, can also have important consequences which are extremely difficult to build into forecasts. Political crisis in the Middle East led to a worldwide 'oil crisis' in the mid-1970s, which significantly altered the design and use of car transport. Disasters such as the Hatfield rail crash of October 2000, and natural events like the Icelandic volcano eruption of spring 2010 that disrupted global air traffic, also create crises of confidence among travellers and transport providers that may affect long-term travel behaviour.

You will see from this list that the factors which shape transport practices and policies are very varied. This suggests that predicting what sort of transport infrastructure should be provided in the future is a rather uncertain, if not risky, endeavour. The transport geographer David Banister summarises this succinctly:

> The important point here, not often acknowledged in much transport analysis, is that travel is a product of changes in existing patterns of demand and the travel generated by new activities. Much of the growth in travel is caused by decisions taken outside

> the transport arena, yet it is often the transport system that has to accommodate to these changes.
>
> (Banister, 2005, p. 212)

Banister's point is that predicting the future only by projecting from existing travel and transport patterns is difficult because it is not always possible to take account of all the external social, economic and environmental influences that may affect future transport demand and use. 'Predict and provide', as an approach to forecasting and planning for the future, tends to think of transport systems as 'closed' systems, so that it is possible to predict future transport use from the careful study of existing transport patterns. Banister, however, suggests that the variables which need to be taken into account in thinking about future mobility patterns are likely to go beyond transport-related factors.

The issue that Banister's warning raises concerns the need to think carefully about the limitations of social science in predicting future patterns of behaviour and action. The point is not, however, that social science should not even be involved in this sort of activity at all. One of the most important uses of social science, across all sorts of sectors, is precisely in providing evidence and concepts with which to estimate and imagine future trends so that they can be better anticipated, planned for, or mitigated. The contested understandings of social science that this chapter looks at all revolve around this basic use of social science and, in particular, around different understandings of the relationships between existing evidence, competing concepts and alternative visions of the future.

2.1 Contesting 'predict and provide'

In the UK, the 1960s were the heyday of 'predict and provide' in transport planning. At this time, a run-down railway network and an outdated road system were increasingly seen as inadequate in the face of the demands made by the growing and increasingly widespread use of the private motor vehicle. Successive governments were faced with the challenge of transforming often outdated infrastructures in light of the seemingly inexorable growth of car ownership.

One of the most important government interventions in transport planning in this period involved a thorough overhaul of the British railway system. Two reports, published in 1963 and 1965, both called

The Reshaping of British Railways, had a fundamental impact on the shaping of personal mobility. Together they are known as the Beeching Report, after their author Dr Richard Beeching, the chairman of British Railways who oversaw the review into the modernisation of the railway system. The Beeching review is an example of the 'predict and provide' approach in practice.

Beeching's remit was to establish the basis for making the British railway system profitable. His answer to this challenge was to recommend sweeping cuts in services and lines – including the closure of up to one third of all railway stations, and the withdrawal of rail services from around 5000 route miles (8000 km). It was estimated this would save £18 million.

Figure 5.2 Dr Richard Beeching

The modernisation that Beeching recommended was, however, based on a particular model of calculating the costs and benefits of railway services, a model that in due course would become a central challenge to the implementation of his review. The 'bottom line' for Beeching was that any service that did not cover its 'direct costs' (the specific financial costs attached to running a particular service) should be cut. This provided the narrow test of 'viability' applied when deciding on all rail closures. Furthermore, Beeching used a particular methodology to predict future levels of rail provision. He calculated traffic levels and flows across the rail system, and compared these with other available provision in terms of road, water or air transport. On this basis, it was claimed that cutting railway lines would not have an adverse effect on individuals' travel and transport opportunities and levels of personal mobility.

Set alongside the motorway building programme in the UK, which began in the same period, the substantial implementation of the recommendations of the Beeching Report was an important moment in shaping the UK as a car-based society (Haywood, 2009).

Beeching's review proved highly controversial, as its implementation reshaped the mobility patterns available to people in different parts of the UK. One of the most important challenges to the logic that underlay the recommendations took place in the 1980s, some two decades after the Beeching Report was originally published. The campaign to save the Settle–Carlisle railway line in the north-west of England is an example of social science being used to contest particular policy proposals and support alternative proposals. The campaign used social science to challenge the methodology and values of 'predict and provide', which informed the recommendation to close this stretch of railway. This case study shows how different approaches to calculating future mobility patterns draw on different concepts and values. In this case, arguments about what kind and level of mobility were desirable became arguments about what kind of world people want to live in.

The Settle–Carlisle line was originally listed for closure by Beeching in 1963. The line runs through some of the wildest, highest and most remote and scenic parts of the English Pennine hills (see Figure 5.3). It also has many bridges, tunnels and engineering structures that are expensive to maintain. It was therefore always vulnerable to the calculations used in Beeching's review. At the beginning of the 1980s British Rail announced that the line would be closed, because of the prohibitive costs of renewing and maintaining this infrastructure of viaducts and tunnels. This decision generated widespread opposition, which formed into a concerted campaign to challenge the planned closure, involving passengers, railway enthusiasts, local authorities, county councils and the National Park Authority (Abbot and Whitehouse, 1990). The campaign used various tactics, not least encouraging more people to actually use the line: when the campaign began in 1983, journeys per year were 93,000, and these increased to 450,000 by 1989.

Figure 5.3 Map of Settle–Carlisle railway route

The campaign against the closure used social science to challenge two sets of assumptions that underpinned the Beeching Report: that closure was justified because the line was not economically viable; and that it would have few negative impacts on social or personal mobility. There are therefore two aspects to the use of social science in contesting the 'predict and provide' forecasting which had led to the recommendation that the Settle–Carlisle line should be closed. First, since the closure was justified on the grounds that the line was not economically viable, the particular economic understanding of how to calculate costs of railways was challenged. Here the terrain of debate remained within the area of economics, broadly defined. Second, however, social science was also used to broaden the understanding of the value of railway transport, beyond narrowly defined economic understandings of value, to include social and environmental costs and benefits. Here social science was used to challenge the claim that the closure would have no negative impacts on mobility patterns.

Let us look in turn at each of these aspects of the use of social science in contested public issues.

In the first use of social science, campaigners argued that the way in which British Rail had calculated costs and revenues biased the results against rail routes that ran through sparsely populated areas, but that provided important connections between other parts of the railway system and provided destinations for leisure travel. This involved challenging the specific ways in which the revenue generated by the line was calculated.

- Income from ticket sales for travellers who used the Settle–Carlisle line, but as part of a longer-distance journey, was ignored in the closure plan.
- Income from travellers originating from urban areas, but who used the line to reach remote destinations for leisure and tourism, was also ignored.
- The assumption that if local feeder services were cut, passengers would continue to use long-distance and intercity services was also challenged. Evidence suggested people were reluctant to change between different modes of transport mid-journey.

In questioning these specific technical features of the economic calculations used to justify the closure, campaigners challenged the narrow understanding of costs and revenues on which decision making about railway closures was based. In this first use of social science, campaigners argued that the understanding of the economic value of the line was too narrowly defined, and tended to exclude revenues that were generated by the line remaining open.

But social science was also used to broaden out the understanding of the value of the line, beyond a restrictively economic definition. In this second use, social science was used to identify how the closure of the railway line would indeed impact negatively on the mobility of different social groups. Contrary to the assumption of the Beeching review that rail closures would just lead to people transferring to other modes of transport, social science evidence challenged the idea that railway closure would be neutral in its impacts on mobility patterns. In their study of the social consequences of railway closures on rural areas in the UK, the sociologists Mayer Hillman and Anne Whalley (1980) had found that only the poorest socio-economic groups readily transferred from rail to bus. Moreover, not only did closure tend to encourage car use over other modes of public transport, but, in areas where lines had closed, over one third of people changed not just their method of travel but also the destination that they had previously reached by train. And one in twelve ceased altogether the activities they had previously undertaken by rail. When it came to the social impacts of railway closures, Hillman and Whalley concluded that 'the impact has been socially regressive, for it is the older people, those without cars and those in blue-collar households, who have cut back most on their activity and those who are the hardest hit. Women have been harder hit than men' (1980, p. 111).

This conclusion was further supported by research undertaken in 1984 by the geographer John Whitelegg. He undertook a survey of 5156 passengers on the Settle–Carlisle route, and found that the number of passengers willing to travel by an alternative bus service was very low. He found that in the event of closure most people would either travel by private car or not travel at all. Whitelegg's research raises the issue of unintended consequences that was discussed in the introduction to this chapter. In this case, he identified the processes by which the closure of the Settle–Carlisle line would impact on the viability of all sorts of other private and public sector activities that reached beyond the immediate focus of the railway itself. Whitelegg argued that the impact of railway closure on promoting car use further reduces support for local services, buses and shops, as people using their cars are prepared to travel beyond their locality for their goods and services. At the same time, line closure and increased car use have an adverse effect on jobs in tourism and the service sector. Since these sectors are a major source of employment in rural areas, line closure would also contribute to the out-migration of young adults, a decline in viable rural communities, and greater second-home ownership. By diminishing the viability of local services and local economic activity, rail closure would ultimately create 'hardship' well in excess of the inconvenience of not having train services.

Whitelegg's argument also relates to Banister's observation (2005, p. 212), quoted earlier in this section – if it is true that growth in travel is caused by factors that do not originate within the arena of transport per se, then the reverse might also be the case: decisions to reduce particular forms of mobility, in this case to close railway lines, might well resonate well beyond the effects on travel patterns. Social science is implicated in these types of debates precisely because it is used to try to calculate and forecast the range of effects, both positive and negative, that specific decisions about transport are likely to have.

It is worth noting that the terms in which the opposition conveyed their arguments drew on a set of challenges to the descriptions, and to the particular concepts and values, of the proponents of closure. This was evident in questions about the appropriateness of predominantly using calculations of 'direct costs' as the main criterion for the decision to close the line, given the significance of other economic models and considerations. It was also evident in broader disputes about whether economic concepts and theories were, on their own, a sufficient basis on which to debate closures – since a whole range of other social and environmental factors needed to be assessed. Above all, opposition to the closure of the line was framed around a set of values that were different from those held by the proponents of closure. Closure was justified on the grounds of a narrow definition of economic efficiency, and in terms that saw car use as an unproblematic expression of individual freedom; opponents of the closure certainly challenged the economics of the case, but above all they sought to promote a vision of the wider public benefits that the railways sustained and supported.

2.2 Using social science to contest public issues

It should also be borne in mind that social science was only one part of the campaign to oppose the closure of the Settle–Carlisle line. Campaigners used all sorts of tactics and resources – legal challenges, media publicity, the lobbying of politicians, and submissions to the public inquiry that was set up. It would be wrong to think that contested public issues of this sort can be neatly 'solved' by appeal to the proper social science. That is not the lesson to be taken from this case study; rather, the important point that it teaches us is that social science is thoroughly implicated in contested issues of this sort, but on 'both sides' as it were. In this case, the economic understandings used to support the case for closure were challenged by alternative understandings of the economics of transport, as well as by broader understandings of the social benefits of public infrastructures like railway lines. In the case of the Settle–Carlisle campaign, closure plans were delayed, and then finally reversed in 1989.

Social science understandings were one resource available to campaigners seeking to challenge plans to close the Settle–Carlisle line. This is one way to think about the use of social science in contested public issues – social science evidence, concepts and understandings provide one means of making claims: of making arguments about what is the case, or what should be the case; but also of claiming to speak on behalf of particular groups of people, or particular constituencies. Campaigners can make claims using all sorts of 'resources': through access to media publicity, or through celebrity endorsement of their cause; by making legal challenges; by mobilising supporters, getting them to vote for an issue, or to take part in a letter-writing campaign, or to go on a march. Social science evidence and argument can be thought of as another form of making such claims, alongside these types of activities. It does not mean that social science, when used in contested public issues, is necessarily 'biased': the value of social science to campaigners, or to policy makers or private companies, lies precisely in the authority it might lend their claims and positions.

In the case discussed in this section, the campaign to oppose the closure of the Settle–Carlisle line, we can see that social science is involved on both sides of the issue. British Rail, and successive governments in the UK, adopted a specific understanding of the economic value of railway services, based on fairly narrow calculations of economic viability. We have seen that these understandings were challenged by campaigners who used social science in two related ways, which can be summarised as follows:

- First, social science was used to challenge the understanding of the economic value of railway services. In the Settle–Carlisle dispute, contested interpretations centred on the definition of some key terms, including 'direct costs' and 'hardship'. Beeching had defined direct costs very narrowly, and the definition of the hardship that would be caused by the closure restricted the range of people who might legitimately claim to be affected by the plans. The campaign against closure challenged these understandings of the costs of railway services, and broadened the range of likely groups of people who would be affected by closure.
- Second, in this respect – broadening the definition of the hardship caused by the plans – campaigners also made use of social science to widen the understanding of the value of railway services beyond narrowly economic calculations. The Beeching Report assumed that if railway lines did not cover their direct costs then they should be

closed. In the face of this apparently self-evident truth, campaigners demonstrated that people would not transfer from train to bus, and that increased car use resulting from rail closure would have a detrimental effect on the local economies and communities of the areas affected by the decision.

Social science was therefore implicated in this contested public issue in different ways. In the dispute, the two sides approached the contest with very different ideas of value. Whereas British Rail and the UK government were concerned with protecting taxpayers' money, eliminating unnecessary expenditure and creating an efficient, wealth-generating society, campaigners against the closure defined value primarily in terms of the lives and lifestyles of rural communities. This was related to a broader contrast between the value associated with personal car use, and an alternative understanding in which public infrastructures of transport – roads, railways, bus services – were viewed as enhancing both the individual and the collective good.

In this section, we have seen how social science is inevitably involved in practices of forecasting, planning and implementing future patterns of social life – in this case, of mobility. We have seen how one way of forecasting future travel patterns, called 'predict and provide', rests on particular assumptions about the causal relationships between current patterns and future trends. But we have also seen that challenges to this way of forecasting use social science to broaden out, and to complicate, the understandings of the causal relationships between transport infrastructure and patterns of mobility. In the next section, we look in more detail at the ways in which different approaches to social science understand the causal relations between transport and travel, and between transport and wider social processes.

3 Contested understandings of causality

As previously stated, this section will consider two aspects of causal understandings of mobility, and the disputes in which they are implicated:

- relationships between the provision of transport infrastructure and future travel patterns
- relationships between transport and travel on the one hand, and a range of other social processes on the other.

3.1 Does building more roads reduce congestion?

The Settle–Carlisle controversy in the 1980s was part of a wider questioning of the assumptions that lay behind transport planning and provision in the UK. In particular, the role of 'predict and provide' transport planning in encouraging the rise of a car-centred society was called into question. The watershed moment for 'predict and provide' transport planning is often associated with the publication of a government White Paper in 1989, *Roads for Prosperity* (Department of Transport, 1989). This included traffic forecasts that simply extrapolated existing trends in motor car and commercial vehicle growth into the future, and therefore predicted an increase in road traffic of between 83 per cent and 142 per cent by the year 2025. Such forecasts suggested that a road-building programme of enormous ambition and cost was needed, which would require an unprecedented expansion in the UK road network.

These forecasts were seized on by environmentalists and anti-road lobbyists as evidence that the UK could not continue to build more and more roads to provide for this growth. One key debate around transport futures that emerged at this time, and which continues today, is the question of whether building more roads is a means of reducing congestion and increasing the efficiency of the transport network, or whether road building actually just generates more traffic without reducing congestion. Social science understandings are implicated in this debate because they can provide different accounts of the relationship between transport infrastructure – roads, railway lines, bus routes – and actual levels and patterns of travel.

As we have seen, 'predict and provide' approaches to transport planning tended to privilege road-building programmes, by using existing growth patterns to predict future demand and assuming that the transport network had to be provided to accommodate that demand. We have also seen, in the case of the Settle–Carlisle dispute, that a fundamental area of contestation concerned the ways in which boundaries are drawn around the costs and benefits of particular means of travel. The Beeching Report drew these boundaries quite tightly, with the effect that many railway lines appeared to be economically inefficient. Campaigners against rail closure sought to broaden these boundaries, in order to bring into view the wider revenues and benefits that railway lines might help to generate or sustain. Since the 1980s, campaigns around environmental sustainability and equal access to transport have argued that the same appraisals of costs and benefits that railways have been subjected to should also be applied to car use. The challenge to conventional wisdom about car use has involved social scientists raising questions about the causal relationships that are assumed to exist between road building and traffic levels.

3.1.1 Road building and induced demand

The primary justification for public expenditure on road building, in the UK and elsewhere, tends to be an argument that road building is necessary to cope with future increases in traffic and to reduce congestion. However, this assumption is challenged by the transport writer Lynn Sloman, for whom car culture is less a matter of choice and freedom, and rather more like an addiction:

> The growth in traffic provides a spurious justification for the Government and local councils to spend billions of pounds on damaging new road schemes. Unfortunately, this leads to a vicious circle: as new roads are built or existing roads and motorways are widened, they fill up with extra traffic and quickly become congested.
>
> (Sloman, 2006, p. 38)

The idea that road building increases traffic, rather than reducing congestion, may appear a little counter-intuitive. But this effect has been demonstrated by a wide range of social science studies. The reason why the building of more roads increases the volume and intensity of traffic, rather than reducing it, is explained by use of the concept of **induced demand**.

Induced demand is the effect of supplying more of a certain good such that it encourages increased usage of that good, rather than redistributing or decreasing the intensity of demand.

Induced demand is a concept from economics which refers to the effect of supplying more of a good such that it encourages increased usage of that good, rather than redistributing or decreasing the intensity of demand. This effect is not anticipated by 'predict and provide' planning, which is likely (in our example) to underestimate the increase in overall traffic levels that follows from providing more roads to cope with increased demand at existing rates. The geographer Susan Owens argues that the concept of induced demand applies to the case of road building, and explains that this requires a much broader understanding of human behaviour, motivation and decision making than is found in conventional 'predict and provide' approaches. She explains the effects of building more roads as follows:

> When travel is cheap, people use mobility to extend their choice of jobs, retail facilities and leisure opportunities, and to improve their residential amenity. Employers, retailers and developers respond appropriately in their locational decisions. The most attractive, rather than the closest facilities are used; and homes are chosen for reasons other than proximity to work. Time and money spent on travelling is readily traded against these other factors. This simple fact makes it difficult to define the most travel-efficient forms of development without making assumptions about future mobility, and therefore about other factors and policies strongly influencing the propensity to travel.
>
> (Owens, 1994, p. 48)

Owens is making the same point that we saw Banister (2005, p. 212) making earlier in this chapter, about the difficulty of factoring in all the variables that help to shape travel patterns. But she is also making a point about how the intentions that guide road-building programmes might not be achieved, because of the complexity of effects that these programmes set in chain. For Owens, road building leads to an increase in choices about where to work, live and undertake leisure, with people being prepared to travel greater distances as more roads are built to accommodate this possibility. Road building therefore does not necessarily ease congestion in the long term, because people see road expansion as an opportunity to undertake more journeys over longer distances, thereby filling up new road capacity.

As already suggested, the idea that building more roads might increase traffic and do little to alleviate congestion may appear counter-intuitive. In order to better understand this effect, consider the graphic representation in Figure 5.4.

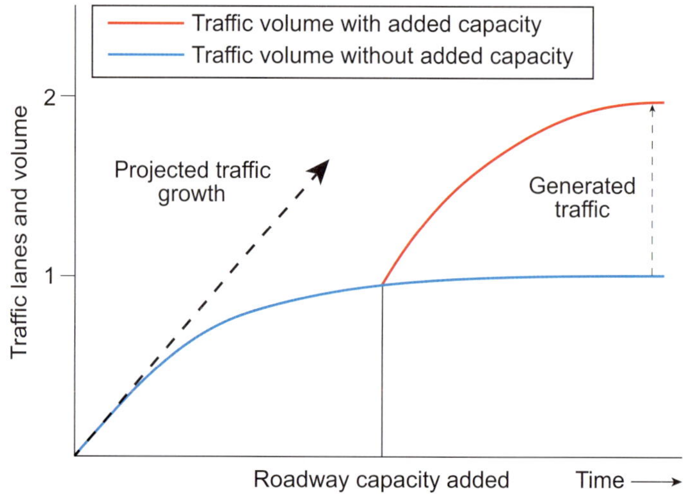

Figure 5.4 How increased road capacity generates traffic

In this figure, the dotted line running at 45 degrees is the projected or predicted level of traffic growth. Consistent with the assumptions used in 'predict and provide' planning, this projection assumes that there is a constant relation between traffic levels and road capacity – 'Traffic lanes and volume'. Now, the blue line indicates the actual pattern of traffic growth over time. You can see that, initially, traffic levels grow unhindered when roads are uncongested. However, as traffic increases and jams become more common, people are increasingly reluctant to make more and longer journeys. This is indicated in Figure 5.4 as the blue line levels off, indicating a balance or 'equilibrium' between traffic and congestion.

It is at this point that it might appear that the best thing to do is increase road capacity. You can see this in Figure 5.4 ('Roadway capacity added'). Now the cycle starts again, as indicated by the red line. Initially, traffic increases once more. Adding new capacity does enable an increase in traffic levels – this is called 'Generated traffic'. It is made up both from some of those additional journeys that would have been taken if there had been less congestion, and from longer trips that are now possible because travelling is easier and faster.

However, you will see that soon enough a new equilibrium is reached – the red line levels off as well, as the increase in traffic levels enabled by adding road capacity generates more and more congestion.

Now, if you compare the dotted line showing the initial prediction of traffic growth with the red line, showing the amount of new traffic accommodated after road capacity is increased, you can see that increasing road capacity will, over time, satisfy only a proportion of total predicted demand for road capacity. Because any increase in traffic resulting from added capacity quickly produces its own congestion, there seems to be an endless dynamic:

- Road capacity is increased, with the intention of accommodating the increasing demand without worsening congestion.
- This actually has the effect of increasing demand to a greater extent than was expected.
- The congestion problem is thereby reproduced all over again.

What this example illustrates is that social science, by developing what might appear to be counter-intuitive understandings of an issue, can challenge a taken-for-granted approach to a problem. In this case, a simple argument that building more roads is the best way to reduce congestion, boost efficiency and accommodate predicted demand is challenged by an alternative approach to economic analysis of the issue. Thinking about road building with the help of the concept of 'induced demand' leads to a different interpretation of the likely effects of road building, where increased road capacity just leads to even greater traffic levels without necessarily reducing congestion levels.

Increasing road capacity therefore has some unexpected outcomes on people's behaviour as car users. Building more roads enables people to travel further and pack more in to the day. This is the simplest sense of the meaning of 'induced demand'. As Owens indicates in the quote above (1994, p. 48), the more we are able to rely on car travel to get us around, the more our lives become shaped by patterns of mobility that are dependent on car travel. This is the idea that Miller's vignette about cars and their slaves (2001, p. 1), quoted in the introduction to this chapter, is meant to capture. People use cars for various reasons: to do the weekly shop, commute to work, go away on holiday and so on. Thus they might come to expect certain levels of mobility as a consequence: car travel becomes associated with being able to go where we want and when we want, without having to worry about timetables or connections. Car travel is, after all, associated with freedom, choice and convenience. On the other hand, the more that patterns of mobility are dependent on car use, the more people might find that they literally cannot do without cars: if the growth of out-of-town supermarkets, for example, negatively impacts on the viability of town-centre or neighbourhood retailers, then the degree of 'choice' available to us might be rather limited after all.

3.1.2 Road building and automobility

Automobility is a term used to capture the dual sense that modern car culture is associated with both freedom and necessity.

The sociologist John Urry (2004) has coined the term **automobility** to capture the dual sense of the freedom and dependence associated with modern car culture. On the one hand, people living in car cultures come to expect and accept the ability to travel when and where they want to, regarding it almost as an individual right. But, on the other hand, as we have seen, the actual ability to be as mobile as we please depends on the availability of complex systems of infrastructure – roads, railways, cars, trains, bridges, viaducts and so on. These systems both enable and constrain – they provide the routes through which mobility can be exercised, but they also define those people and places who are less well served by such opportunities.

The social science concepts discussed above, such as 'induced demand' and 'automobility', have become important in discussions about future mobility in a period when the inexorable growth of car transport has been called into question on economic, social and environmental grounds. The programme of road building in the UK projected in 1989 by the *Roads for Prosperity* White Paper (Department of Transport, 1989) predicted 2700 miles (4300 km) of new or improved trunk roads plus 150 new bypasses being built over ten years, at a cost of £23 billion at 1989 prices. This programme generated widespread opposition, both among locally affected communities and among national and international campaigners. High-profile protests against road building, such as opposition in the early 1990s to the proposed cutting of the M3 through Twyford Down, near Winchester (Hampshire), focused attention on the procedures for assessing the costs and benefits of such major construction projects. At Twyford Down, the new road threatened two Sites of Special Scientific Interest, two Scheduled Ancient Monuments and an Area of Outstanding Natural Beauty. This site, and the protest around it, crystallised a dispute between narrowly economic calculations of the benefits of road building, and a growing anti-roads movement which argued that wider environmental and social costs should be considered as part of the decision-making process for new road schemes.

Figure 5.5 Protestors at Twyford Down

High-profile cases such as the Twyford Down protest have been associated with the emergence of what has been called a **new realism** in transport planning, as the simple assumptions that lay behind 'predict and provide' have come to be seen as unable to cope with the complex causal relations that shape transport, travel and mobility. The idea that individual travel could expand unhindered in the future without costs or consequences has become more and more difficult to sustain. Banister summarises the difficulties that now must be faced when thinking about forecasting and planning for future systems of mobility:

New realism is an approach to transport planning that emerged in the 1990s, emphasising improvements in public transport, better provision for cyclists and pedestrians, and urban planning which minimised the use of private vehicles.

> Predicted increases in travel demand cannot be met. The expectations that new capacity could be provided, either through new construction or through traffic management, to meet that growth has now been firmly rejected. Even if it were possible, it would be undesirable. The land required for new infrastructure is at a premium in many countries, and the environmental and social costs involved make it unacceptable, particularly if a solution is only temporary. In many transport systems working close to capacity, additional increases in that capacity will be immediately

> taken up by 'latent' demand with previous or even worse levels of congestion being quickly re-established.
>
> (Banister, 1994, pp. 210–11)

In this section, we have seen that the same sorts of arguments that were made in the Settle–Carlisle case study concerning opposition to railway closures have also been used to challenge the ascendancy of car transport and road building as the models for future mobility. In both cases, social science is used to bring into focus the complex relationships between the provision of transport infrastructure on the one hand, and, on the other, the actual patterns and levels of travel that those systems of transport sustain and generate. What both cases underscore is that forecasting future mobility is very difficult, because mobility is not simply a function of transport systems alone.

This brings us to the second aspect of social science understandings of causality that inform disputes about mobility – the question of how to understand the relationship between transport and travel on the one hand, and a range of further social processes on the other.

3.2 Car use: poison or cure?

As we have seen already in this chapter, contested understandings of future mobility rest on models and theories of causality. The assumptions involved might be quite limited – for example, the idea that closing railways will just lead people to switch to other transport modes without changing the patterns of their travel. Or they might be more expansive – for instance, the idea that car use is a basic requirement for economic growth. We have seen how disputes about mobility often revolve around contested understandings of the costs and benefits of different transport modes, and, again, how these costs and benefits can be calculated in narrow or broad terms. But you will also recall Banister's argument (2005, p. 212), quoted in Section 2, that patterns of mobility do not arise simply because of decisions made within the arena of transport per se; to put it in the terms introduced in Chapter 1, the variables that help to shape patterns of mobility are not restricted to transport issues, such as road capacity or numbers of railway lines. A whole host of factors is involved, and understanding how these factors interact to generate patterns of car use, or levels of railway journeys, is a complex matter.

In this section, we consider this issue of how to think about the complex range of causal factors that shape mobility by using one particular tool of causal thinking, which is called 'counter-factual analysis'. Chapter 1 discussed understandings of causality produced by testing a hypothesis through experiments. Counter-factual analysis works in the opposite way. Rather than asking whether B or C will happen if you do A, it asks what would have happened if some action or intervention had not taken place: what would have happened if A had not been done. Counter-factual analysis is a mode of imaginative reasoning that tries to compare what actually happened with what would have happened under different circumstances. This type of reasoning is useful because it can help social scientists question assumed relationships of cause and effect: so, for example, rather than just assuming that increased car use causes the decline of town centres or the growth of suburbs, it might help provide new perspectives on the factors shaped by and shaping car use over time.

The example of counter-factual analysis we are going to look at in this section comes from the work of the historical geographer Colin Pooley (2010). Pooley asks what would have happened to personal mobility in the UK if use of the private car had been severely restricted at the start of the twentieth century. This is an important question to raise if we are to be able to find out what role car use has actually played in shaping patterns of mobility. As suggested above, counter-factual analysis is 'imaginative' in the sense that it is trying to establish what might have happened in different circumstances. But Pooley's analysis isn't just made up. Rather, he draws on a wide range of historical evidence, including travel statistics, government papers, business archives, newspaper reports, previous studies of historical commuting behaviour, and residential mobility and leisure patterns. He also uses evidence from the built environment relating to the shape and form of towns and suburbs. He draws on all this evidence to raise questions about some taken-for-granted assumptions about the effects and benefits of car use, as well as some questions about the supposed negative impacts of car use.

An important starting point for Pooley's counter-factual analysis of car culture is provided by two observations he makes, based on the historical evidence. First, many people travelled freely over long distances before the development of mass car ownership, and a significant minority of people today choose not to own a car and manage to travel easily over long distances despite the much-diminished

British public transport system. Second, most everyday travel undertaken by individuals in Britain is over a relatively short distance, often less than 2 km (1.25 miles), and for such trips other forms of transport can readily be substituted for the motor car – indeed, a car may not be the quickest or most effective means of transport for many such journeys in large urban areas (Pooley, 2010, p. 271). So, Pooley establishes that car use is not essential to mobility even over long distances, and that quite a lot of journeys are actually over short distances. These two observations raise the question of whether car use is quite as necessary to modern living, and to personal mobility in particular, as might be supposed. But they also bring into view the question of whether increased car use should be thought of as a cause of wider social changes, or as an effect of those changes.

Reading 5.1 is taken from Pooley's discussion of personal mobility.

As you read through this extract, consider the ways in which Pooley uses different sorts of evidence to raise questions about possible causes of social change, and the ways in which car use is ascribed either negative or positive effects.

Reading 5.1

Personal mobility

There have been significant changes in the journey to work in Britain over the twentieth century, with the mean distance travelled to work (males and females) increasing from around 4 km [2.5 miles] in 1900 (with about half of all trips on foot) to just under 15 km [9.3 miles] in the 1990s (with fewer than ten per cent of trips on foot and 50 per cent by car). However, the time spent travelling to work has increased much less. By the 1920s the mean time taken to travel to work was 30 minutes and in the 1990s this had increased slightly to 35 minutes. It is argued, and supported by research elsewhere, that travel time is far more important than distance, and that the motor car has allowed people to travel further but has not in other respects changed travel-to-work patterns. Moreover where public transport provision is good, most notably in London, car use has remained at a low level for the journey to work. Thus, it can be suggested that if access to private motor vehicles had been restricted the time spent travelling to work would have changed little, and the distance over which people travelled would depend primarily on the effectiveness of the public transport system.

Evidence from an analysis of the everyday travel of children aged 10/11 from the 1940s to the present suggests that there has been even less change in personal mobility over the past 50 years. Thus in Manchester in the 1940s children aged 10/11 travelled on average some 3,500 km [2200 miles] in a year, with the average trip distance just 1.3 km [0.8 mile]. By the start of the twenty-first century, children of the same age in Manchester travelled further in total (some 4500 km [2800 miles]) but the average trip distance remained very low at 1.5 km [0.93 mile]. If we focus on the most common event – the journey to school – in the 1940s in Manchester the mean distance for children aged 10/11 was 1.3 km [0.8 mile] and in 2000 the mean distance was 1.4 km [0.875 mile]. There is thus convincing evidence that despite the widespread use of the car during the second half of the twentieth century, most everyday travel for children living in a city such as Manchester remained short distance. It can thus be argued that the widespread adoption of the motor car has had surprisingly little impact on the everyday mobility of children and their parents and that, if car use had been restricted, patterns of individual everyday mobility would have remained much the same.

Perhaps the group that has seen most change in their mobility over the past half century are the relatively elderly. In the 1940s many people in their 60s were considered old and/or infirm and would have travelled little beyond their immediate neighbourhood. Today most people of the same age can travel widely. Indeed several elderly respondents in c.2000 suggested that they had more mobility in their 60s than at any other time in their lives. However, this increased mobility has little to do with the availability of motor transport. Primarily it is a reflection of improved health, increased leisure time following retirement, and surplus income. Some older people do drive but many prefer not to, and discounted fares on trains and buses encourage those over 60 to use public transport. It can be suggested that the elderly have experienced significant mobility change over the past century, but that it would have been much the same with or without the motor car.

Personal mobility and transport infrastructures both play an important part in shaping the city and in turn reflect urban structure. Spatial expansion and suburbanisation are characteristic of twentieth-century British cities, and it might be assumed that suburban sprawl was dependent on the availability of the motor car, and that in a landscape without cars cities would be both high density and compact to facilitate movement between different activities. However, there is little direct evidence to suggest that the motor car caused suburbanisation or that the lack of access to a car prevents urban sprawl.

Substantial suburbanisation in large British cities began in the second half of the nineteenth century, long before the development of the motor car as a form of mass transport. At that time it occurred largely independently of transport developments: railways mostly followed suburban development, and the affluent who suburbanised could afford the journey into town by existing means (horse-drawn omnibus, tram or private carriage). A second phase of suburbanisation occurred in the 1920s and '30s as those on lower incomes moved to newly-built suburban private and social housing estates. However, few of the houses built at this time were provided with a garage (or space to build a garage) and the expectation was that people would travel easily from the suburbs to the city by tram or motorbus. Given that most people seek to minimise travel time and distance, it is likely that other aspects of urban structure may have been different if access to private motor transport had been restricted. In the 1950s, when most people still did not have access to a car, there was much better provision of neighbourhood facilities including shops, schools and social activities. One of the key trends of the late twentieth century has been the closure of local facilities and the concentration of services (especially retailing) in large peripheral complexes. These are usually predicated on the assumption that people have access by car. If car use had been severely restricted it seems likely that the growth of out-of-town shopping complexes would also have been much less, with provision of good public transport to those that were developed, but also the retention of far more neighbourhood facilities. Lack of access to a car would probably also have restricted the extent of counterurbanisation that occurred in Britain from the 1960s.

In contrast, it can be argued that a landscape without cars would produce a much cleaner urban environment and, potentially, a more healthy urban population. Following the impacts of deindustrialisation (which led to the closure of much potentially polluting industry) and the enforcement of the Clean Air Act in 1956 (which regulated both domestic and industrial smoke emissions in urban areas), the vast majority of air-borne pollutants in towns and cities in Britain have been generated by motor vehicles. For instance, it is estimated that in the UK on average over 50 per cent of nitrogen dioxide and 75 per cent of carbon monoxide is emitted by motor vehicles, and there is clear evidence of the health effects of living near a main road. However, even without private motor transport, an increased number of urban buses could have a significant impact on pollution and, as early as the 1930s, the MoH [Ministry of Health] in Salford was expressing concern about the impact of diesel fumes. A town full of diesel buses could be just as bad as one congested with cars, and thus arguments to convert public transport to less polluting technology would not have been diminished.

It is more difficult to ascertain the full impact of a town without cars on human health. While removal of cars would have created a cleaner environment, and potentially would have improved human health, the combined effect of other lifestyle factors including diet, exercise, smoking and alcohol consumption arguably all have a much bigger influence on individual health today. However, again the evidence is limited. High levels of exercise, including walking and cycling, are more closely correlated with income and lifestyle than with car ownership. Thus lack of access to a car does not necessarily mean that people walk and cycle more, and beneficial impacts of restricted car access on exercise and health are likely to be highly spatially variable and probably concentrated in those areas which already have a good health record.

(Source: Pooley, 2010, pp. 271–4)

The picture that emerges from Reading 5.1 is quite a complex one. For example, Pooley points out that, over time, increased mobility among older people might be due to car use, but might also be ascribed to general improvements in healthcare. Likewise, he indicates that the relationship between car use and processes of suburbanisation is not a straightforward one.

What Pooley does in Reading 5.1 is to take 'facts', drawn from various forms of evidence, and place these alongside other facts, or alongside assumed causal relationships. In so doing, he is able to question some of the simple understandings of the causal effects of car use. The overall aim of Pooley's counter-factual history is to contribute to debates about sustainable transport futures, but his careful analysis of facts and concepts actually reveals a complex set of possible understandings of the relationship between transport systems and social change.

From Reading 5.1, it is possible to develop an argument *against* the car, but also to muster some evidence that would *support* car use in certain ways. The 'anti-car' and 'pro-car' aspects of Pooley's argument are listed in the accompanying box.

Pooley's argument

Anti-car argument

This is probably the easier of the two arguments to make because it is reading with the grain of what Pooley is trying to say. His position is that public transport can play and has played a substantial role in enabling individual mobility, and that therefore the car is not a necessary prerequisite for the current high levels of personal mobility. The points brought out here stress both that we could have high levels of mobility without the car and that a car-free environment would be cleaner and safer.

The key points are:

- Travel time is far more important than distance and has remained much the same since use of the car became widespread.
- Where public transport provision is good, car use has remained at a low level for the journey to work.
- '[I]f access to private motor vehicles had been restricted the time spent travelling to work would have changed little'.
- Evidence from Manchester suggests most everyday travel for children living in cities remains short distance.

- Today people over 60 years of age travel widely, with increased mobility primarily 'a reflection of improved health, increased leisure time following retirement, and surplus income', rather than a result of car ownership.
- In the UK, on average, over 50 per cent of nitrogen dioxide and 75 per cent of carbon monoxide is emitted by motor vehicles, and 'there is clear evidence of the health effects of living near a main road'.
- An almost car-free city would have a major impact on the level of air pollution in urban areas, and would certainly make cities much more pleasant places in which to live and walk.

Pro-car argument

Though this is the more difficult of the two arguments to make, Pooley still presents plenty of material in favour of the car. The main thrust is that the car is not responsible for some of the negative consequences of modern urban life often attributed to it. Additional points reinforce the idea that the absence of the car would cause inconvenience and curtail freedoms, such as the choice of where to live. Pooley also makes use of social science evidence that indicates that health, fitness and well-being have a more direct causal relationship with income levels and prosperity than with car ownership.

The key points are:

- '[T]here is little direct evidence to suggest that the motor car caused suburbanisation or that the lack of access to a car prevents urban sprawl.'
- The motor car did not cause economic decentralisation. This had much more to do with changing industrial processes, 'deindustrialisation' and land prices; the car was simply a convenient means of transport at the time.
- 'A town full of diesel buses could be just as bad as one congested with cars'.
- The combined effect of lifestyle factors, including diet, exercise, smoking and alcohol consumption, may have been a much bigger influence on individual health than motor vehicle use.
- 'High levels of exercise, including walking and cycling, are more closely correlated with income and lifestyle than with car ownership.'

Pooley's counter-factual analysis of the history of car use in Britain places the questions about the costs and benefits of such use in a much wider context than the discussion in Section 3.1 did. Here it is not just a question of whether road building generates traffic or reduces congestion. It is a matter of placing car culture in a broad social and historical context, to understand how this particular activity is shaped by and helps to shape a range of other social activities. This returns us once again to the theme introduced by Banister in Section 2, the idea that transport is not a closed system. This is why 'predict and provide' approaches to forecasting future mobility have come to be seen as being of limited value on their own. Transport issues are parts of wider processes, and this is why forecasting future mobility is so difficult. A number of different factors need to be taken into account in deciding where to build roads, whether to build new airports, whether to invest in new railway infrastructure. Social science is involved in these sorts of issues not just because they are complicated, however. It is also because these issues are hotly contested – these decisions raise questions about the uneven distribution of the costs of new investments, the unequal impacts of closing existing services, and the unanticipated effects of developing new technologies. Transport issues are more than merely technical issues – they inevitably involve different visions of the future patterns of social life, and they inevitably draw social science into debates about future mobilities.

4 Conclusion: contested understandings of the future

This chapter began by comparing two views of modern car culture, one in which mobility is presented as a realm of freedom and choice, and a contrasting view that presented people as so dependent on their cars as to appear like slaves. The contrast dramatises the social science issues that arise around attempts to understand future trends of transport use and travel patterns – issues that revolve around the complex questions of how lots of separate decisions and action combine to generate aggregate, collective outcomes. You have seen, above all, that understanding the likely outcomes of decisions around transport use is a complex task, involving the gathering of evidence, but also the use of concepts and values. Social scientists such as Banister and Owens have been shown arguing that the range of factors shaping transport systems and travel patterns go far beyond the realm of transportation per se. Because of the difficulty of forecasting future mobility patterns, social science is inevitably implicated in debates about how best to take action now, in the present, to achieve effects in the future. And because these decisions can affect the livelihoods and life chances of different people in different ways, this also means that social science becomes involved in deeply contested public issues.

The chapter has investigated how social science is used in attempts to forecast future transport demand and travel patterns, taking the examples of railway policy in the UK from the 1960s to the 1980s, and more recent debates about the future of car transport. In Section 2, the limitations of 'predict and provide' models of transport forecasting were discussed, looking at the case of the Settle–Carlisle dispute to show how social science was used to challenge the understandings of cause and effect that had informed the Beeching programme of railway modernisation. One thing that is clear from that discussion is that the use of social science in contested public debates is, in the end, about more than just getting the facts straight and the explanation correct. By virtue of being used to support or challenge policy making and decision-making programmes around the provision of transport – to support rail closures and more road building, or to challenge these programmes – social science becomes involved in *enacting* social worlds. The debate about the future of the Settle–Carlisle line was certainly informed by social science; and the outcome of the debate, to keep the line open, indicates that social science in turn had a part to play in *shaping* social worlds too – the social worlds of the north-west of England look very different today, because of the success of the campaign to keep the line open, than they would have done if the line had been closed.

The same theme emerges from Section 3, which looked at the way social science understandings are used in contemporary debates about the sustainability of car transport systems. In this section, we saw how social science is used to produce counter-intuitive understandings of the causal relationship at work in transport processes – to question whether road building will lead to a more efficient system, or whether car transport is essential for enhanced personal mobility. Here, too, the concepts and understandings used by social scientists have been developed to inform policy and public debates about transport futures and, as a result, in so far as these understandings are used to decide on whether or not to build more roads, they too help to enact certain outcomes in the world. This relationship between contested understandings and the enactment of social worlds will be developed further in the next chapter.

4.1 Chapter summary

In this chapter you have learned that:

- social science is used to support and challenge forecasts of levels and patterns of travel in the future
- public debates about forecasting and providing for future mobility raise questions about how best to understand relationships between individual actions and collective outcomes, and between intended and unintended outcomes of decisions
- the provision of transport infrastructures is costly and has wide social impacts, and thus it is often highly contentious. Social science therefore is often found at the heart of hotly contested public debates, on both sides of the same issue
- the case of 'predict and provide', from the Beeching Report to the Settle–Carlisle dispute, illustrates this use of social science in public debate, but also indicates that social science does not provide a neutral solution to such debates – rather, it is used to support and challenge different positions and perspectives

- social science becomes involved in these contested public issues because of the difficulty of establishing two sorts of causal relationships: the relationships between the provision of transport infrastructure and future travel patterns; and the relationship between transport and travel on the one hand, and a range of further social processes on the other
- social science develops counter-intuitive understandings and counter-factual analysis in order to raise questions about the cause-and-effect relationships shaping transport, travel and mobility
- because of its role in informing and shaping policy debates and public debates about mobility, social science descriptions and understandings are also implicated in the enactment of future mobility patterns, both anticipated and unanticipated, planned and unplanned.

References

Abbott, S. and Whitehouse, A. (1990) *The Line that Refused to Die: The Story of the Successful Campaign to Save the Settle and Carlisle Railway*, Hawes (North Yorkshire), Leading Edge.

Banister, D. (1994) *Transport Planning* (2nd edn), London, Spon.

Banister, D. (2005) *Unsustainable Transport: City Transport in the New Century*, London, Routledge.

Beeching, R. (1963) *The Reshaping of British Railways*, London, British Railways Board.

Beeching, R. (1965) *The Development of the Major Railway Trunk Routes*, London, British Railways Board.

Department of Transport (1989) *Roads for Prosperity*, London, HMSO.

Haywood, R. (2009) *Railways, Urban Development and Town Planning in Britain: 1948–2008*, London, Ashgate.

Hillman, M. and Whalley, A. (1980) *The Social Consequences of Rail Closures*, London, Policy Studies Institute.

Merton, R. (1936) 'The unanticipated consequences of purposive social action', *American Sociological Review*, vol. 1, no. 6, pp. 894–904.

Miller, D. (2001) *Car Cultures*, Oxford, Berg.

Owens, S. (1994) 'From "predict and provide" to "predict and prevent"?: Pricing and planning in transport policy', *Transport Policy*, vol. 2, no. 1, pp. 43–9.

Pooley, C. (2010) 'Landscapes without the car: a counterfactual historical geography of twentieth-century Britain', *Journal of Historical Geography*, vol. 36, no. 3, pp. 266–75.

Sennett, R. (1977) *The Fall of Public Man*, London and Boston, MA, Faber and Faber.

Sloman, L. (2006) *Car Sick: Solutions for our Car-addicted Culture*, Dartington, Devon, Green Books.

Smith, A. ([1776], 1999), The Wealth of Nations – Books I–III, London, Penguin.

Urry, J. (2004) 'The "system" of automobility', *Theory, Culture and Society*, vol. 21, nos 4/5, pp. 25–39.

Whitelegg, J. (1984) 'Rural railways and disinvestment in rural areas', *Regional Studies*, vol. 21, no. 1, pp. 55–63.

Chapter 6
Contesting the place of music

Jason Toynbee

1 Introduction 229
1.1 Structure of the chapter 230
1.2 Aims of the chapter 231
2 Understanding people and music on the move 232
2.1 *Musique Afro* and the value of authenticity 233
2.2 Understanding travelling cultures 237
2.3 Death metal in Bali 241
3 Understanding audiences and markets for music 249
3.1 Managing uncertain audiences 255
3.2 Enacting music markets 258
4 Conclusion: how social scientists understand contested mobilities in music 264
4.1 Chapter summary 265
References 266

1 Introduction

On a warm summer evening I walk through a street in Hillfields in the English Midlands city of Coventry. It's only about a kilometre to the city centre where there are modern shopping malls, and on display all the consumer goods of international capitalism: mobile phones, computers, clothes, cosmetics, sports gear and on and on. Here in Hillfields it feels completely different. The environment looks traditional and British: narrow streets with small brick houses from the early twentieth century joined together in solid terraces. Yet at the same time I get a strange sense that this place is a crossroads at the centre of the modern world. Then I realise: it's the soundscape telling me this. Balkan Gypsy music drifts from an upstairs window, a North African café on the corner pumps Algerian *rai* into the evening air, someone is watching a Bollywood musical on their TV, and then a car drives past with a thumping, dance-hall bass line made in Jamaica.

What I am hearing around me are the sounds of a mobile world, seemingly all gathered here in this neighbourhood. It is no accident that I am hearing these sounds right here. Hillfields is typical of many places in Europe and North America: places where economic migrants, asylum seekers and others from around the world have settled. A deprived urban area with relatively cheap housing, Hillfields is the kind of place that attracts mostly poor people who leave their homelands to seek a better life. And as people move, they bring their music with them. Music moves with people, who bring their own tastes and skills with them as they arrive in new places. But music also moves on its own, as it were, circulating around the world in the form of **commodities** to buy and sell. Since the development of sound-recording technology in the 1880s, music has circulated in various material forms. By the early twentieth century, record companies were exporting discs made in Europe and the USA around the world, as well as recording music in Asia, Africa and South America for sale to local populations (Gronow and Saunio, 1998). Subsequent technological developments, such as the digitalisation of sounds, have made music even more portable.

A **commodity** is an item that can be bought and sold on the market, and, in particular, a product made specifically for that purpose.

This chapter investigates how social science has sought to make sense of the meanings that people attach to the music they listen to, and in particular how social science has sought to develop understandings of the mobility of music. Developing the theme introduced in the last chapter, it will focus on how these understandings are linked to *contestation*, in two distinctive senses. The first is the way in which social science has sought to develop understandings of the role of music in enabling people to negotiate and challenge the forms of marginality, inequality or discrimination that they face. This aspect of the relationship between music and contestation will be examined by looking at two case studies of **ethnographic research**: Parisian *musique Afro*, and 'death metal' in the Indonesian island of Bali. Second, there are contested understandings of the proper role of social science research on music. On the one hand, the type of ethnographic research that will be discussed in the chapter is associated with the idea that social science can help in 'giving voice' to the concerns of its research subjects by providing better understandings of their practices. On the other, the type of research on music discussed in the third section of this chapter is associated with a different model of the use of social science, one in which social science is used instrumentally to help companies sell music more effectively to consumers.

Ethnographic research is a qualitative approach to research which aims to describe and understand the experience and knowledge of a cultural or social group. It often uses interviews and observation as methods.

These are contrasting, and contested, positions on what social science should be used for. And central to debates about these two positions, as well as to internal debates about ethnography or applied social research, is the dual value of music as both a practice and a commodity – as something that is central to the meaningful activities of people's everyday lives, and something that is produced, bought and sold for profit. Sometimes, these two values of music can seem to be incompatible; sometimes, as this chapter will show, they might be seen to be consistent with each other. As you will see, social scientists disagree about the proper relationship between these two sets of values.

1.1 Structure of the chapter

In Section 2 of the chapter, you will explore how social science understands mobile music through the use of ethnography. The section looks both at the music that moves *with* people as they move to new places, and at the music that moves *to* people from far away. Ethnography uses qualitative methods and involves spending lengthy periods with the people you are studying, and becoming sensitive to the things that are important in their lives, in order to produce **thick descriptions** of particular cultural practices. The ways in which ethnography conceptualises the mobility of culture is also discussed.

A **thick description** is a style of ethnographic representation based on the detailed study of people's actions and interpretations, which seeks to place those actions in a context that gives them meaning.

Section 3 provides a contrast, focusing on social science research in the form of music industry market research. While it too is concerned with finding out about how people use and make sense of music, market research does this for a different reason: in order to sell musical commodities. A key issue here is the way the industry tries to make predictable markets that tend to be highly uncertain. The essential difference between the two approaches to mobile music is that ethnography seeks to do justice to people's own understandings of their cultural practices, often in the name of 'giving voice' to their research subjects; while market research is concerned with 'giving people what they want', but it might also be seen to actively shape the conditions under which people express their tastes and preferences. Section 3 therefore introduces the idea that social science research can combine descriptions and understandings in order to *enact* social phenomena in new ways.

1.2 Aims of the chapter

This chapter aims to:

- examine how social science understands the ways that music moves with people and to people, using examples from ethnography and market research
- explore how social science contributes to understandings of the ways in which people use music to negotiate, challenge or contest their marginal social status or positioning
- explore contested understandings about the proper or appropriate role of social science music research
- develop the idea that social science research can contribute to the enactment of social worlds.

2 Understanding people and music on the move

Because mobile music raises the issue of how music matters in the fabric of people's lives, social scientists have found ethnography to be a particularly useful way of researching it. Ethnography is a qualitative research methodology, associated in particular with anthropology but increasingly used across the social sciences, including sociology and human geography. As you read in Chapter 1, ethnographic study involves researchers immersing themselves in a particular social setting, often in a distinct place, and, through in-depth observation and engagement with the activities of a particular community, making sense of the practices of that group of people. Ethnography can involve employing a range of methods for the generation of empirical materials, and can include in-depth qualitative interviews, conversations, participant and non-participant observation, and even covert observation of interactions. But ethnography is not just about providing very detailed accounts of specific activities or events. It puts a premium on interpreting why things happen by trying to understand what activities mean to the people involved in them: as a result, ethnography is inherently interpretative, and therefore informed by concepts and theories.

So ethnography refers both to a way of generating data about social phenomena, and also to a way of interpreting and writing about those phenomena. This double sense is captured most famously in the term used by the anthropologist Clifford Geertz in his *The Interpretation of Cultures* (1973), when he refers to his own ethnographic work as a form of 'thick description'. This term is meant to capture the idea of ethnography as a close-up investigation of the actions and interpretations that shape people's everyday lives, and as a way of placing those actions into the context that gives them meaning. It is an approach that is most effective in taking seemingly mundane rituals of life – in Geertz's case, for example, the practice of cockfighting on the Indonesian island of Bali – and showing how they serve as arenas in which people work through and engage with the tensions, contradictions and power relations of the social world of which these rituals are one small part.

In this section, we look at two case studies of ethnographic research on music cultures, both of which take as their examples situations where music plays an important part in enabling people to find a place within contested social contexts. In the first case, the focus is on the meanings that music has among people who have arrived in a new place; in the second case, it is on the meanings that music that has arrived from somewhere else takes on among locally situated groups of people.

2.1 *Musique Afro* and the value of authenticity

Figure 6.1 *Coupé-décalé* dancers and musicians

In our first case study, the ethnographer Laura Steil (2011) is writing about the *musique Afro* scene in Paris in which she participated as a dancer for two years in the mid-2000s. Steil describes how in this period black African and Caribbean youths, the sons and daughters of migrants to France, were moving away from a fascination with hip hop and were 'returning' to African-influenced music. Using the example of *coupé-décalé*, a new musical genre of dance music from Côte d'Ivoire, she argues that this shift represented more than just a shift in musical taste:

> *Coupé-décalé* started to reshape the way young people spoke, dressed and carried themselves as well as modifying the soundtrack, *ambience* and texture of their leisure time. Speaking with an African accent became a source of pride rather than an object of scorn, and those who could not put on a convincing accent were

> disconsolate. Wearing baggy clothes and sports brands lost its appeal, and young people began to don Versace and Dolce and Gabbana imitations. Fast excited gestures were replaced by slow, broad ones, especially in walk and conversation.
>
> (Steil, 2011, p. 57)

In making sense of this emerging *musique Afro* scene, Steil focuses on interpreting it in terms of one particular concept, which she sees as central to giving it the significance it has to its participants: the concept of *authenticity*. Reading 6.1 is an extract from her account of her participation in two dance troupes, where she begins to draw out the relevance of authenticity to this music scene.

As you study Reading 6.1, try to focus on the values and motivations that are at stake for participants, and how Steil interprets these as throwing light on the meaning of authenticity.

Reading 6.1

Authenticity in the *danse Afro* scene

The popularity of African music brought about a positive acknowledgment of the African dimension of the young people's lives, and added new layers of meaning to 'authenticity'. First, public displays of affection and attachment to the *quartier* ('hood') no longer sufficed to perform 'authenticity'. The culturally intimate African dimension of young people's lives had to become visible. Second, poverty and wealth were invested with new significance. French young people who had cultivated a romantic attachment to the manners and lifestyle of the 'ghetto' were confronted by the energy their African peers deployed to leave, or at least appear as if they had left, poor living conditions. Indeed, the key figures in *coupé-décalé* and *n'dombolo* [another new African musical style, from Zaire] were actors who put forward an image of success and wealth. Moreover, other meanings of the 'ghetto' became available. For many Congolese, for instance, 'ghetto' meant a way of dealing with things rather than a place; it referred to the 'hustling' and 'working the angles' that pervaded the music business. It was thus possible to 'hustle' and belong to the 'ghetto' while simultaneously living in a huge mansion, wearing authentic designer clothes and producing mainstream music. Aspirations to a better life on the one hand and 'authenticity' on the other were not contradictory to African artists. This may explain their appeal to dancers who ardently wanted to make it but did not want to let go of their 'authenticity'.

'Realness' was intimately tied to authenticity. What the dancers insisted on was loyalty to individuals (manifest through physical presence, phone calls, text messages or Internet chats) and to artistic norms (evident in dance moves that were identical to the African originals in name and execution). But being 'real' (*vrai*) also required a certain degree of rupture and irreverence. Indeed, a dancer's status depended on possessing a style, a unique and original signature to apply to routines. Friendships that were too close could hinder the development of a personal style, since dancers who constantly hung out and rehearsed together tended to mimic one another's habits unintentionally. Being 'fake' (*faux*) denoted the exact opposite: social isolation, disrespect or ignorance of artistic norms, and a lack of personal style. The two dance groups considered here represented two extremes in terms of status. The VIPs were greatly admired; their fan-base and their opportunities grew as the year unfolded. They were considered 'real'. The Glamorous Chicks were either unknown or deliberately ignored, and remained so throughout the year, their rare performances subject to mockery. They were considered 'fake'. My idiosyncratic profile as a white, yet not French, woman, in mostly black and African-descended groups gave me an excellent vantage point from which to approach the issue of 'realness'. 'Realness' had actually as much to do with attitude, behaviour and 'morality' as with race, ethnicity and cultural capital. Indeed, '*vrai*' meant not only 'real' but also 'true', while '*faux*' denoted 'fake' as well as 'wrong'. The implication of these double meanings was that 'realness' had to do with some kind of moral correctness.

The leader of the VIPs was a handsome, stylish and disarmingly charismatic man of 23 years. Jordan was at once the group's choreographer, manager and most talented dancer. His unusual haircut – chemically straightened hair sculpted into a Mohawk – reflected his creativity and boldness. Jordan was living proof that the spirit of the 1980s *sapeurs* [a Zairean youth culture] lived on in

> the present. As the only permanent fixture in the group, he aimed to become a star, and the group's popularity ultimately depended on his own.
>
> (Source: Steil, 2011, pp. 61–3)

Let us consider the issue of how Steil uses the concept of authenticity to make sense of the importance of this music and dance culture. This concept has long been an important theme in research into popular music. Across many different musical cultures, researchers have suggested that values of authenticity – of being real, of being true to a community, or perhaps to ideals of artistic expression – are hugely significant. In the case of mobile music, authenticity takes on an added dimension, of being true to the place where the music has its origins. Perhaps the most interesting thing about the description that Steil provides is the paradoxical nature of the practices in which authenticity seems to be at stake. On the one hand, there is faithfulness to Africa, the following of original names and dance moves. That's one version of authenticity. On the other hand, we learn of the need to be creative and for dancers to develop their own style, to be authentic in relation to their own skills and vocation as dancers, to be 'real'.

Steil also notes a contradiction between a culture of ostentatious wealth, or more often pretend wealth, and the idea that you should still be attached to the ghetto. She suggests it is resolved because the 'ghetto' becomes 'a way of dealing with things rather than a place', and refers in particular to the sort of 'hustling' common in the music business. This reinforces another point about authenticity. As Steil notes, '"Realness" had actually as much to do with attitude, behaviour and "morality" as with race, ethnicity and cultural capital.' In other words it is a value that depends on what people do within the subculture of *danse Afro*, and not merely on the social position that they bring with them from the outside. We get a strong sense that Jordan, leader of the VIPs, embodies just this paradoxical sort of authenticity in his own practice. What counts is the way he conducts himself, and negotiates the various tensions involved in being authentic.

You can see, then, that in Reading 6.1 Steil is using authenticity as a concept with which to understand the activities she observes, both in terms of what they mean to the participants and to make sense of them for outside observers as well. You can see this dual emphasis in Steil's use of the concept. She quotes her research subjects using terms like 'real' and 'fake'. Yet her own use of 'authenticity' depends very much on going beyond these terms, and placing them in an alternative interpretative framework. In this way, Steil provides an understanding of the importance that this musical culture plays in the lives of its participants, as one means through which they make sense of their own position in society as migrants.

2.2 Understanding travelling cultures

Steil's ethnographic account of African music cultures in Paris depends on both immersion in a particular milieu, on getting up-close and taking part in the practices of dance that make up this world; but also on adopting a certain sort of distance, by using concepts to provide a social science understanding of participants' actions. This movement between immersion and distance is one way in which ethnography itself might be thought of as a 'mobile' method.

Classically, ethnography is a method associated with social scientists travelling to a different place, settling down for a while to get to know that place, and then returning with their new understanding of a distant culture (Clifford, 1992, p. 99). As such, it has often found it difficult to break free from its historical origins in European colonialism in the nineteenth century as a means of recording and cataloguing the cultures and habits of 'exotic' peoples as a precursor to subjecting those people to colonial and imperial rule. One of the most important features of traditional ethnography was the idea that different 'cultures' inhabited their own particular places – that's why you needed to travel far away to study them. It is an idea closely associated with the notion of 'fieldwork' as a method of data collection. One of the founders of modern ethnographic fieldwork was the anthropologist Bronisław Malinowski, who in the early twentieth century pioneered ethnographic approaches to **participant observation**, in which researchers lived among their research subjects, learned their language and became involved in their daily lives. This is an approach, then, that depends on travelling to another place and then dwelling there for some time, in order to develop understandings of the culture of that place. The historian and anthropologist James Clifford suggests that, in this regard, ethnography as it developed in the twentieth century is itself a 'practice of modern travel' (1992, p. 97).

Participant observation is a research method which involves intense involvement on the part of the researcher(s) in the way of life of the social or cultural group being researched.

This approach to ethnography, in which it is assumed that cultures are fixed in place, has come to be widely criticised. Clifford himself uses an image from one of Malinowski's own books to draw out some of the problems with this approach (see Figure 6.2). The picture shows Malinowski, in profile, sitting in his tent, in 'the field', with his research subjects – residents of the Pacific islands of Trobriand – looking on. In the 1920s, when Malinowski was writing about the culture of these islanders, this image indicated his own distinctive research practice, of living alongside his subjects – it showed that the authority of his account of their lives rested on his 'being there'. Today, when we see such pictures, Clifford suggests (1992, p. 98) we might be inclined to ask different questions, not least, questions about what relations of power are involved in these sorts of practices of observation.

Figure 6.2 Malinowski's tent – inhabitants of Omarakana, a village in the Trobriand Islands, look on

The point of Clifford's critique of traditional ethnography is to draw attention to the extent to which social science descriptions and understandings depend on a whole series of practices and technologies that are not neutral. This leads Clifford (1986) to argue that ethnographic writing is not merely the translation of observations into findings, but is in part a creative process. By trying to make visible the ways in which the authority of ethnography depends on technologies like 'the tent' and the creativity of written description, Clifford and other critics seek to do three things.

First, they encourage a greater degree of **reflexivity** among ethnographers and other social scientists. 'Reflexivity' refers to the ways in which social scientists reflect on the conditions that make their research possible, to be produced, distributed and made public. This process of reflection can focus on various issues, including the personal biography or social identity of the researcher, and the institutional relationships in which the researcher and researched are bound.

Reflexivity means reflection on the conditions through which knowledge is produced, distributed and made use of.

Second, they seek to transform how we understand the object of this sort of social science – 'culture'. As already suggested, traditional ethnography depended on the idea that cultures were 'local', but that these local places were closed in, fixed and available for study *in situ*. Increasingly, however, ethnography is concerned with an alternative focus on 'travelling cultures' – on the ways in which ideas, meanings and values move around, circulate and are translated from place to place (see Gupta and Ferguson, 1997).

The two case studies we are looking at in this section are both illustrations of this new sense of ethnography as a methodology that investigates the mobility of culture. Although Steil is an outsider to the music culture she studies, she is not investigating a culture in a 'faraway' place but in a modern metropolitan city, Paris, and she is concerned above all with understanding how people make sense of the place they are in by drawing on resources and meanings from all sorts of other places. Likewise, the next case study is about how people in one place draw on music cultures from other places to make sense of their own local situations. The cultures that both cases look at are mobile cultures, and the local places they focus on are not closed in, but better thought of as nodes in a whole set of flows and movements and circulations.

The third thing that the critique of traditional ethnography does is to give much greater attention to the ways in which cultural practices, like the mobile cultures of music, are infused with relations of power. It is no longer assumed that ethnography just helps us to understand how people make sense of their own situations; it is common for contemporary ethnography to focus on the ways in which more or less marginalised or disempowered groups resist and negotiate the power relations in which they find themselves located. We can see this emphasis in Steil's account of music culture. One of her motivations for wanting to get close to her subjects is because she identifies with their lives, both in their suffering and in their flourishing. Elsewhere in her account, Steil describes the recent history of migration to France, the racist attacks on black people, and the way in which Africans and their sons and daughters struggle to send back money to poor relatives in their countries of origin. And, as she points out, 'a number of studies have shown that stigmatised groups tend to encourage collective rather than individual survival' (Steil, 2011, p. 61).

This is the context in which Steil locates her own analysis of music, dance and the efforts of an artist like Jordan to become successful while remaining authentic. For him, this dance culture is not just fun, or mere play. It is part of his efforts to find a place in what is often experienced as a hostile social environment. He is simultaneously trying to stay faithful to the group to which he belongs and to express himself as an individual. What emerges strongly from Steil's account is her desire to understand the key values of the African community in Paris, and the factors that have given rise to them. This involves not only finding out the *facts* about these values, but also appreciating them *as values.* To put it another way, in order to understand a social world where circumstances press down hard on people, Steil has to get up-close to them to better appreciate their ways of making sense of the world.

So we can see that the sort of ethnography that Steil presents is quite distinctive, in its focus on mobile cultures and on contested power relations, from more traditional styles of this research method. But in certain respects it still exemplifies the strengths of ethnography as an approach to developing social science understandings of everyday life. Steil uses qualitative research methods to learn about and to better understand the meanings that shape the cultural life of her subjects. She provides a 'thick description' of this culture because she seeks both to make sense of the surrounding context in which these meanings take on their full significance, and also to provide an account that makes sense to an outsider.

You can see this relationship between proximity and distance in Steil's account. She wants to get close to her research subjects in order to be in the best position to find out about them; observation depends on physical proximity and the need to get your subjects to 'open up'. One key factor here is that Steil is herself a dancer; she can participate in this specialist activity. What is more, her gender and ethnicity, as a woman and white, give her a particular advantage in terms of access to the subculture she is studying, as she points out in Reading 6.1. But while Steil is clearly empathetic in her approach, she also emphasises the advantages that distance can bring. As she puts it, '[m]y idiosyncratic profile as a white, yet not French, woman, in mostly black and African-descended groups gave me an excellent vantage point from which to approach the issue of "realness"'. Here, then, we get a sense that there is tension involved in ethnographic understanding. You need to be close enough to see and feel what matters to people, yet far enough away to recognise social patterns and relations that are not part of common-sense understanding in that culture. In these respects, Steil's account illustrates a general point about ethnographic research summarised by the anthropologist Sherry B. Ortner: 'Ethnography of course means many things. Minimally, however, it has always meant the attempt to understand another life world using the self – as much of it as possible – as the instrument of knowing' (1995, p. 173).

2.3 Death metal in Bali

Musique Afro represents an example of mobile music being used by people to make sense of the places they find themselves in, as a second generation of migrants remakes the connection with their parents' home culture of Africa. Now, however, we are going to look at another case study, where the subjects of research are not migrants – they are 'at home'. The example of death metal in Bali concerns young men from the local middle class, on the face of it very much at home on the island, who have adopted a style of music that has been imported *from outside*. The ethnographic research of Emma Baulch (2008), a cultural studies scholar, is based on fieldwork in the late 1990s, and presents localness in this music scene as a product of the ways in which musicians and audiences 'gesture elsewhere' to other places. So, we have here another example of the focus of contemporary ethnography on the ways in which musical practices move around the world, and on the way in which local places are made up from flows and circulations of mobile cultural practices.

Extreme metal, of which death metal is a sub-genre, originally emerged in the 1980s as a punk–heavy metal hybrid which, as the sociologist and music critic Keith Kahn-Harris puts it, 'eschewed melody and clear singing in favour of speed, down tune guitars, and growled or screamed vocals' (quoted in Baulch, 2003, p. 200). Although the style originated in the USA and Europe, it soon spread to and further developed in places as diverse as Chile, Malaysia and Israel. Here its circulation depended on informal networks built out of the exchange of letters, cassette tapes, small label recordings and fanzines. For Baulch, approaching the scene as a social scientist, the research problem is how to understand the particular ways in which death metal was appropriated in Bali at a key moment of political tension and contestation in Indonesian history.

You might stop for a moment and ask yourself what, if any, image you have of Bali. You may, for instance, have come across the 1958 Hollywood film musical *South Pacific*, which includes lyrical descriptions of Bali Ha'i, a fictional volcanic island, close to a larger Pacific island occupied by US troops in the Second World War. The island represents an exotic, but unattainable, paradise to the troops for whom it is off-limits. 'Bali Ha'i' was also the title of a hit song from the musical. The film, and the song, fixed in place a stereotype of 'Bali'.

Figure 6.3 *South Pacific*: unobtainable paradise or exoticist stereotype?

Exoticist signifies the way in which a judgement is made in one culture about the strangely desirable, but also inferior, nature of another culture.

Actually, the real Bali – without the 'Ha'i' – is not in the Pacific at all but over a thousand kilometres further west, part of the island chain that makes up the state of Indonesia. But despite its inaccurate and **exoticist** portrayal in the film, 'Bali Hai' has been taken up as the name of an Indonesian beer brewed in Jakarta, the capital of Indonesia and located on the much bigger island of Java, to the west of Bali. The point worth drawing out here is that as music and media circulate around the world their meaning can change. For the brewers and drinkers of Indonesia it seems that using the name Bali Hai, even though it is part of an inauthentic Hollywood fiction, is just fine. Perhaps it might even be a source of ironic amusement.

Baulch is concerned with the same process, but in a different context – with the way in which music that originates from elsewhere can be appropriated in a particular place in order to bolster a sense of local identity. What is notable about her example of the appropriation of death metal, however, is that it situates this process of appropriation in a context of local contestation. During the period in which she was undertaking her fieldwork, Indonesia was undergoing political upheaval. The 'New Order', the repressive regime of President Suharto that had been in power since 1966, was coming under increasing pressure from opposition groups, including regionalists in some of the Indonesian islands like Bali. Suharto would be finally forced out of power in 1998. Baulch shows how metal **subculture** not only provided a focus for an alternative subculture based on opposition to, or difference from, the official regime, but also became implicated in the growing turmoil that eventually led to its downfall. For instance an opposition party, the PDI, adopted the heavy metal symbol of the devil's horns in the 1992 presidential election campaign. In 1993 there were riots at a concert by Metallica, an international thrash metal band, when poor youths in Jakarta objected to the high price of tickets, forced their way in and looted the surrounding streets.

A **subculture** is a group of people who share a common set of practices, tastes, and values, which sets them apart from or differentiates them from the wider society of which they are a part.

In Reading 6.2, Baulch provides an account of how belonging to this subculture depends on negotiating the meanings of music and other cultural products from elsewhere. As you read it, you will notice that, like Steil, Baulch makes use of the concept of authenticity. Does she use it in the same way? She also makes use of two other social science concepts: the idea of **territorialisation**, and the idea of **performative vocabulary**.

Territorialisation means making a space your own, often by marking out clear boundaries.

Performative vocabulary refers to the range of actions, particularly in terms of style and deportment, used to establish and publicly display one's identity.

What points is Baulch making about music and mobility when she uses the terms authenticity, territorialisation and performative vocabulary?

Reading 6.2

Balinese death metal and the 'absence' of authenticity

Denpasar's [capital city of the province of Bali] death metal scene had its roots in a radio programme, called 1921 in reference to its twice-weekly slot (19hrs–21hrs, every Saturday and Sunday), and broadcast on a local community radio station, Radio Yudha. Begun in the late 1980s as a heavy metal show, following the developing tastes of its announcer Agus Yanky, and many of its listeners, 1921 gradually became dedicated to thrash metal, and following that death metal, before it was wound up in 1994. As Agus Yanky (interview, 6 February 1998) recalled, when 1921 broadcast songs by thrash metal bands increasing numbers of enthusiasts responded to the new show by visiting the studio at the time of the broadcasts. In this way, 1921 … operated as a call to prayer, sucking disparate enthusiasts from family compounds scattered all over Denpasar, and bringing them together in a space in which fixity was achieved through tape swapping, information exchange, the production of self-designed black tee shirts and the kind of uniquely Balinese drinking rituals that serve to knit male solidarity. It was thus that a death/thrash fandom became territorialised.

The importance of territory was affirmed by the way in which death metal enthusiasts began to stake out public and bodily spaces for the display of symbols of death/thrash fandom once they had established the Yudha studio as a home territory. Categories of belonging and group identification were established when the people who gathered there began to adopt the universal death metal aesthetic, and to perform this aesthetic in a public arena. [Black] tee shirts were emblazoned with the names of death metal and thrash bands, unmistakeable for their illegibility, thus drawing attention to the practice's desire to veil literal meaning in mystery. The tee shirts served as 'performative vocabulary' (Bell and Valentine 1995, p. 143), for they were worn as the death thrashers began to stage exhibitions in more public arenas, such as the Kumbasari market and the cassette store, Istana Musik, both located in central Denpasar.

Enthusiasts' recollections are particularly revealing of the significance of this performative vocabulary. That black tee shirts were meant to demonstrate pride in a marginal status is evident in Age's [one of the fans] recollection of how, in the years between

1990 and 1994, 'others would be in their trendy get-ups, we'd be different. We'd wear all black with holes in our clothes. We didn't care, we'd come together en masse, ride around in convoys, en masse. Maybe it was a kind of exhibition, to show that we were a community'. Community, then, was performed by means of a uniform aesthetic.

In line with the equality conveyed by the death/thrashers' uniform aesthetic, tangible resources were relatively equally distributed – album fetishisation was scorned, as was that of guitars. Ensuring equal distribution of cassettes, and discouraging individuals from amassing personal collections, was indeed one of the functions of the gatherings at Radio Yudha. As Moel [another fan] recalled, after the scene extended its links to Malaysia, enthusiasts formed a death metal organisation to help formalise distribution channels:

> We used to gather at the studio and make tee shirts … Then, a friend from Malaysia came to visit. In Malaysia, they had a [death metal] organisation to maximise access to the information they received. To prevent individual people from amassing personal collections, we also formed a death metal organisation.

But maintaining a coherent deviance requires at once exclusion and unity, and whilst tangible resources appear to have been shared, intangible ones became the basis for exclusion and hierarchy; power and seniority within the Balinese scene were based on virtuosity and archival knowledge. In this way, the scene actively sought to maintain a marginal status by employing exclusionary tactics. [Indeed], the predominance of cover bands in the early- and mid-1990s was due to their role as a realm for necessary skill enhancement and a rite of passage, for newly formed bands who attempted originals were scorned as upstarts. For death/thrash enthusiasts, therefore, authenticity appeared to lay in an absent elsewhere which could only be reached by diligently rehearsing foreign repertoires. In this quest, the present and the locale became secondary concerns, as the authentic self was determined by an absent truth.

Reference

Bell, D., and Valentine, G. (1995) 'The sexed self: strategies of performance, sites of resistance', in Pile, S. and Thrift, N. (eds)

Mapping the Subject: Geographies of Cultural Transformations, London, Routledge.

(Source: Baulch, 2003, pp. 196–204)

As with Steil's ethnography, Baulch presents authenticity as an achievement that requires people to juggle between, on the one hand, the place they find themselves in and, on the other, the distant locations from which 'their' types of music and cultures have arrived. More so perhaps than in Reading 6.1, in Reading 6.2 authenticity is very strongly presented as a means of identifying with another place. Baulch suggests that the marking out of community in this subculture involved a democratic, inclusive form of social practice – an expression of agency, in the terms used in Chapter 4. Enthusiasts shared cassette tapes and formed organisations to spread the word. Yet at the same time there was a hierarchy based on 'archival knowledge': the different things enthusiasts knew about the genre on a global basis. Indeed the value of authenticity in the scene had to do very much with staying close to the repertoire of the international genre. Cover versions of material that originated outside Indonesia were *de rigueur*; original compositions were frowned upon.

There is an interesting comparison to be made with Steil's study in relation to authenticity and mobility. In both Parisian *danse Afro* and Balinese death metal, authenticity seems to have involved a tension between home and away, between what you are now and what you might become. To be successful, you have to negotiate these tensions. But it seems that 'home' was an even more ambiguous value in the Balinese scene than in *danse Afro*. It depended on using objects and symbolic markers like T-shirts to communicate to others that which marked out a local space, yet at the same time 'gestured elsewhere' to a global thrash metal scene.

In Reading 6.2, this achievement of authenticity among death metal enthusiasts in Bali is explained by Baulch through the concept of 'territorialisation'. This is the term she uses to describe the practices by which the circulation of music and meanings from elsewhere was brought down to the ground, as it were – practices of swapping and exchanging and of making T-shirts. Although the radio show, 1921, was a mediated 'call to prayer' that brought in new members of the scene, what counted most was the physical space of the Radio Yudha studio.

Death/thrash fans congregated there and through talk, swapping cassette tapes and, just as important, the wearing of black T-shirts emblazoned with illegible band names, they generated and creatively developed a set of shared rituals of agency and belonging, specific to the subculture. These practices of territorialisation are then linked by Baulch to how these men displayed their identities as members of this subculture in the public spaces of Denpasar. Baulch uses the term 'performative vocabulary' to describe the meanings associated with the wearing of the T-shirts in public. The word 'performative' suggests a sense of display and demonstration – of theatricality even; it is meant to draw attention to the degree to which wearing these T-shirts was a way of doing something, signalling pride in their marginal status. By saying that this made up part of a performative *vocabulary*, Baulch is indicating that this particular practice was perhaps just one among a range of actions that were available to these men to signal their identity in a public space – it was one part of a repertoire of actions they had available to them.

Figure 6.4 Leading Balinese guitarist Ari Phobia in his room

Like Steil, Baulch therefore uses social science concepts to make sense of, and do justice to, the full significance of the seemingly arcane, everyday features of a particular subculture of musical enthusiasts. By providing a situated interpretation, and drawing out how and why music matters to her research subjects, she shows how this set of practices needs to be understood in a broader context, which includes the social and political environment of Indonesia at the time of her study.

Both of the case studies looked at in this section have focused on how music moves – how it moves with people, and how it moves to them. And both have focused on how people make sense of mobile music in the places in which they live, and not least in relation to the contested relationships of power and privilege that they have to negotiate in those places. You have seen how ethnographic research makes use of strategies of immersion to get up-close to research subjects, but also makes use of concepts in order to make sense of cultural practices as if from the outside. It is this movement between inside and outside perspectives that marks ethnography as an approach to generating social science understanding. Where once ethnography was associated with travelling to distant places to understand local cultures, now it is regarded as a method that is very well attuned to understanding how meaning is made through the movement of people, things and movements to different places.

Ethnography is one social science approach for understanding why music matters to people in their everyday lives. We have seen that it can throw light on how mundane activities might play a role in helping people negotiate their ways around contested, conflicted, power-laden social worlds. And we have also seen how this approach has itself developed through a contested process of criticism and adjustment, as the colonial heritage of traditional ethnography has been transformed by an emphasis on reflexivity and travelling cultures. In the next section, we look at another style of social science research that also seeks to understand what people like about music and why they like it. But this style of social science draws into explicit focus something that has so far been in the background in the ethnographies discussed in this section – the status of music as a *commodity*, something produced in order to be bought and sold. In both of the case studies discussed in this section, the meanings of mobile music cultures have been closely associated with the movement of culture as a commodity – with designer clothes, with cassette tapes and records. These ethnographies show how people make their own meanings out of these circulating commodities. In the next section, you will look at the ways in which social science is involved in actually making possible the circulation of music as a commodity, and at debates about whether authentic meaning can really be found in music cultures dependent on **commodification**.

Commodification is the process of transforming something into a commodity, e.g. land, food, music.

3 Understanding audiences and markets for music

Studying what meanings ordinary people give to their everyday activities, like watching television, listening to music, or going to the shops, has become an established field of social science research across many disciplines. But the idea that social science could and should study everyday life, and do so from the perspective of what matters to ordinary people, has not always been widely accepted. One of the periods in which such research was pioneered was the 1930s and 1940s, when social scientists in the USA developed a set of empirical methodologies, such as surveys and focus groups, for investigating the audiences for new forms of popular culture such as the movies, radio and magazines. This is a style of social science research that is interesting not least because, over time, it has become the basis for various uses of social science by commercial organisations; and, because of this, it is a style of social science whose legitimacy has sometimes been contested and challenged.

These new forms of empirical social science developed in a period in which popular culture itself was transformed into a major industrial sector. The music industry illustrates this more general process. By the late 1930s the production of popular music had effectively undergone an industrial revolution in the USA. Using the new federal highway system to move across the country, big swing bands were constantly on tour, playing to dancers in ballrooms and dance halls. Often their performances were broadcast live on radio networks such as CBS and NBC, which by now had a national reach. At the same time the record industry was recovering from its near collapse in the Great Depression, boosted in part by the rapid take-off of a new piece of technology, the juke-box. In cinema the development of sound after 1927 had enabled the massive growth of the screen musical. It also quickly became the norm for all feature films to have a musical soundtrack. In effect, then, by the end of the 1930s, music making and dissemination were being carried out by a large-scale multi-media industry, which brought music into people's lives through multiple channels and contexts. The result was that music became ubiquitous, which it had never been before.

As new mass media developed, so public interest in understanding the effects of media also grew. In the USA in 1937, the Rockefeller Foundation funded a programme of research into the new mass media, focusing on radio. The Radio Project, as it became known, was one of the first attempts by social scientists to make sense of the ways in which media technologies reshape everyday life. The project was headed by Paul Lazarsfeld, a pioneer of empirical social science. Lazarsfeld developed a programme of social research – **administrative research** – that combined methods such as surveys, focus group interviews and experiments. This approach was, he argued, a way of generating useful social science knowledge about particular problems, which could be used by both policy makers and commercial clients. Research into radio also made use of a device called a 'programme analyser'. This collated responses to radio programmes from people who had been invited into the CBS studio: 'At pre-selected moments, signalled by a light, they were asked to indicate by pressing a red or green button on their chair, whether they did or did not like what they were hearing at that moment' (Scannell, 2007, p. 17).

Administrative research seeks to generate useful social science knowledge about particular problems, and can be used by both policy makers and commercial clients. It is associated with Paul Lazarsfeld but criticised by Theodor Adorno, who distinguished two types of administrative research: benevolent and exploitative.

One of the other participants in the Radio Project was the German Jewish philosopher Theodor Adorno, who, like Lazarsfeld, was an exile from Nazi-controlled Europe. Adorno oversaw the research into the impact of the broadcasting of music on the new medium of radio. But the primary outcome of his involvement in this project was to call into question the legitimacy of undertaking empirical research that attempted to collate and measure people's responses to cultural forms such as popular music. It is worth looking in some detail at the basis of Adorno's 'critique of radio music' (1945), because it represents a sceptical perspective on the idea, discussed in Chapter 1, that people can actively appropriate cultural commodities to give them new meanings of their own.

Figure 6.5 Theodor Adorno

Adorno's involvement in the Radio Project led him to develop a sustained critique of the effects of mass-mediated culture, and also to criticise the whole programme of administrative research. For the radio music study, he had been asked to find out 'how can "good music" be conveyed to the largest possible audience' (Adorno, 1945, p. 209). ('Good music' was here assumed to be the canon of European classical music.) What he provided instead was a critique of the very possibility of posing such a question. Adorno would eventually help to develop an argument about the effects of the 'culture industry', an argument in which mass-mediated consumer culture was seen to be irretrievably tainted by its dependence on commodities and markets. For him, media such as radio were better understood as channels of propaganda rather than channels for the dissemination of high culture to the masses. In Reading 6.3, Adorno outlines his criticism of the Radio Project's empirical methodology.

As you study the reading, consider what sorts of questions Adorno thinks are most important to ask about 'radio music'.

Reading 6.3

Adorno's critique of administrative research

Some would approach the problem of radio by formulating questions of this type: If we confront such and such a sector of the population with such and such a type of music, what reactions may we expect? How can these reactions be expressed statistically? Or: How many sectors of the population have been brought into contact with music and how do they respond to it?

What intention lies behind such questions? This approach falls into two major operations:

(a) We subject some groups to a number of different treatments and see how they react to each.

(b) We select and recommend the procedure which produces the effect we desire.

The aim itself, the tool by which we achieve it, and the persons upon whom it works are generally taken for granted in this procedure. The guiding interest behind such investigations is basically one of *administrative* technique: how to manipulate the masses. The pattern is that of market analysis even if it appears to be completely remote from any selling purpose. It might be research of an *exploitative* character, i.e. guided by the desire to induce as large a section of the population as possible to buy a certain commodity. Or it may be what Paul E. Lazarsfeld calls *benevolent* administrative research, putting questions such as, 'How can we bring good music to as large a number of listeners as possible?'

I would like to suggest an approach that is antagonistic to exploitative and at least supplementary to benevolent administrative research. It abandons the form of question indicated by a sentence like: How can we under certain conditions, best further certain aims? On the contrary, this approach in some cases questions the aims, and in all cases the successful accomplishment of these aims under the given conditions. Let us examine the question: how can 'good music' be conveyed to the largest possible audience.

What is 'good music'? Is it just the music which is given out and accepted as 'good' according to current standards, say the programs of the Toscanini concerts? We cannot pass it as 'good' simply on the basis of the names of great composers or performers, that is, by social convention. Furthermore, is the goodness of music invariant, or is it something that may change in the course of history with the technique at our disposal? For instance, let us take it for granted – as I do – that Beethoven really is good music. Is it not possible that this music, by the very problems it sets itself, is far away from our own situation? That by constant repetition it has deteriorated so much that it has ceased to be the living force it was and has become a museum piece which no longer possesses the power to speak to the millions to whom it is brought? … Does a symphony played on the air remain a symphony? Are the changes it undergoes by wireless transmission merely slight and negligible modifications or do they affect the very essence of the music? … And as to the large numbers of people who listen to 'good music': *how* do they listen to it? Do they listen to a Beethoven symphony in a concentrated mood? Can they do so even if they want to? … Or do they listen to it as they do to jazz, waiting in the introduction of the finale of Brahms's First Symphony for the solo of the French horn, as they would for Benny Goodman's solo clarinet chorus? Would not such a type of listening make the high cultural ideal of bringing good music to large numbers of people wholly illusory? …

None of these or similar questions can be wholly resolved in terms of even the most benevolent research of the administrative type. One should not study the attitude of listeners, without first considering how far these attitudes reflect broader social behaviour patterns, and even more, how far they are conditioned by the structure of society as a whole.

(Source: Adorno, 1945, pp. 208–10)

Adorno starts by ruling out empirical 'administrative research' into radio music, and indeed mass media more generally. His assumption is that such research is simply there to 'manipulate the masses', whether it is 'exploitative' (designed to sell commodities) or 'benevolent' (designed to be useful or helpful to existing society). The Himmelweit study on television and children discussed in Chapter 1 would be, in Adorno's terms, an example of benevolent administrative research. It was not driven by commercial considerations, but rather by a concern to investigate the social impact of television. Nevertheless, from Adorno's perspective it fits the model of a focus on specific 'effects' without homing in on how these might be 'conditioned by the structure of society as a whole'. In the terms used in Chapter 4, Adorno's understanding of mass media holds to a structural interpretation, in which the real significance of this sector is determined by the social relations of capitalist commodity production around which it is organised. The appearance of 'agency' provided by asking people what music they like or dislike is merely a way of hiding these structural relations from view.

But in Reading 6.3, Adorno goes to great lengths to raise difficult questions about how to understand the culture of radio music. What is it about this medium that he is most concerned by? It is worth noting that Adorno was himself an accomplished, classically trained musician and a great champion of contemporary avant-garde music, associated with composers such as Arnold Schoenberg and Alban Berg. This was music that was *difficult* to listen to, and was meant to be. If you look at Reading 6.3 again, you can see that what Adorno objects to is the idea that the key problem is how 'good music' is 'conveyed'. Getting people to listen to 'good music' does not appear to be the main issue for him. The issue is *how* people listen to 'good music' – now easily broadcast, made accessible in the spaces of everyday life, the home or office, by the new technology of radio.

Adorno is often criticised for holding to rather lofty standards of 'proper' aesthetic taste (and this is certainly evident in Reading 6.3). But his critique of radio music is more substantive than that. The reason that Adorno thinks the empirical questions about the effects of radio music are not worth pursuing is because he thinks that the image of the active listener, able to choose between this or that piece, able to express an opinion, is really an indication of the transformation in the conditions for the circulation of culture. He views this transformation negatively. He actually thinks that people are really being manipulated and conditioned. We have already seen an alternative, more positive interpretation of the scope for 'agency' that mobile music opens up. As you saw in Reading 6.2, the Balinese death metal enthusiasts in Baulch's (2003) study took recordings made by the multinational record companies, copied them on to cassette tapes and circulated them to other enthusiasts, outside the sphere of the market. They made use of music for their own purposes, creatively 'gesturing elsewhere', as Baulch put it.

We seem to have a stark difference here. Adorno seems to think that the agency of listeners is really rather superficial, really an expression of a deeper level at which people are in fact manipulated and conditioned by 'the culture industry'. However, in ethnographic styles of social research, the active role of audiences in appropriating commodified music is celebrated – sometimes in rather heroic terms.

But, actually, the choice between these two positions might not be so simple. Commercial actors, for example, do not necessarily think that audiences can be easily manipulated and conditioned. Let us now look in a little more detail at how the meanings of musical commodities are understood in what is sometimes called the **culture industry**.

The culture industry was a phrase coined by Adorno to emphasise how popular culture is made on an industrial basis for profit, resulting in standardised musical commodities.

3.1 Managing uncertain audiences

Adorno's critique had no effect in stopping the onward march of radio and music research. After the Second World War, at a time of rapidly expanding commercial and governmental interest in media research, Lazarsfeld and his colleagues at Columbia University in the USA developed a long-term research programme into mass communication effects and the problem of persuasion. Questions that recurred in this period concerned the extent to which the media had effects on their audiences, and how these were to be understood.

Lazarsfeld and his colleague Elihu Katz used the new technique of the social survey to address these questions (it's worth noting that their sample included only women, although no reason was given for this; rather like Alfred Kinsey, whose research you read about in Chapter 2, their approach to sampling was unusual by today's standards). Their conclusion was that the media had limited effects. Moreover, these effects were produced indirectly. The authors explained this in terms of **personal influence** and **two-step flow**. These concepts refer to the process whereby a 'primary group' of opinion leaders influence the interpretation of media messages by the people around them (Katz and Lazarsfeld, 1955). This has been a hugely important finding in communications studies, suggesting that the mass media are not all-powerful, that audiences are not homogenous and that a constructive role is played by their more active members. This is an optimistic, democratic understanding, which in certain respects anticipates the emphasis in contemporary ethnographic research into popular culture on active meaning-making. If you recall the Balinese death metal scene described in Reading 6.2, then the musicians at its heart, hanging out in

Personal influence is a concept of Elihu Katz according to which our understanding of the media is shaped by our communication with other people.

A **two-step flow** signifies the dissemination of ideas from the media, via key opinion leaders, to others who are influenced by them in a community.

the Radio Yudha studio, might be said to belong to a primary group of opinion leaders.

While the new field of communication studies was establishing its academic credentials within social science, the media industries were developing their own approach to market research. In effect, as mass culture grew so too did the demand for what Adorno had bluntly called 'exploitative' research – knowledge that might boost sales or help deliver audiences to advertisers. For Adorno, of course, such research was simply instrumental, reinforcing the process whereby audiences were led to desire the very standardised commodities that the culture industry was geared up to deliver, and to imagine that their desire was really an expression of their free choice.

3.1.1 The 'infinite variety' of cultural markets

However, the idea that cultural markets can simply be manipulated in order to generate guaranteed profits has been called into question by economists specialising in cultural commodities. As the economist Richard Caves (2001) argues, cultural commodities are 'experience goods'. In other words, consumers can tell whether or not they like them only *after* they have read, watched or listened to them. This is because, far from being standardised, they are actually highly complex and given to variation.

Take the example of a pop song. You may think of this as the archetypal formulaic cultural commodity. But no two songs are exactly alike. Play one now – or, better, just play a favourite song back 'in your head'. Ask yourself, 'What do I like about it?' The singer's voice might be one reason. Then there is the melody. And you will probably be thinking about how you are responding to the rhythm, or beats. Actually, each of these aspects could be broken down further, and countless other attributes could be added. The song might have special meaning to you, because of when you first heard it for example. Every one of these factors might, or might not, play a part in your judgement of the song.

Caves uses the expression 'infinite variety' to describe this complex and multi-dimensional quality of cultural products. It is infinite variety, he suggests, which makes it so difficult for media and cultural organisations to predict in advance what audiences will like (Caves, 2001, p. 6). The same quality also helps to explain the mobility of cultural products, especially music. Its multi-faceted nature means that it can be valued in different ways by those who listen to it in different places, and taken up and adapted by musicians across the world in new ways. *Musique Afro* and Balinese death metal are cases in point.

Far from being standardised, then, from this perspective of the infinite variety of cultural forms there arises the problem of uncertainty of consumer demand. This helps to account for some of the distinctive structures and strategies of media organisations and cultural markets. In these cultural sectors, there is a commercial premium on having the best possible knowledge about the likely popularity of new products, so as to avoid launching expensive flops. In a radically uncertain market, you try to reduce uncertainty.

3.1.2 Market testing

This problem of uncertainty, because of the difficulty of predicting cultural taste, is confronted in rather different ways in different cultural sectors. For media that are capital-intensive, like film and television, 'sunk' costs per unit are high: in other words the costs of filming, say, cannot be recovered if the production process ceases. So rather than committing to making a whole television series or a complete film, and risk losing all your investment, 'pre-testing' may be employed. Pre-testing is a form of audience research carried out before production is complete and major resources have been committed. The US television industry uses it extensively. The procedure is to select an audience sample and then show a 'pilot', usually the first episode in a series, to the members of that sample, either in a theatre or at their homes. Feedback is collected electronically in the theatre (through a modern-day version of Lazarsfeld's programme analyser), or through interviews at home. It is then possible to respond to the feedback by making changes to scripts or other production values. If the feedback is very negative, production can be halted altogether and the programme dropped. Similar methods are used in music radio research. For instance, the 'call-out' involves playing small segments of songs to respondents over the telephone, and then collecting feedback. Larger-scale changes to a whole radio 'format' (the particular profile of records and music styles played by a station) are tested through a combination of survey and focus group methods.

But pre-testing is not used in all media sectors. In some markets, such as the music industry and book publishing, there are very high rates of innovation. Recorded music turns over quickly in the charts and the number of individual titles is high – this is the 'repertoire' published or released by companies. It is not necessarily assumed that all singles or albums will be hits, or that all books will be best-sellers. But by having a wide repertoire, the chances are that some will be, and that these will more than cover the costs of those that aren't. In the recorded music market, it is impossible to pre-test because of the sheer quantity of records that are released every month. Instead the industry relies on post hoc knowledge of the actual rather than the potential market. Traditionally the charts – the Top 100 or Top 40 – provided sales information about this. But they were never very accurate and may well have been corruptly rigged by record companies at various times. These days there are computerised, electronic point of sale (EPOS) systems in record shops that log every item sold. Music downloads from the internet (at least the ones you pay for) are logged too. And in the USA an independent market research company, SoundScan, collates all this information to produce the published charts, with breakdowns of sales according to genre.

In a market where pre-testing is impossible, the only other option is to try to make sense of trends in existing sales in order to predict which styles and artists are going to be popular in the future. That way, in principle at least, firms can respond to what people are likely to want in the future on the basis of what they are choosing now. We have already seen a version of this sort of forecasting at work in Chapter 5, and you will recall from that discussion that, actually, basing future forecasts on present trends can itself be a little risky. This way of trying to manage uncertainty in audience taste allows commercial companies to present their industries as ones in which consumers determine what will happen in the music market, and in which those firms that follow emerging demand will have a competitive advantage. But this does not quite answer the problem of uncertainty adequately. It does not quite account for how commercial actors are able to respond to innovations in cultural styles and tastes. To understand that, we need to rethink what we understand a 'market' to be in the field of cultural commodities.

3.2 Enacting music markets

Of course, the model of using existing patterns of taste to decide future production is exactly what Adorno criticised. This appears to be how popular music becomes standardised: the music industry gives people what they have already demonstrated they want. But rather than thinking of markets as standardising culture (as Adorno does), or as media in which competition, informed by knowledge, drives a virtuous cycle of supply and demand (as commercial actors themselves are prone

Tell us how we did today! Visit www.tellaldi.com to complete our survey and be in with a chance to win £100 in Aldi vouchers

argue that the information generated in
: does not just reflect existing tastes, but
ıe markets it is ostensibly describing.

markets has been developed by the
l and the sociologist Richard
e that markets can be understood as social
that the music market is made up of a range
;anisations all focused on a common purpose
elling records. The 'field' that is focused on
ɪr its effectiveness on knowledge about music
l and Peterson describe the way this knowledge
ıated as 'field-wide information regimes' (2000,
ms try to deal with uncertainty in music
:ing and then *sharing* information – as in the case
e recently the sophisticated analysis of sales
provided by EPOS devices. However, Anand and Peterson point out that an 'information regime' of this sort does not simply reflect an external market – it both produces and reproduces the market.

Another way of putting it is that rather than simply describing the music market (a difficult enough task), market research helps to enact the market for music. In Reading 6.4, Anand and Peterson explain the idea that market information regimes enact music markets, using the example of US music industry market research.

As you read this, look in particular at the difference in music markets that the reading ascribes to the development of SoundScan in the 1980s, and consider how this might be an example of research 'enacting' new music markets.

Reading 6.4

Music and market information regimes

A market information regime comprises regularly updated information about market activity provided by an independent supplier, presented in a predictable format with consistent frequency, and available to all interested parties at a nominal cost. The culture industries, dependent on satisfying consumer tastes that change rapidly, develop market-defining measures such as the *New York Times* bestseller list in the commercial book-publishing field and the Nielsen ratings for television programming.

Sensemaking and the construction of market information regimes

... In competitive market fields, performance-related information is the raw material from which organisational actors make sense of their environment. The outcome of this process is an enactment of a 'market.' Market information regimes are the medium through which producers observe each other and market participants make sense of their world. What is more, the regular collection of specific information focuses the attention of field participants on those reports. The existence of a particular market information regime conveys the impression that the information is valid and vitally important, and its availability creates demand for its use in interpreting their environment.

Sensemaking devices comprise cues and connections embodied in routine organisational activities (Weick, 1995). In market information regimes, information typically takes the forms of sales reports, inventory information, trade magazine reports of 'hot selling' items, newspaper articles, rumors or gossip with connections to past, present, and future courses of action. The framing of market information can vary in terms of the scope of information collected, the methodology for compiling information, and the political tone with which the information is presented.

The SoundScan revolution

In the mid 1980s record store chains began introducing barcode-reading sales registers that automatically communicated each purchase to a computer. Scanners were introduced in stores primarily to facilitate the stores' own supervision and inventory control needs. ... [A] company [called SoundScan] proposed to aggregate sales information from record stores and sell it back to interested decision-makers in the commercial music field. SoundScan Inc. would make possible direct weekly retail sales figures, and when aggregated in a computer database, the information could not only help control inventory better, but also be asked to answer detailed market research questions on the consumption patterns of record buyers.

The introduction of SoundScan was intended to affect only the methodology of the *Billboard* [magazine] market information regime as represented in the album chart, without changing the substance of the chart itself. From the first week, however, it seemed clear that changing the methodology changed the content of the chart as well, and these changes directly implicated *Billboard* in the politics of presenting market information to the field. … In order to test whether the new basis of collecting data for the chart did, in fact, make a difference in the distribution of genres on the *Billboard* album chart, we carefully compared the weekly charts for 13 weeks before and after the advent of the SoundScan methodology. We recorded similarity and difference in trends for chart dynamics and relative share of various categories of artists and genres.

The introduction of SoundScan led to three major changes. First, there was a change in the relative strengths of various music genres represented in the chart, with country music making spectacular gains largely at the expense of pop music. Second, a greater number of albums reached the much-vaunted number-one chart position, and reached peak chart position more swiftly. Third, specific types of records were advantaged or disadvantaged. In particular, there was a fall in the number of independent labels and new artists appearing in the chart.

Conclusions

First, market information regimes provide a common focus of attention that serves to interlock disparate actors into a common field. … In the field of commercial music, the creation and weekly dissemination of information showing the relative success of the most popular phonograph records made it possible for field participants [industry and consumers] to structure their beliefs about the success or failure of particular recordings, artists, and sub-genres by reading the performance charts. Market information regimes facilitate continuity in ongoing fields by providing a focus of attention around which participants can cohere.

Second, we established that the constitution of fields is information regime-dependent, because reframing the scope, methodology, or tone of a market information regime creates a cognate change in participants' understanding of the field itself. Initially, SoundScan seemed a mere change in methodology for compiling the album chart. However, embedded in its methodology is a fundamentally different view of the scope of the field, one that involved field-wide focus on absolute counts of album sales rather than just the relative ranking of a preselected list of albums.

Third, we showed that the inclusion of new categories of market information can itself spur the formation of new niches within a field. In the early 1970s, for example, the dance music called 'disco' was being performed in small urban clubs by inventive discotheque disc jockeys, but the form was invisible to all those outside the specific club scene. *Billboard* gave it coverage, created a chart for the current hot dance tracks, and sponsored several national conventions that brought together club owners, disco DJs, industry executives, and academic scholars.

Reference

Weick, K. (1995) *Sensemaking in Organizations*, Thousand Oaks, CA., Sage

(Source: Anand and Peterson, 2000, pp. 271–82)

In Reading 6.4, Anand and Peterson effectively turn upside down conventional understanding in economics, business studies and the music industry itself about the nature of the market. They suggest that it is not simply people who want to buy recorded music, but rather the 'market information regime' that creates and establishes patterns of taste and demand. Admittedly, the market knowledge at stake here is partly derived from previous and existing music sales, but, more important, the information regime also *creates* new knowledge about what the market is and how it operates. This leads to further enactment in the form of new marketing plans and commercial strategies based on this acquired and developed knowledge. What is more, the market information regime makes for continuity in the field, ensuring that common focus and understanding – what Anand and Peterson call 'sensemaking' – tend to persist over time. When change *does* happen in the field, the authors attribute this to change in the regime. As they put it, 'the constitution of fields is information regime-dependent, because reframing the scope, methodology, or tone of a market information regime creates a cognate change in participants' understanding of the field itself'.

The case that Reading 6.4 discusses in detail is the advent of SoundScan in the 1980s. It is the best example of how this 'regime' enacts music markets. SoundScan changed the whole nature of the music market, increasing the sales of some genres, notably country music, while reducing the sales of others. Independent record companies' sales also suffered under the new regime. But there is also the example of disco. Here the music industry trade magazine *Billboard* turned a kind of dance music played in clubs and largely invisible to the mainstream audience into a specific genre. *Billboard* writers discussed the music in articles, a special chart was created for it, and the magazine brought together key players in the disco scene. In effect, a major part of bringing disco into existence as a genre was the way knowledge of it was produced by *Billboard* magazine. In the cases of both disco and SoundScan, we have examples of the argument that Anand and Peterson make, of how the strategic description and understanding of music practices give rise to the enactment of new media markets.

Anand and Peterson were writing about music markets before the rapid rise of internet music downloads, both paid for and unpaid for, which raises questions about how far their argument still holds. SoundScan still exists, compiling retail CD and online sales. It is still the main agent in the information regime, in other words. But internet-based forms of distribution transform the information regime in significant ways. They might allow for even more fine-tuned, real-time tracking of information about music tastes. Record companies themselves can gain more direct knowledge of the market through their own download websites. However, knowledge is also exchanged by music consumers in new ways. Recent research has focused on 'e-Mavens': music downloaders and fans who spread information about music – what's new, what they like, what they don't like and so on (Walsh and Mitchell, 2010). In effect, e-Mavens are a virtual version of the opinion leaders identified by Katz and Lazarsfeld in the mid-1950s. From the perspective of Anand and Peterson, they reshape the market information regime, raising the possibility that the 'music field' is now more open to the influence of active consumers.

4 Conclusion: how social scientists understand contested mobilities in music

This chapter has developed the theme of mobility, by looking at the way in which music moves *with* and *to* people. It has discussed how music becomes embedded in contested situations in the social worlds through which it moves, but also how music is the subject of contested debates among social scientists about how best to understand the significance of mobile music. As you have seen, understandings of the way people make and use music can diverge radically – for instance, from the open, people-oriented perspective of ethnography to the music industry's self-interested market research.

The recurring issue that the mobility of music raises is how to understand the active role of listeners in making sense of cultural products. Ethnographic research focuses on the creative appropriation of music, as one means by which people negotiate the often difficult social situations in which they find themselves. Commercially oriented market research also acknowledges that audiences are creative, but understands this in terms of a problem of uncertainty that has to be managed. In this latter example in particular, you have seen how the description and understanding of music markets can also be instrumental in the enactment of social phenomena. Research for the music industry produces an 'information regime' that involves not just a description and an understanding of music consumption, but the active construction of a whole social world of music: the making of a market, agreement between competing record companies about how it should be framed, the creation and marketing of some genres at the expense of others, and so on. The ways in which social science research knowledge helps to enact social worlds will be further elaborated in the remaining two chapters of this book.

The chapter has also sought to draw out the relationship between music, mobility and contestation, in two senses. In Section 2, the role of music in enabling people to negotiate the forms of marginality, inequality or discrimination they face was discussed, and the ways in which ethnographic research understands these processes was investigated. In Section 3, the use of social science research instrumentally, to help companies sell music more effectively to consumers, was discussed. Common to both fields of research is a focus on the meanings that ordinary people ascribe to cultural commodities. In one example, commodities are the background to practices of active, creative meaning-making; in the other, people's varied tastes provide a challenge for those seeking to produce and distribute music for profit. But these two strands of social science research represent contrasting and contested models of what the uses of social science should be.

4.1 Chapter summary

In this chapter you have learned that:

- through 'thick descriptions', music ethnographers like Steil and Baulch use concepts and values derived from theoretical frameworks to make sense – from the inside and the outside – of the meanings that music has for ordinary people
- contemporary ethnography focuses on understanding 'travelling cultures', emphasising the ways in which practices in particular places are shaped by flows and circulations from all over the world
- contemporary ethnographic analysis emphasises the ways in which active appropriation of mobile music is a means of negotiating contested, power-laden terrains of everyday life
- an alternative tradition of social science research on cultural practices, associated with a tradition of 'administrative research', seeks to provide useful social science knowledge – for both 'benevolent' and 'exploitative' purposes
- music markets, and other cultural markets, are characterised by uncertainty, which means that commercial activity in these sectors is shaped by the need to predict and manage uncertain demand
- while market research purports to describe music markets so that commercial actors can respond to consumer demand, an alternative social science perspective argues that commercial actors enact the market for music through the coordination of 'market information regimes'.

References

Adorno, T. (1945) 'A social critique of radio music', *Kenyon Review*, vol. 7, no. 2, pp. 208–17.

Anand, B.N. and Peterson, R. (2000) 'When market information constitutes fields: sensemaking of markets in the commercial music industry', *Organization Science*, vol. 11, no. 3, pp. 270–84.

Baulch, E. (2003) 'Gesturing elsewhere: the identity politics of the Balinese death/thrash metal scene', *Popular Music*, vol. 22, no. 2, pp. 195–215.

Baulch, E. (2008) *Making Scenes: Reggae, Punk, and Death Metal in 1990s Bali*, Durham, NC, Duke University Press.

Caves, R. (2001) *Creative Industries: Contracts between Art and Commerce*, Cambridge, MA, Harvard University Press.

Clifford, J. (1986) 'Introduction: partial truths' in Clifford, J. and Marcus, G. (eds) *Writing Culture: The Poetics and Politics of Ethnography*, Berkeley, CA, University of California Press.

Clifford, J. (1992) 'Travelling cultures' in Grossberg, L., Nelson, C. and Treichler, P. (eds) *Cultural Studies*, New York/London, Routledge.

Geertz, C. (1973) *The Interpretation of Cultures*, New York, Basic Books.

Gronow, P. and Saunio, I. (1998) *An International History of the Recording Industry*, London, Cassell.

Gupta, A. and Ferguson, J. (eds) (1997) *Culture, Power, Place: Explorations in Critical Anthropology*, Durham, NC, Duke University Press.

Katz, E. and Lazarsfeld, P. (1955) *Personal Influence: The Part Played by People in the Flow of Mass Communication*, Glencoe, IL, Free Press.

Ortner, S. (1995) 'Resistance and the problem of ethnographic refusal', *Comparative Studies in Society and History*, vol. 37, no. 1, pp. 173–93.

Scannell, P. (2007) *Media and Communication*, London, Sage.

Steil, L. (2011) '"Realness": authenticity, innovation and prestige among young *danseurs afros* in Paris', in Toynbee, J. and Dueck, B. (eds) *Migrating Music*, London, Routledge.

Walsh, G. and Mitchell, V-W. (2010) 'The effect of consumer confusion proneness on word of mouth, trust, and customer satisfaction', *European Journal of Marketing*, vol. 44, no. 6, pp. 838–59.

Chapter 7
Enacting elections

Richard Heffernan

1 Introduction 271
1.1 Structure of the chapter 274
1.2 Aims of the chapter 274
2 Collecting and generating evidence about elections 276
2.1 Social science and general elections in the UK 278
3 Explaining participation and non-participation in elections 282
3.1 Explaining turnout in elections 284
4 Social science theories of voting decisions 289
4.1 The class-based theory: a sociological explanation of voting 290
4.2 The party-identification theory: from a sociological to a social-psychological explanation of voting 292
4.3 The valence-politics theory: an issue-based explanation of voting 294
4.4 Description and understanding in the evaluation of theories of voting 297
5 Enacting elections: informing and shaping public debate 300
6 Conclusion: making sense of participation 303
6.1 Chapter summary 303
References 305

1 Introduction

This chapter introduces the idea that social science not only describes and understands social worlds, but it also helps to enact them – by seeking to *inform* public debates and policy making, social science helps to *shape* the ways in which processes and practices work. The chapter explores this idea by using the example of how social science investigates one particular type of participation; that is, participation as a citizen in elections. Voting is often thought of as a basic form of participation in the political life of the communities where people live. Voting in an election is a means by which people participate in two ways: by making their voice heard, expressing their support for one candidate or party, making demands for certain policies or actions; and also as a way of expressing membership of a political community – a locality or a nation, perhaps – as a civic duty undertaken as a citizen.

Figure 7.1 Political party tellers observing and monitoring the counting of votes cast in the Ceredigion constituency at the General Election, 6 May 2010

This chapter looks at the ways in which social science is used to make sense of two related aspects of elections:

- first, the use of social science to explain why some people vote and why others do not

- second, the use of social science to try to account for why people vote in the ways they do.

In both of these respects the chapter will show how social science understandings of participation in elections help to inform public debates about politics and shape efforts to enhance participation levels.

Elections are a focus of social science investigations partly because they are, of course, important. They are a means by which governments are chosen, and in turn held to account. They are also one of the largest rituals of participation in the modern world – they are occasions when thousands, hundreds of thousands, or millions of people all engage in the same event, often on the same day, to help decide on who will represent them. Voting in an election is a particular form of participation. In democratic elections people vote in private, but each person's individual vote is made into an expression of the public's will by being combined with all the votes cast. In this way, each individual voter becomes part of a collective. By having their own vote counted as part of the overall vote, the individual act of each voter becomes meaningful by being aggregated alongside others. Elections, by enabling people to participate in political processes, are understood as expressions of the 'popular' will and one way of measuring public opinion. David Butler, one of the best-known social scientists to have studied elections in the UK, goes so far as to suggest that 'history used to be marked off by the dates of kings. Now it is marked by the dates of general elections' (1998, p. 454).

Elections generate lots of data – the results of an election take the form of numerical outcomes, tabulating how many people voted for each candidate or party. The results of an election are therefore determined by the voting decisions of lots of people. But as to what elections *mean* – why some parties win, why others are defeated, why some candidates are or are not successful, beyond the mere fact of winning or losing – the results of an election don't tell us this. Social science is one of the ways in which the background processes that led to particular outcomes are explained, interpreted and made meaningful. Social scientists seek to explain why some people vote and others don't, and why those people who do vote cast their ballots in the way they do. They use social science methodologies such as surveys and interviews to find out these things, and generate theories to make sense of elections.

This chapter looks at the history of social science explanations of voting in general elections in the UK since 1945. These are the elections that determine the composition of national governments in Britain. The formal study of elections is called **psephology**, and social scientists who study elections are often called psephologists. The term originates from the Greek word *psephos*, which means 'pebble', because the ancient Greeks used pebbles as ballots to enable them to cast votes to choose a candidate for public office. As you will see in this chapter, elections are studied by social scientists from a number of disciplines – political scientists, sociologists, psychologists, geographers and others. They seek to understand various issues involved in elections: for example, how citizens make their electoral choices and cast their vote for one party rather than another; or how the outcomes of elections might vary depending on just how individual votes are aggregated. You will see that, over time, social scientists have developed different theories as to why people participate in elections, and why those who do vote in the ways they do. And you will see that these different theories can be evaluated in relation to evidence and concepts.

Psephology is the formal study of elections.

The chapter will show how social science informs and shapes public debate about the meaning of elections and voting. The focus is primarily on academic social scientists who investigate electoral processes. But academic social scientists are not the only people trying to make sense of elections. Polling organisations and pollsters seek to map, measure and assess public opinion before, during and after elections. Polling organisations are commissioned, both by parties and especially by news organisations, to take regular measures of public opinion and, using combinations of sophisticated statistical tools and qualitative methods like focus groups, to predict how electors will vote and to try to call the outcome of an election in advance of it happening. So social science plays an important role in the activities of pollsters too. These two forms of social science, academic and non-academic, feed into wider public debates that include pundits and journalists, politicians themselves, and members of the general public – all of whom have a variety of reasons for wanting to have better knowledge of what voters are thinking, who particular segments of the population might be more or less inclined to vote for, or why particular elections produced the outcomes they did. It is as part of this wider public conversation about the meanings and motivations behind voting decisions and election outcomes that social science, as used by both academics and non-academics, helps to enact the meaning of this form of political participation.

The chapter illustrates the role of social science in describing, understanding and enacting participation in elections by focusing on two sets of questions.

- The first relates to how election analysts seek to uncover and explain levels of electoral participation. Here they ask: who is entitled to vote? And who actually does vote, why and when?
- The second set relates to how social scientists seek to describe who votes for different parties or candidates, and to understand why people chose to vote for the party or candidate which they did vote for.

1.1 Structure of the chapter

Using the UK as a case study, Section 2 outlines how social science considers electoral behaviour, and looks at the generation of data about elections. The data about elections are the basic means through which social science descriptions of political participation are generated. Sections 3 and 4 then address two issues that social science has attempted to explain by collecting evidence, developing concepts and proposing theories. The first issue, examined in Section 3, is the question of why some people don't vote in elections – the issue of **turnout**. The second, considered in Section 4, is the question of why people vote in the way they do. This section looks at different theories of electoral behaviour which social scientists have used to explore electoral outcomes in order to better understand them, and perhaps to predict future behaviour based on evaluations of past behaviour. Section 5 elaborates on the way in which social science descriptions and understandings of elections also help to enact social worlds by informing and shaping public debates about politics, participation and public life.

Turnout refers to the number of people who vote in an election as a proportion of the total number of people who are eligible to vote.

1.2 Aims of the chapter

This chapter aims to:

- introduce the social science investigation of elections, and its role within wider public debates about politics and participation
- consider the ways in which social scientists describe and understand non-voting, helping to inform and shape debates about participation

- consider the ways in which social scientists describe and understand the individual motivations and social variables affecting voting decisions and electoral outcomes
- show how social science is used by academics and non-academics to inform and shape public debates about elections, helping to enact social worlds.

2 Collecting and generating evidence about elections

As we have already seen, one reason that social science investigates elections is because they are important processes. But there is also something about elections that makes them particularly well suited to social science investigation. In one sense, the outcome of any election is normally easy to establish – the results take the form of lots of numerical data.

Table 7.1 shows the results of the general election held in the UK in 2010. As you look at it, consider the different types of data used to describe the outcome of this election.

Table 7.1 describes the results in different ways. For example, the Conservative party gained 10,726,614 votes in total; the Labour party 8,609,527. It also shows that this represented 36.1 per cent and 29 per cent of the total votes cast, respectively. The table also has information about the increase in votes, both in total and as a percentage share of the vote since the previous election in 2005, as well as the numbers of seats won by different parties.

But the table doesn't tell us much, if anything, about *why* voters cast their ballots in the way which, when aggregated, generated this overall picture. That is the thing about elections: they produce lots of numbers, but the information provided by these numbers, the election results, is actually rather 'thin' – it records only who millions of different individuals voted for, but not why. It doesn't even tell us who voted for different parties – for instance, how many women voted for the Conservatives, how many middle-class professionals voted for Labour? You can't tell this from looking at the results of an election on their own.

Table 7.1 The results of the 2010 UK general election

Party	Seats	Gain	Loss	Net[1]	Votes	%[2]	+/-%[3]
Conservative	**307**	100	3	+97	10,726,614	36.1	+3.8
Labour	**258**	3	94	-91	8,609,527	29.0	-6.2
Liberal Democrat	**57**	8	13	-5	6,836,824	23.0	+1.0
Democratic Unionist Party	**8**	0	1	-1	168,216	0.6	-0.3
Scottish National Party	**6**	0	0	0	491,386	1.7	+0.1
Sinn Fein	**5**	0	0	0	171,942	0.6	-0.1
Plaid Cymru	**3**	1	0	+1	165,394	0.6	-0.1
Social Democratic & Labour Party	**3**	0	0	0	110,970	0.4	-0.1
Green	**1**	1	0	+1	285,616	1.0	-0.1
Alliance Party	**1**	1	0	+1	42,762	0.1	+0.0
UK Independence Party	**0**	0	0	0	919,546	3.1	+0.9
British National Party	**0**	0	0	0	564,331	1.9	+1.2
Ulster Conservatives and Unionists – New Force	**0**	0	1	-1	102,361	0.3	-0.1
English Democrats	**0**	0	0	0	64,826	0.2	+0.2
Respect–Unity Coalition	**0**	0	1	-1	33,251	0.1	-0.1
Traditional Unionist Voice	**0**	0	0	0	26,300	0.1	
Christian Party	**0**	0	0	0	18,623	0.1	
Independent Community and Health Concern	**0**	0	1	-1	16,150	0.1	+0.0
Trade Unionist and Socialist Coalition	**0**	0	0	0	12,275	0.0	
Scottish Socialist Party	**0**	0	0	0	3,157	0.0	-0.1
Others	**1**	1	1	0	321,309	1.1	0.0

1. Change in number of seats from the previous election.

2. Percentage share of the votes cast.

3. Percentage change in share of vote since previous election.

Source: BBC, 2010

Elections are 'informationally thin' in this way because voting is undertaken in secret. The secret ballot is actually quite a new practice in the long history of elections, dating back to the nineteenth century. But it is now understood to be a quite basic requirement of democratic elections that people get to cast their ballots in secret, free from observation by or influence from other people. One result of this is that the data that are generated as an output of an election – the results – tell us very little about the inputs that led to those results. The task of social science in describing and understanding elections lies in trying to get behind the results, finding out further facts about who voted and who didn't, and who voted for whom, and, perhaps above all, to try to explain why people voted in the ways they did. And it is by doing this, by filling in the blanks behind election results, that social science helps to make sense of electoral processes as public events.

2.1 Social science and general elections in the UK

The UK has a parliamentary political system. At general elections, its citizens elect Members of Parliament (MPs) to take seats in one part of the legislature, the House of Commons. The government emerges by being in possession of a majority of seats there. So, for example, in 2010 the government was formed by two parties, the Conservatives and the Liberal Democrats, agreeing to set up a coalition that could command a majority in the Commons by combining the seats they had won between them – giving them 364 seats, out of the overall total of 650 seats in the Commons. The prime minister, rather than being directly elected by UK voters, is the party leader who is able to 'lead' the Commons majority.

In the UK, general elections are just one sort of election in which citizens are able to participate. For example, a resident of London could, in a period of five years, participate as a voter in elections to choose the following representatives:

- an MP
- a Member of the European Parliament (MEP)
- the London mayor
- a London Assembly member
- local councillors, who are usually elected in multi-member wards.

Meanwhile, an elector in Scotland, Wales or Northern Ireland has the opportunity to vote for:

- an MP
- in Scotland, two Members of the Scottish Parliament (MSPs); in Wales, two Assembly Members (AMs); in Northern Ireland, up to six Members of the Legislative Assembly (MLAs)
- MEPs
- local councillors.

So in the UK voting is a means of participating quite regularly, about once a year, in political life. But how do social scientists go about studying all these elections?

In the UK, the systematic study of elections dates from the period following the end of the Second World War in 1945. This was the year of publication of the first of the Nuffield Election Studies, a series of scholarly works on British general elections. The series was founded by Robert McCallum, the social scientist who popularised the term psephology. For many years, up until 2005, it was co-authored by David Butler, the social scientist specialising in electoral analysis who was quoted above. Over time, Butler became a public intellectual, regularly appearing on television around elections.

Figure 7.2 Psephologist David Butler on election night, 1974

Each Nuffield study explores both the election outcome and the election campaign, and surveys the chronology of the previous Parliament before the election. The first aim of the election studies set up by McCallum and developed by Butler was to be descriptive – to provide a historical record of elections. But its second aim was to be explanatory – to answer questions such as 'why did voters vote as they did?' (McCallum, 1954). This aim of developing better understandings of elections is a more complex matter. Butler's particular contribution to the series was the development of rigorous statistical analysis, in which the relevance of different variables in shaping electoral behaviour was assessed. And election studies of this sort also had a third aim – to inform and shape public debate:

> Not only is the study of elections valuable for historical record, it may also guide and clarify the ideas of the active politician. It is a time for stocktaking, for reviewing methods and policies. To the extent that an election survey is accurate and objective and informed with some degree of political imagination, the active worker and political journalist may profit by it.
>
> (McCallum, 1954, p. 511)

The Nuffield Election Studies are one example of how social science has sought to describe and understand elections in the UK. Data from surveys, along with data from other sources such as censuses, are used to identify patterns and correlations between electoral outcomes and different variables. Elections studies use information and evidence collected before, during and after elections, as well as across successive elections.

Much of the evidence now used to analyse elections in the UK is produced by the British Election Study (BES). This was first set up by Butler and the political scientist Donald Stokes in preparation for the expected 1964 election. They conducted the first national survey of voters in the early summer of 1963. Two more election surveys were carried out at the elections of 1964 and 1966. This research helped prompt the theories of electoral behaviour discussed in the next two sections of this chapter. The BES is now carried out routinely around each general election.

The BES is based on a large-scale post-election interview survey, which is conducted among a representative sample of voters. Surveys are conducted among the same respondents after successive elections. In this way, the BES generates data about people's motivations for voting, and about changing patterns of voting over time. The BES is the longest-running survey of electoral behaviour of its kind in the world. It is actually one of the longest-running social science surveys of any kind.

It is funded by the Economic and Social Research Council (ESRC), the public body responsible for funding and promoting social science research in the UK. The goal of the BES is 'to understand why people vote, and why they vote the way they do' (Economic and Social Research Council, 2010). Each BES examines long-term trends in British voting behaviour; explains the election outcome, party choice, and turnout; and examines the consequences of elections for the operation of democracy more generally (ibid). Having accumulated data for each general election held over a period of more than four decades since 1964, the BES is an example of social science data being used to facilitate the study and analysis of long-term changes in voting behaviour. Above all, it is used to describe and understand the factors which influence the outcome of elections, and to understand long-term changes in the nature of participation and voter choice. The BES informs further research and analysis conducted by academics, polling organisations and news journalists. In this way, it provides the basic reference point of evidence and data for developing understandings of the dynamics of voter participation and voter choice in the UK. Public debates about the meanings of any given election, in terms of what has changed over time and what factors have influenced outcomes, are fundamentally dependent on the information generated by the BES and other social science data sets. We shall now move on to look at each of these issues in turn, in Sections 3 and 4.

3 Explaining participation and non-participation in elections

In a democracy such as the UK, the level of participation in elections is a vital feature of the legitimacy of their outcomes and of the governments formed on the basis of the results. Democracy is meant to be a system in which all the people (or at least a majority of them) have a say in how governments are formed. If only small numbers of people actually vote, then this condition is not being met through elections. Furthermore, if some groups systematically don't vote, or if fewer of their members vote compared with members of other groups, the inclusive, democratic functions of elections might be called into question. For example, in the UK turnout has tended to decline most markedly over time among young people. Does this constitute a problem, a challenge to the legitimacy of the electoral system?

The issue of voter turnout, then, is vital to the value ascribed to elections as part of democratic government. In most countries voting is a voluntary act, although in some (Australia, for instance) it is compulsory; citizens are expected by law to participate and incur a fine if they do not. Where voting is voluntary, as in the UK, the first step is for individuals to be registered to vote, by being included on an electoral register. In some countries, such as the USA, it is up to the individual to place themselves on the register; in others, such as the UK, local government workers proactively seek to register electors. Voter registration is the first stage at which issues of differential participation in elections arise – some groups tend to be systematically under-represented on electoral registers, for a variety of reasons. For example, social science research shows that relatively mobile population groups – including students and those living in temporary rental accommodation – are less likely to be included on local electoral registers in the UK (Electoral Commission, 2010).

When social scientists mention turnout, they are referring to the number of people who actually do 'turn out' to vote in a particular election as a proportion of the total number of people who are eligible to vote. Table 7.2 shows turnout at different types of elections in the UK, excluding Northern Ireland, in the period between 2005 and 2011, including local elections, general elections and elections to the European Parliament.

As you look at the table, you will see that the figure ranged from a low of 34.5 per cent (in the European Parliament elections of 2009), to a high of 65.1 per cent (in the general election of 2010). Can you identify any correlation between voter turnout and type of election across the table?

Table 7.2 Turnout in UK elections, 2005–2011

	%
General election 2005	61.3
English locals 2006	36.6
Scottish Parliament 2007	53.9
Welsh Assembly 2007	46.4
English locals 2007	38.3
English and Welsh locals 2008	35.6
London Mayor 2008	45.3
English locals 2009	39.3
European Parliament 2009	34.5
General election 2010	65.1
Scottish Parliament 2011	50.4
Welsh Assembly 2011	41.4
English locals 2011	39.2

Source: adapted from Denver, 2011

One thing social scientists have argued is that turnout rates vary according to different types of elections. Table 7.2 appears to provide some evidence for this. Elections can be categorised as either 'first-order' or 'second-order' elections: this is a way of indicating the relative importance to voters of the different elections they might be able to vote in. In the UK, general elections that determine the composition of the House of Commons, and therefore elect the national government, are considered to be first-order elections. They have higher turnouts than other UK elections, such as those for devolved government in Wales and Scotland, for local government and for the European Parliament. These all appear to be second-order elections.

First-order elections such as the general election of 2010 (with a turnout of 65.1 per cent) have a very high public profile. These, being national events, are fiercely contested by the parties and attract overwhelming news media and public attention. We have already noted that the lowest turnout in Table 7.2 was for the much less important European

Parliament elections in 2009 (34.5 per cent), and indeed these elections have always had lower turnout rates than other kinds of elections.

So it seems that one thing that affects turnout, or in other words participation in elections, is the relative degree of importance ascribed by people to different elections. Clearly, then, electors do not consider every election to be equally significant. The likelihood of voting increases according to the perceived importance of the body that is being elected.

But participation in elections also varies across social groups at the same types of elections. Some groups of people are more likely to vote than others; and, furthermore, there appears to be evidence of a long-term decline in the overall level of voter turnout in the UK. How do social scientists seek to understand these processes?

3.1 Explaining turnout in elections

There is a widespread perception, in the UK and elsewhere, that there is a crisis in political participation in liberal representative democracies. One reference point for this perception is the declining levels of turnout in elections. For example, Table 7.3 shows the level of turnout in general elections in the UK since 1945.

Can you identify any trend in turnout at general elections below?

Table 7.3 Turnout in UK general elections, 1945–2010

Year	%	Year	%
1945	72.6	1974 (Oct.)	72.7
1950	83.8	1979	75.9
1951	81.9	1983	72.6
1955	76.7	1987	75.3
1959	78.7	1992	77.7
1964	77.1	1997	71.2
1966	75.8	2001	59.1
1970	71.9	2005	61.3
1974 (Feb.)	78.8	2010	65.1

Source: adapted from Denver, 2011

You can see that in 1945, turnout was 72.6 per cent. In 2010, however, it was 65.1 per cent. More than 24 million people voted in 1945; slightly fewer than 30 million in 2010. More people voted in the latter year, but turnout was down, because in 2010 a smaller proportion of those people eligible to vote actually did so.

If you look at Table 7.3 a little more closely, you will see that turnout rates at general elections were actually quite steady between 1945 and 1992, averaging 75 per cent, and peaking in 1950. But since then they have plummeted. A post-war low of 59.1 per cent in 2001 was followed by only a slight increase to 61.3 per cent in 2005. Even the 2010 election, a closely fought event where the outcome was always in doubt (a factor which ought to increase turnout), only saw an increase to just 65.1 per cent.

Figure 7.3 A polling place in Glasgow during the 2012 local council elections

So the evidence suggests a complex picture of very high turnouts in 1950 and 1951 followed by a stable trend, only for turnout to slump dramatically in 2001 and then remain below the average for the post-war period. How have social scientists accounted for this decline, and how do they seek to explain non-voting? We can identify six types of explanation.

1 The first is that election turnouts reflect the competitive nature of the election. Uncompetitive elections, where it is expected – from polling data – that one party is going to win easily, tend to have lower turnouts than elections where a close outcome is predicted. Many commentators suggest that this explains the fall in turnout in both 1997 and 2001, when Labour, as was long expected, swept the electoral board; and in 2005, when Labour was expected to be re-elected with a smaller Commons majority. This did not happen, however, in 1983, when the Conservatives won a long-expected substantial majority on a respectable turnout of 72.6 per cent. However, in 2010, at an election in which no single party won an overall majority of seats, the result proved too close to call throughout the election campaign. But turnout rose by only 3.8 per cent over 2005 to 65.1 per cent (still some 10 per cent below the average for 1945–92). Such a fact, for many commentators, calls this explanation into question.

2 The second explanation suggests that the propensity of an individual to vote is a reflection of their perception of the personal and social benefit, or utility, they will derive from voting. Turnout will be greater when electors incur fewer 'costs' and receive greater 'benefits' from voting. But this explanation actually has trouble explaining why people do vote. On its own assumptions, since each individual vote is highly unlikely to make a material difference to the electoral outcome, it is not clear why any individual would bother to vote at all. So this approach has limited value in explaining why some people do vote and others do not.

These two explanations tend to explain turnout in a narrow way, either focusing on the nature of elections and campaigns, or thinking of voters as individuals who make 'rational choice' decisions, similar to the approach you came across in Chapter 4.

3 The third explanation emphasises the social circumstances of individual voters. Social scientists have shown that turnout varies in different constituencies at the same election. For example, in the 2010 general election turnout ranged from just over 44 per cent (in Manchester Central) to almost 78 per cent (in East Renfrewshire). Geographers have demonstrated that Britain has long been divided into constituencies with relatively high turnouts (such as rural or suburban, middle class and relatively affluent places) and those with lower turnouts (such as urban, working-class and poorer areas) (Johnston and Pattie, 2006).

These variations reflect differences in the socio-economic circumstances of different people. Levels of education, access to information, having time – all these factors tend to determine people's participation in civic activities of all sorts, including voting in elections. Because these resources are unevenly distributed across different social groups, this explanation helps to suggest why certain types of people are more likely to vote than others.

In the terms used in Chapter 4, this explanation emphasises the structural factors that shape people's likelihood of voting.

4 The fourth explanation focuses on the political 'supply side', by suggesting that electors respond both favourably and unfavourably to the ways in which parties seeking votes try to engage with and mobilise them. From this perspective, variations in turnout can be explained by the extent to which the parties are perceived as offering significantly different choices (Clarke et al., 2004, pp. 261–74). Voters are more likely to vote when they think that very different policies would be pursued by the different parties, especially when the outcome of a close election is considered to be in doubt.

None of these four explanations helps, however, to completely account for the long-term trend of declining voter turnout.

5 A fifth explanation suggests that declining turnout is because feelings of apathy and alienation play an important role in people being either not motivated enough to vote, or alternatively actively motivated to not vote – in other words, to abstain. Electoral apathy is as old as the hills; bear in mind that even back in the 'good old days', when some 75 per cent of electors turned out to vote – as was the case between 1945 and 1992 – this means that around 25 per cent did not. Compared with apathy, voter alienation can be seen to be both positive and assertive. Alienation – if reflected in turnout falling below the established average – testifies to the fact that more electors than ever before respond unfavourably to the ways in which parties seeking votes try to engage with and mobilise them.

6 A sixth, related explanation holds that there is a declining association between voters and political parties. This phenomenon, known as 'partisan **dealignment**', refers to the fact that electors are far less likely than in the past to vote automatically and relatively unthinkingly for a particular party. If you strongly support a party you will be more likely to turn out to vote, because partisans are more likely to vote than those with no alignment. Given that voter

Dealignment is a concept used in political science to describe the trend whereby voters abandon previous attachments and affiliations to particular parties.

> partisanship has been declining for some time, this argument can help explain why turnout has trended downwards over a long period of time. However, the evidence demonstrates that while the strength of electoral partisanship declined from the mid-1970s onwards, turnout did not begin to fall until 1997 and fell markedly only in 2001, thereafter rising somewhat in 2005 and 2010. This explanation is related to the theory of **valence-based voting**, discussed further in Section 4.3.

Valence-based voting is a model of voting which suggests that the strongest factor influencing voter choice is judgements about the competence and performance of politicians.

You can see, then, that the explanations that social scientists have presented to account for declining electoral participation and falling turnout are quite varied. Some focus on specifically electoral issues, some on broader issues of political behaviour, some more broadly on patterns of social difference as a whole. Different approaches support different programmes to address the matter. In Section 5 we shall return to these issues to see how the different approaches to understanding turnout can inform attempts to enhance participation and reverse the decline in voter turnout.

In this section we have seen how social science attempts to use concepts of different sorts to explain why people do or do not vote at elections, and how these explanations are evaluated in relation to the evidence on turnout that is available. In the next section we move on to see how social science seeks to explain why people who do vote, do so in the *particular* ways they do.

4 Social science theories of voting decisions

As with voter turnout, discussed in Section 3, social scientists have developed different theories to understand why people vote as they do in elections. In this section we look at three influential explanations, or theories, of electoral behaviour and examine the forms of evidence and evaluation that are used to support or criticise them.

We have already seen that the formal and systematic study of elections in social science is a relatively new endeavour. Only since the 1940s have social scientists had the means to collect and analyse survey data, and to make use of other aggregate data from censuses or other databases, in order to develop theories of voter decision making. For example, the sort of data generated by social science research programmes such as the BES enable social scientists to do two things:

1 to describe voting patterns, by establishing who voted for which party and by making comparisons over time about the changing nature of those who vote for different parties

2 having described the voters who support different candidates or parties, to develop explanations of why people vote as they do, and what influences their voting decisions.

In pursuing these two aims, social scientists build models that help them to hypothesise different causal relationships between variables and voting decisions. The explanatory theories that social scientists develop enable the conceptual exploration of the phenomenon under study, allowing the better understanding of the phenomenon that they have described, and also making it possible for them to predict future behaviour based on their evaluation of past behaviour.

In the following sections, we look in turn at three different theories which have been developed to explain voting decisions:

- a *sociological* theory, which examines the relationship between social characteristics such as class and voting
- a *social-psychological* theory, which examines the relationship between voters' partisan self-images and voting, and is sometimes known as the party-identification theory
- an *issue-based voting* theory, also known as the valence voting model, which suggests that voters make their choices based on their

perception of issues, party appeal and, increasingly, their estimation of party leaders.

These three theories have been used to better understand and predict electoral outcomes. They have formed the basis both of social science analysis of elections, and of the ways in which wider public debates frame the meanings of electoral results and the process of electoral politics. But as we look at them in turn, we shall also see that each theory can be subjected to evaluation in terms of its conceptual coherence, its empirical adequacy, and the degree to which it is comprehensive in addressing all possible factors and variations.

4.1 The class-based theory: a sociological explanation of voting

In election studies in the UK after 1945, the predominant theory of voting was a sociological model that suggested that class-based variables were the most important factors shaping electoral behaviour. In this sort of theory, electoral choice was understood as a function of a voter's individual position within various social structures – the class position of their parents, or their own occupational status, level of educational attainment, or form of housing tenure. On the basis of these factors, it was said, people develop long-term identifications with particular ideologies represented by political parties.

In the post-war period in the UK, this sort of explanation appeared to have some validity. It suggested that by being working class, an elector would more likely than not vote Labour; by being middle class, the elector was more likely to vote Conservative. In the two-party system that dominated in this period, relatively few votes were cast for parties other than Labour or Conservative. The theory of class-based voting was championed by Butler and Stokes (1974), who argued that the links between class and partisanship – that is, strong identification with a particular party – were strongly supported by the evidence. Class voting, perhaps tinged with other forms of social identity, was the dominant electoral theory in the UK from the 1940s through to the 1960s. It led the political scientist Peter Pultzer to suggest that 'class is the basis of British party politics; all else is embellishment and detail' (1967, p. 98). The class-based theory of voting has three core ideas.

The first is that relatively fixed social characteristics, such as social class, work through long-term socialisation processes to predispose

> individuals to support one party rather than another. Second, the results of these socialisation processes can be either reinforced or undermined by the individual's social context – for example, by the kind of work the individual does, the sort of neighbourhood he or she lives in, and the informal groups to which he or she belongs. The third idea is that social characteristics and social contexts produce a distinctive set of affiliations and senses of solidarity around parties. Over time, and again largely as a result of socialisation, most individuals tend to develop stable and enduring attachments to particular political parties. These party identifications serve both to colour the ways in which individuals interpret political information and to predispose them to vote for the same party in successive elections.
>
> (Clarke et al., 2004, p. 5)

This theory explains voting primarily with reference to structural factors – people's positions within various social structures lead to stable identifications that are reflected in their electoral choices:

> The approach never claimed that all variation in voting preferences would be determined by social structure. Other contingent factors, such as the condition of the economy, specific issues, perceptions of party leaders, or events, would cause some people to switch their votes between elections. But, most people would continue to vote according to their structural positions and their party identifications and this, in turn, would be associated with relative electoral stability.
>
> (Clarke et al., 2004, p. 5)

In later theories, the relationship between people's structural position, the specific contexts in which they live (geographical location, for example) and party identification is understood to be much more fluid than in this sociological theory. Over time, evidence showed, for example, that significant numbers of working-class people did vote for the Conservative party, and that the Labour party drew support from significant sectors of the professional middle classes. In terms of the theory, these were 'deviant voters', because their behaviour deviated from the pattern expected by the voting theory. The predictive ability of the theory came increasingly to be questioned, and it was also pointed out that the model lacked widespread application – it seemed very much shaped by the UK pattern of class, whereas in other parts of Europe, for example, religious affiliation has often been a predominant factor shaping electoral behaviour.

The decline of the class-based theory reflected, in part, changes in the social structure itself, as the traditional industrial working class shrank, and white-collar and service sector employment grew. As the nature of class in the UK changed, so too did the idea that class completely underpinned electoral behaviour. Social scientists describe this process as 'class dealignment', whereby both the form and the nature of social class changed at the same time as class failed to retain the close association with voter choice which social scientists had previously suggested that it had.

4.2 The party-identification theory: from a sociological to a social-psychological explanation of voting

As we have just seen, the primary claim of the sociological theory of class-based voting is that the relationship between class and party identification is a predictable and a stable one. The notion that electors identified with a certain party was seen to be the explanation for the fact that significant numbers of voters consistently voted for the same party across several elections. Voters with a weak or no party attachment were considered to be among the 'swing' voters whose votes would decide a tight election between the two main competing parties, Labour and Conservative. In this theory, it was argued that:

> the voter's choice of party was largely based on class and party identification … Most people were brought up to think of themselves as supporters of one party or another (with upwards of 40 per cent of the electorate describing themselves as *very strong* party supporters) and thus developed an enduring loyalty to a party which they would support, for the most part, through thick and thin. The emphasis in this explanation is on stability – class and party identity didn't change much and so most people always

> voted for the same party – rather than volatility. Electoral change would be slow and gradual.
>
> (Denver, 2011, p. 86)

The validity of this theory was called into question in a two-step process. First, by the late 1970s, in spite of some residual linkage, social class was no longer a very good predictor of party support. The process of class dealignment, whereby the link between social class and voting began to fracture, was first noted in the early 1970s and continued unabated in the 1980s and 1990s (Clarke et al., 2009).

From the 1970s onwards electoral analysts began to play down the explanatory power of sociological factors like class structure. Instead, a new theory was advanced, one which argued that people were linked to parties for reasons other than class identity. This social-psychological theory still held that there was a firm and enduring linkage between electors and a particular political party – it held to the idea that party identification was the key factor in electoral behaviour. But it suggested that this identification was shaped by other factors rather than social class alone.

The development of this theory reflected in part a response to evidence, but also a conceptual shift in focus. Rather than assuming that a person's social position (in the labour market or housing market, for example) would determine their voting behaviour, this approach sought to explain why individual party identifications, where they existed, proved so resilient over successive elections. It was suggested that, once established, a person's identification with a particular party formed a stable and enduring emotional or psychological bond. Party identification therefore sought to explain why electors had *internalised* a strong, stable and long-term attachment to one party rather than another. It also explained why an elector would consistently vote for that party, because it posited that they were committed to what was described as their 'normal vote'. Casting a vote was, in this view, akin to supporting a football team: someone formed an attachment and it was rare for them to abandon this attachment and change allegiance, even when their 'structural' circumstances changed.

In this account, then, a particular conceptualisation of the importance of personal, psychological identity is considered the key explanatory factor in determining people's voting behaviour over time.

Second, having weakened the link between class and voting by deepening the understanding of the process of party identification, social scientists were subsequently led to revise this new social-psychological theory in light of further evidence which suggested that, in fact, party identification was lessening in importance over time. Electoral surveys showed that party identification declined markedly from 1964 onwards. Writing in 1974, Butler and Stokes found that 45 per cent of electors 'strongly identified' with either the Conservative party, the Labour party, or, to a lesser extent, the Liberal party. And they found that these identifications had remained relatively stable over several election cycles and would usually harden with age. However, by the late 1990s it was found that only 9 per cent of electors would consider themselves to be 'strong party identifiers' (Clarke et al., 2009). So, if the social-psychological theory had weakened the link between class and identification, in turn the importance of party identification based on internalised attachment was called into question.

Social scientists now tend to view the UK electorate as decoupled from class and partisan bases, and consequently as having become more volatile and unstable – more difficult for politicians to take for granted, and more difficult for social scientists to predict. As a result electoral behaviour is no longer consistent and stable. Voter support is now often considered to be less a form of partisanship and more an expression of temporary association. Today, far fewer voters can be classified as strong partisans, firmly committed to supporting one party over another at every election. And it was strong, stable partisans, not weak occasional ones, that lay at the heart of the sociological and social-psychological models of voting behaviour. Over time, then, the number of floating voters, those unattached to a specific party by either social class or partisanship, has been seen to have substantially increased. This is in part a shift driven by the generation of new data and evidence about voter behaviour and characteristics. But it is also a conceptual shift – away from structural explanations of voting, towards theories which ascribe much more agency to voters in explaining electoral behaviour. This shift is indicated in the third theory discussed in this section, known as the 'valence-politics' theory of voting.

4.3 The valence-politics theory: an issue-based explanation of voting

Valence politics refers to the idea that voters make their decisions about who to support based on their evaluative judgement of the *competence* and *potential competence* of different parties. The development of this approach reflects a shift away from theories in which electors and parties are linked together by strong ties of attachment, towards a theory in which voters make electoral decisions based on how they, their families and perhaps their neighbourhoods are affected by major contemporary conditions and their assessment of how successful or not the government has been in either creating or tackling those conditions. This theory, one in which people vote on issue-based grounds, argues that voters are more likely to vote for a party of government when it has been economically successful and has been able to deliver prosperity to them as individuals.

In this theory, it is assumed that people broadly agree about what the government should be elected to do: it should effectively and carefully manage the economy; secure economic growth; achieve and maintain low rates of inflation and unemployment; ensure national and local security and the rule of law; and provide a wide range of well-funded, efficient and effective public services: 'Voters, because they focus on such "valence issues", vote for the political party (but also, increasingly, the party leader or prime minister) that they consider can do the job of government best and so better "deliver the mix of policy outcomes that are widely seen as good things"' (Clarke et al., 2009, p. 5).

It has been suggested that this theory focuses too narrowly on economic issues, neglecting other key issues of importance to electors, and therefore to parties seeking votes. Nevertheless, the idea that elections are determined by valence politics – by voters' judgements about issues and competence – is now widely accepted in electoral studies.

The valence-politics approach represents a significant shift in how electoral politics are conceptualised by social scientists. It suggests that elections are primarily determined not by 'position' issues, on which different people are likely to have very different opinions, but by issues where people tend to be in agreement with regard to the overall aim – issues like crime, or corruption, or economic growth. These latter are valence issues because their importance is agreed on – so the key factor in voter choice becomes a matter of judging which party is best equipped, most competent, to actually deliver the sought-after ends. The idea of valence voting has strong similarities with the theory of individualisation discussed in Chapter 4. Both argue that agents increasingly make judgements and choices that diverge from the predictable patterns once associated with traditional positions of class, gender, occupation, or other structures of social relations.

From this perspective, voters support one party rather than another because of the evaluation they make of a party's ability – or that of its leader – to deliver on the policies they value. They can also punish those parties – usually the party in government – that have not delivered on these policies. Voter identification can be either positive or negative. And it can, obviously, change over time in response to political, economic and social trends.

The emergence of this theory is in part a reflection of a change in how social scientists conceptualise voting behaviour. As the geographers Charles Pattie and Ron Johnston observe, a valence-politics approach 'radically reconceptualises party identification, seeing it not as long term psychological attachment to a party, but as a running tally of a government's performance' (2009, p. 468). According to this theory, governments lose elections when electors feel that their delivery has not been satisfactory *and* when the opposition is considered to offer a credible alternative – when 'potential' wins over 'performance' because the government's 'performance' is considered by enough voters to be inadequate.

One important implication of the shift to theories of valence politics is the argument that a key determinant in voter behaviour is the assessment of party leaders:

> Leadership is a valence issue in that few of us would want to elect a prime minister with no leadership skills. Perceptions of leadership competence have independent effects on party choice, even after controlling for factors such as underlying party identification and evaluations of the economy. Leaders matter, and can be an electoral asset for their party (as [Tony] Blair was for Labour in 1997) or a liability (as, arguably, Gordon Brown rapidly became [for Labour] in early 2008). Other valence issues of importance in influencing party choice include voters' evaluation of competence in handling major public services such as the NHS and education, benefits such as pensions, and public problems such as crime and security.
>
> (Pattie and Johnson, 2009, p. 470)

Figure 7.4 In the run-up to the 2010 UK general election, the leaders of the three main parties appeared in a televised debate for the first time

The valence-politics theory thus posits a significant shift away from fixed or strong identifications towards active evaluation as a core consideration in how electors make choices and cast their votes. In turn, this means that election campaigns matter more than ever. Social science descriptions and understandings of the increasingly fluid and unpredictable nature of the voting process have helped inform a shift in the broader public understanding of how elections are won and lost. This is a key form of social science enactment – evidencing change over time and influencing the behaviour of parties seeking votes, who increasingly recognise that they have to ceaselessly campaign for votes by emphasising their appeal and criticising that of their opponents (see Figure 7.4).

4.4 Description and understanding in the evaluation of theories of voting

We have seen how social science has shifted from one theory of voting behaviour to another, depending on the degree to which a particular theory is able to predict or explain electoral outcomes and patterns of change across successive elections. See Table 7.4 for a summary of the main features of each of the three theories of voting discussed here.

Table 7.4 Three social science theories of voting

	Theory of action	Basis of voting decision	Nature of voter–party relationship	Strength of attachment over time
Sociological theory	Structural explanation	Rational utility – class interests	Partisan	Stable and predictable
Social-psychological theory	Structure and agency	Emotional attachment – identification with party	Partisan	Stable and predictable
Valence-politics theory	Agency	Judgement of competence – issue-based	Dealigned, weakened partisanship	Fluid, temporary, unpredictable

You can see that the three theories can be differentiated along four dimensions:

- the theory of action which underlies their accounts of voting
- the basis of voting decisions they each identify
- the nature of the relationship between voters and parties
- the assumptions made about the strength of the attachment between voters and parties over time.

The shifts from one approach to another have not been driven simply by testing theories against evidence. The changes are also related to important conceptual shifts. For example, consider this quote from Johnston and Pattie, describing the view of voter behaviour that is now widely accepted under the valence-politics approach:

> Voters are increasingly open to alternative claims for their support, and identification with individual parties has become weaker, a process called partisan dealignment. Their decisions are largely influenced by evaluations of current conditions (dominantly but not solely economic) and the perceived performance of parties and candidates in government, by their expectations regarding the future, and by their assessments of the potential governance offered by rivals.
>
> (Johnston and Pattie, 2004, p. 47)

One thing to notice about this description of valence-based voting is that it still assumes, like the class-based theory which was ascendant previously, that economic factors play a crucial role in explaining electoral outcomes. But the difference lies in how these are conceptualised. In the class-based approach, the assumption is that people's economic interests are determined structurally, by their position within stable patterns of class, employment, housing and education. In the valence-politics approach, economic factors are considered to be just as important, but they are now understood in terms of 'issues' in relation to which voters make judgements regarding parties' relative performance and competence.

So whereas class-based and party-identification theories both emphasise voters' stable structural position and associated loyalties, valence theories see voting as a much more fluid process, with voters making short-term judgements about past performance and future potential. This shift in theory, then, is partly due to empirical shifts in voter behaviour – for example, the observable decline of strong, partisan identification in the UK since the 1970s. And it is partly to do with how these new descriptions of voter behaviour have in turn led to new theories of the agency of voters.

5 Enacting elections: informing and shaping public debate

In Sections 3 and 4 we have seen how social science investigations of elections generate descriptions and understandings of voting that fill in, as it were, the blank spaces that the raw materials of an election result produce. By digging beneath election results, comparing electoral data with other data sets, conducting surveys and doing interviews, social scientists seek to make sense of elections and voting decisions – to make sense of them as indicative of changing expressions of the popular will, or as reflections of changing patterns of socio-economic division, or as indicative of new fissures or identities.

Even in this simple sense, then, social science helps to enact elections – social science allows election results to be placed into narratives, not least by providing comparative and historical perspective. This is just one way in which social science informs and shapes how elections are thought about and conducted. Social science research is used, for example, to inform campaigns by parties to better target those people most likely to vote for them. But it's also used in campaigns to increase participation – or voter turnout – across the board, as a generally agreed civic duty, by helping to target groups who are highly represented among non-voters. And as already suggested, it is not only academics who use social science to make sense of, and to describe and understand, elections – it is also used by non-academic polling organisations, by journalists and by pundits, and social science in turn informs and shapes public debates about the meanings of elections and of political processes more broadly.

Social science analysis of voting and elections is interesting not least because it helps us see that the enactment of social worlds does not have to take the form of direct influence on policy making. There is more to 'the uses of social science' than having a direct, observable 'impact'. Electoral studies demonstrate a more diffuse contribution to public debates. For instance, by evaluating the formal theories of electoral behaviour discussed above, social scientists have demonstrated that political parties in the UK now face two significant challenges:

- the changes in the 'sense of belonging' among established electorates, from which parties draw support – something reflected in declining levels of party identification

- the rise of evaluative judgemental voting based on valence politics – which obliges parties to pay ever closer attention to leaders, images and issues.

These changes reflect the conditionality with which voters now cast their ballots. The idea that issue-based competition has become more important is based in part on social science analysis of evidence; but it also relates to a shift in how voting behaviour is conceptualised. The idea that voter evaluations of party policies and of the quality of party leaders play an ever larger part in voter choice has become widely accepted – not only among social scientists, but among politicians, pollsters and pundits, and among voters themselves (Heffernan, 2009).

Social scientists are, then, part of a broader public conversation about politics, voting and election. Sometimes they inform and shape public debates indirectly – by influencing other expert and elite actors, such as journalists or policy makers. Social scientists often act as experts who are consulted by government and are invited to serve on commissions of inquiry. Election experts, for instance, are often asked by government to advise on ways in which voting may be made easier.

But sometimes social science can have a very visible public role in debates about politics. This is nowhere more the case than in the field of electoral studies. Perhaps surprisingly, given the sometimes highly technical, statistical nature of social science research on voting, psephologists have been among the best-known public intellectuals in British cultural life. We have already seen how David Butler helped to pioneer the study of elections in Britain, through the Nuffield Election Studies and then the BES. But from 1950 to 1979 Butler was also the public face of academic electoral studies, along with another academic, Robert MacKenzie. These two became crucial parts of the BBC's election broadcasting as it pioneered the televised coverage and analysis of elections. They, and other academics, served as expert analysts, providing in-depth analysis and historical context, and identifying trends as results came in on election night. This type of expert analysis has now become a staple feature of news coverage of elections, but Butler and MacKenzie pioneered innovative ways of making their complex analysis and predictions accessible to the general public. Most famously, MacKenzie is associated with the 'invention' of the swingometer (see Figure 7.5), a simple graphic device that represented how a given swing in the percentage of votes cast for one party or another would translate into shifts in the number of seats held by each party in Parliament (BBC, 2011a; 2011b).

Figure 7.5 MacKenzie with the swingometer on election night, 1964

Butler and MacKenzie's role as 'media dons' is a well-known example of a much more routine way in which social science enacts social worlds as well as describing and understanding them – by communicating their findings, interpretations and explanations in the public sphere. Writing in 2001, Butler himself helps us see this dimension of enactment, in a reflection on his own career in broadcast coverage of UK elections. Having studied each election since 1945, Butler observes that elections 'have been transformed in the past half-century'. He goes on to suggest that 'The real turning point came in 1959, with the coming of television and opinion polls. We've now moved to 24-hour electioneering from stately middle-of-the-day events' (BBC, 2001).

Here Butler encapsulates two of the ways in which social science has informed and even shaped how elections are organised and made sense of – through the widespread use of social science methods such as opinion-polling, used by academics, news organisations and campaigns; but also by noting the importance of television in reshaping how elections are organised. Because if television has played an important role in shaping elections, then social scientists like Butler, MacKenzie and others have themselves been important actors in shaping how television has transformed the meaning and conduct of elections.

6 Conclusion: making sense of participation

In this chapter we have seen how social science seeks to describe voting behaviour at elections through the generation of data about who votes and who they vote for, and also how it seeks to explain why some people vote and others don't. You have seen that in relation both to turnout and to voting decisions, social science theories are evaluated in relation to evidence, but also in terms of changing concepts of what counts as a plausible explanation. For example, the shift from theories of class-based or social-psychological voting to more issue-based theories is in part a response to evidence of changing patterns of voter behaviour and identification. But it's also a result of a conceptual shift away from theories focusing on stable, structural factors, towards theories which conceptualise voting in much more fluid and more agency-oriented ways.

This chapter has also shown how social scientists' analysis of voting helps to inform and shape public debates about elections and politics more broadly. It does so in a variety of ways. Social science descriptions and understandings inform policy making and policy reviews around issues of improving electoral registration, increasing turnout, considering electoral reform and other matters. Social science is integral to how news organisations report elections and how parties devise strategies to win them. And electoral studies has, perhaps surprisingly, successfully made itself one of the most visible examples of social science in the public sphere – as expert analysts on television or radio or in newspapers, social scientists are routinely asked to predict, explain and interpret results, trends and patterns. If voting is an important way of participating in social worlds, then social science has a key role in informing and shaping the terms in which such participation is practised.

6.1 Chapter summary

In this chapter you have learned that:

- voting is a basic form of participation, in terms of expressing both partisan demands and shared identity as citizens

- social science generates data and evidence about voting and elections, in order to make sense of the large amount of 'thin' information that election results provide
- social science addresses the question of participation in elections through analysis of issues of voter turnout
- various explanations of turnout can be evaluated in terms of their empirical adequacy, conceptual coherence and scope of application
- social science explanations of why people vote as they do have shifted over time, from more structural approaches towards more agency-centred approaches
- the rise of valence-based theories of voting behaviour reflects both responses to new evidence about voting, and conceptual shifts in how voting is understood
- social science enacts voting and elections in various ways: by making sense of complex electoral outcomes; by providing expert opinion; and by contributing to public conversations about the meaning of elections, the determinants of voting decisions, and the trends of changes over time.

References

BBC (2001) 'Sultan of swingometers', 7 June [online], http://news.bbc.co.uk/1/hi/uk/1369188.stm (Accessed 28 March 2012).

BBC (2010) 'Election 2010' [online], http://news.bbc.co.uk/1/shared/election2010/results/ (Accessed 28 March 2012).

BBC (2011a) 'Profile of David Butler' [online], http://www.bbc.co.uk/archive/swingometer/11203.shtml (Accessed 9 January 2012).

BBC (2011b) 'MacKenzie's lore: the king of the swingometer' [online], http://www.bbc.co.uk/archive/swingometer/11204.shtml (Accessed 9 January 2012).

Butler, D. (1998) 'Reflections on British elections and their study', *Annual Review of Political Science*, vol. 1, no. 2, pp. 451–64.

Butler, D. and Stokes, D. (1974) *Political Change in Britain: Forces Shaping Electoral Choice*, London, Macmillan.

Clarke, H., Sanders, D., Stewart, M. and Whiteley, P. (2004) *Political Choice in Britain*, Oxford, Oxford University Press.

Clarke, H., Sanders, D., Stewart, M. and Whiteley, P. (2009) *Performance Politics and the British Voter*, Cambridge, Cambridge University Press.

Denver, D. (2011) 'Elections and voting' in Heffernan, R., Cowley, P. and Hay, C. (eds) *Developments in British Politics 9*, London, Palgrave Macmillan.

Economic and Social Research Council (2010) 'British election study' [online], http://www.esrc.ac.uk/_images/BES_tcm8-2690.pdf (Accessed 16 November 2011).

Electoral Commission (2010) *The Completeness and Accuracy of Electoral Registers in Great Britain*, London, Electoral Commission.

Heffernan, R. (2009) 'Political parties' in Flinders, M., Gamble, A., Hay, C. and Kenny, M. (eds) *The Oxford Handbook of British Politics*, Oxford, Oxford University Press.

Johnston, R. and Pattie, C. (2004) 'Electoral geography in electoral studies: putting voters in their place' in Barnett, C. and Low, M. (eds) *Spaces of Democracy*, London, Sage.

Johnston, R. and Pattie, C. (2006) *Putting Voters in their Place: Geography and Elections in Great Britain*, Oxford, Oxford University Press.

McCallum, R. (1954) 'The study of psephology', *Parliamentary Affairs*, vol. 8, no. 4, pp. 508–13.

Pattie, C. and Johnston, R. (2009) 'Voting and identity' in Flinders, M., Gamble, A., Hay, C. and Kenny, M. (eds) *The Oxford Handbook of British Politics*, Oxford, Oxford University Press.

Pultzer, P.G. (1967) *Political Representation and Elections in Britain*, London, Allen and Unwin.

Chapter 8
Giving people a voice

Vicki Squire

1 Introduction 311
1.1 Structure of the chapter 313
1.2 Aims of the chapter 314
2 Describing, understanding and enacting participation 315
3 Principles of participatory action research 321
3.1 The values of participatory action research 321
4 Participatory action research in practice 326
4.1 Case study 1: refugee and immigrant healthcare 327
4.2 Case study 2: young 'womyn of color' in New York City 330
5 Evaluating participatory action research 337
6 Conclusion: enacting social worlds 342
6.1 Chapter summary 343
References 345

1 Introduction

This final chapter of *The Uses of Social Science* focuses on issues of participation, as did Chapter 7, but it moves the analysis of this topic along in two ways. First, Chapter 7 looked at participation in political processes, using the example of voting in elections. However, there is more to participation than participating in these sorts of formal arenas of citizenship alone. There is a whole range of ways in which people seek to express their demands, identities and grievances – to publicly articulate their 'voice'. What is more, certain groups of people might find it difficult to participate in the more formal arenas of public life, because of lack of resources, or discrimination, or exclusion. For people unable to participate fully and equally in these formal arenas, it is likely that the issues that concern them will remain private, hidden and in the shadows. For these groups, finding other ways of expressing their voice, of making their troubles heard more widely, is particularly important.

This chapter looks at the ways in which social science seeks to describe, understand and intervene in processes of participation, and focuses specifically on the use of social science by marginalised groups of people.

This leads us to the second way in which Chapter 8 develops further the themes introduced in the previous chapter. Previously, you have seen how social science descriptions and understandings can help to enact social worlds by informing public debates or policy making. Chapter 7 looked at how social science research into participation helped to inform such debates. This chapter considers how people actually participate *in* social science, and how this illustrates a further dimension to enactment – how social science can be used to give voice to the concerns of marginalised, relatively disempowered groups of people.

The chapter develops these two themes – of participation in a wide range of activities, and of social science helping to give voice to people – by looking at **participatory social science**. Participatory social science seeks to give the subjects of social science research – the people interviewed, surveyed or counted – a more active role in shaping the descriptions and understandings of the social worlds under investigation. This is achieved not just by giving research participants an active voice in the research process, but also by seeking to give them a voice in the wider world through the uses made of their social science research. The

Participatory social science means research in which the subjects of social science research are directly involved in the process of designing, carrying out, analysing, disseminating and acting on the findings of research.

chapter uses one specific example of participatory social science to elaborate on these issues, an approach known as **participatory action research** (referred to as PAR throughout the chapter).

Participatory action research is a type of participatory social science that is orientated towards addressing a specific problem in the life of those involved in the research process.

There are two reasons why social scientists make use of participatory methodologies. The first is relatively instrumental: it is assumed that having people actively involved in research about their social worlds is a better way to generate accurate, reliable descriptions and understandings. But the second reason draws out the degree to which social science descriptions and understandings always involve values too. Social scientists who make use of participatory approaches point to the importance of marginalised groups 'having voice', in order to challenge or transform the conditions and processes that lead to their exclusion. The theme of 'having voice' is central to this chapter. Participatory approaches such as PAR see one role of social science as assisting marginalised social groups to challenge the relations of *power* in which they find themselves positioned – and these approaches also tend to presume that formal rights of citizenship might not be an adequate means to do this. So participatory social science seeks to intervene in or change the realities that it tries to describe and understand – that is, it seeks to enact them in new ways. Often social science research seeks to enact them in new ways in pursuit of certain values – values of inclusion, equality or social justice, for example.

PAR is one example of participatory social science. It combines an emphasis on practical application (as action research) and an emphasis on embedding participation within the research process (as participatory research).

- *Action research* is orientated towards solving practical problems and fostering change. It entails a close relation between action and reflection, with theory 'developed and tested by practical interventions and action' (Kindon et al., 2007a, p. 10).
- *Participatory research* is orientated towards including the researched in the design and implementation of the research. It entails an emphasis on a 'participatory worldview', which serves as a vehicle for 'increasing citizen voice and power' (Kindon et al., 2007a, p. 11).

PAR is an interdisciplinary approach to social science, influenced by developments in social psychology and used widely in fields such as development studies and educational research. The following definition captures the sense of PAR combining a strong value orientation with a strong sense of practical application:

> PAR is rooted in principles of inclusion (engaging people in the research design, process and outcomes); participation; valuing all local voices; and community driven sustainable outcomes. PAR is a process and a practice directed towards social change with the participants; it is interventionist, action-oriented and interpretive. It involves a commitment to research that develops partnership responses to developing purposeful knowledge (praxis); includes all those involved where possible, thus facilitating shared ownership of the development and outcomes of the research; uses innovative ways of consulting and working with people and facilitates change with communities and groups.
>
> (O'Neill and Harindranath, 2006, p. 46)

This definition emphasises the *values* of inclusion and transformation; it emphasises the importance of researchers and researched participating together in the *co-production* of social science knowledge; and it emphasises the interventionist, practical *application* of such knowledge. The elements of inclusiveness, co-production and intervention give a good sense of how PAR seeks to enact social worlds in new ways.

1.1 Structure of the chapter

Section 2 of this chapter raises the question of what sorts of activities might reasonably be considered forms of participation through which people express their voice, and discusses the role of social science in giving voice to people even in the most contentious of situations. Section 3 discusses the principles behind PAR. It emphasises the aim of ensuring that the subjects of social science research 'have voice' through the research process. The section goes on to explore the uses of PAR, setting these out in terms of the different forms of enactment developed throughout this module. This section looks at the theory of PAR, introducing various models of PAR in terms of what the approach is designed to achieve. Section 4 then looks at two case studies of the use of PAR. Issues surrounding the degree to which these examples match the models presented in Section 3 are explored here. Questions about how the success of a participatory social science approach such as PAR can be evaluated are further examined in Section 5.

1.2 Aims of the chapter

This chapter aims to:

- introduce the idea that participation can take many forms
- introduce the principles and aims of PAR
- illustrate how PAR is used in practice to assist in facilitating people to 'have voice'
- consider the different ways in which the aims and practice of participatory social science can be evaluated
- consider the ways in which participatory social science combines description and understandings in order to enact social worlds in new ways, often in relation to specific values.

2 Describing, understanding and enacting participation

> I did see the riots coming and the government should have seen it coming, too. Jobs are hard to get and, when they do become available, youths don't get the jobs. There is nothing to do, they are closing youth clubs so the streets are just crazy. They are full of people who have no ambitions, or have ambitions but can't fulfil them.
>
> (Chavez Campbell, youth and amateur boxer from London, *The Guardian*, 12 August 2011)

> In big cities, you might expect this, but not here ... And they didn't look hungry or deprived. They were wearing designer clothes ... Opportunist thugs. The UK's gone soft. Too many do-gooders.
>
> (Sham Sharma, shop owner from Wolverhampton, *The Guardian*, 12 August 2011)

These two quotes refer to the riots that occurred across a number of towns and cities in England during the summer of 2011. They are comments from two people who are not social scientists, and they were printed in a newspaper immediately after the events took place. They provide very different perspectives on these events, and they contain descriptive elements (what is the case, what happened, who was involved) as well as elements of understanding (why these events took place). And implicitly, at least, they suggest different views of what should be done in response to these events.

The riots of 2011 were major events involving acts of looting and arson, and sparked wide-ranging debates regarding the situation of youth in contemporary Britain. The Parliament at Westminster was recalled during the August break in order to debate issues relating to the riots. Five people died in the violence associated with the events, damages to property were estimated at hundreds of millions of pounds, and thousands of people were arrested and subjected to unusually harsh criminal convictions in light of the perceived seriousness of the riots. The events also sparked large-scale inquiries into and consultations over matters such as policing and gang culture.

Figure 8.1 Rioting started in Tottenham, London, on the night of Saturday, 6 August 2011

Lying behind the debates set off by these events was the question of whether the riots were merely expressions of criminality, or whether they raised wider issues about inequality, injustice and exclusion – even if rioting represented a form of political expression by marginalised or alienated groups. The remarks by Sham Sharma, quoted above, dismiss the latter view out of hand. Chavez Campbell does not defend the rioters, but he does provide an explanatory account of why the rioting happened; an account that points to issues of inequality, exclusion and disempowerment.

These descriptions of the riots raise questions about how to explain and interpret these events. In particular, they raise the issue of how far such events are appropriately understood as throwing into question the legitimacy, fairness and equity of existing configurations of socio-economic opportunity, and political or social participation. The way in which the actions of those involved in the riots are described and understood can differ significantly, depending on the interpretation of the conditions under which the events took place, or their causes.

Similarly to Campbell and Sharma, social scientists have also presented various accounts of why the riots occurred. Some indicate that they were the outcomes of long-standing failures of policing practices. Others suggest that they can be understood as a consequence of processes of social exclusion, and as reflecting the difficulties that some groups encounter in actively participating in society. Still others suggest that the rioters had been participating in the wrong sort of activities – they were too involved, for example, in urban gang cultures.

These different accounts, from both non-academics and social scientists, raise questions about how people who may be excluded from participation in ordinary aspects of social life – from opportunities to work, from formal political processes, from cultural life – can effectively express their concerns. Different ways of describing these sorts of events can have very different implications in terms of what should be done in response to them. Are the 2011 riots best described in terms of exclusion, inequality and protest, or in terms of criminality, social breakdown and lack of respect for authority? Depending on which of these descriptions is favoured, quite different interventions would seem to follow. In fact, we can see that these accounts are not merely descriptions at all. They also contain elements of explanation and interpretation – of understanding, as well as description.

If we return to the two quotes from the newspaper that began this section, you can see how different accounts of the 2011 riots combine description and understanding. The quotes were published in two articles in the same newspaper on the same day, yet provide very different interpretations of the events that occurred. Each quote invokes a different description of the youths involved in the riots; each implies a different understanding of issues of participation or non-participation; and each suggests the need for quite different interventions, or what we might think of as potential enactments. Look again at the quotes, and consider whether the descriptions provided might reflect the different positions of the two people quoted – one a 'youth'; the other a shopkeeper. Campbell is a London youth who may well know some of those involved in the riots, whereas Sharma is a Wolverhampton shop owner whose business was damaged in the riots.

Now you know more about the positions of the two interviewees, it is perhaps unsurprising that they provide such different descriptions and understandings of the same events and groups. Taking each one on its own, consider how valid you think each of these interpretations is.

The differences in the way that each of these interviewees describes the riots and the youths involved are stark. Campbell suggests that the events were unsurprising in light of the lack of involvement of youths in employment, or in other community activities – in his view, they have nothing to do, no jobs and no way of fulfilling their ambitions. By contrast, Sharma suggests that these events were surprising occurrences outside of major cities, and reflect the spread of anti-social behaviour in contemporary society, rather than any material deprivation. For him, the youths involved were opportunistic, taking advantage of the UK having 'gone soft'.

For Campbell, then, the riots highlight the problems that arise where youth cannot participate fully in society. For Sharma, by contrast, they highlight the problems that arise where youth does not participate in terms that fit with established rules or societal norms. If you agree with Campbell, then you might think the best response to the riots is to redirect resources to youth groups as a practical intervention, and to invest in job creation and training. If you agree with Sharma, you might think the best response is to harden how the criminal justice system treats such behaviour. These two very different descriptions and understandings have important implications for the ways in which the riots are presented as public issues requiring practical responses or policy interventions – important implications, in short, for how these events are enacted as events of public significance.

It is worth slowing down here, and looking at the different ways in which these two responses to the riots by non-academics relate to enactments of social worlds. In one sense, they relate to enactment because the descriptions and understandings provided by Campbell and Sharma represent viewpoints that inform debates about particular interventions of a practical or policy-orientated nature. But there is another sense in which these comments enact social worlds. The two viewpoints imply very different ways of relating to the people involved in the riots, which reflect different social analyses of the same events or phenomenon. It would be too easy to suggest that here the difference is between forgiving and condemning. Actually, both Campbell and Sharma suggest responsibility lies not only with the rioters – it also lies either with 'government', which has not done enough to address the underlying causes, or with a society that has 'gone soft'. But these two perspectives do present 'youths' in very different ways: Sharma defines the youths involved in the riots as opportunistic criminals and relates to them as such, while Campbell suggests that they are better defined as those whose legitimate ambitions and expectations are unrealised.

Campbell's and Sharma's are just two voices on this issue. They illustrate how descriptions, understandings and evaluations of events are inevitably mixed up. But what is particularly important about them, from the perspective of this chapter, is that they reflect different social analyses of the same phenomena or event. The relationship between social science and public perception is in this sense an intimate one. Indeed, one of the important points to draw out for the purposes of this chapter is that qualitative social science takes the opinions of people who are not social scientists very seriously. It does not necessarily seek to confirm one of these perspectives rather than the other – to demonstrate either that the causes of the riots were economic, or that anti-social behaviour was the most important underlying factor. Rather, from the perspective of the sort of engaged social science discussed in this chapter, it is assumed that in order to understand an event like the 2011 riots, it is necessary to find out what people involved, on all sides, thought about what went on and why.

This can be a controversial approach to social science, no doubt. Shortly after the riots, a social science research project was set up in partnership between *The Guardian* newspaper, social scientists at the London School of Economics, the Joseph Rowntree Foundation and the Open Society Foundation – the latter two both important funders of social science research. In this combination of media, academics and research foundations, the project was very explicitly meant to use social science research to inform and shape public debates about the causes and consequences of the riots. The programme was called *Reading the Riots*, and it claimed to be 'the only research study into the causes and consequences of the summer riots involving interviews with large numbers of people who actually took part in the disorder' (Lewis and Newburn, 2011). When the project published its first findings, very soon after the riots, they caused no small amount of public furore:

> Widespread anger and frustration at the way police engage with communities was a significant cause of the summer riots in every major city where disorder took place, the biggest study into their cause has found.
>
> Hundreds of interviews with people who took part in the disturbances which spread across England in August revealed deep-seated and sometimes visceral antipathy towards police.
>
> (Lewis et al., 2011)

The report became part of an ongoing debate about the causes of the riots, and about whether seeking to explain these causes was tantamount to excusing those who had been involved in the destruction of property and people's livelihoods, and, in some cases, in causing injury and death. From the perspective of this chapter, what is most notable about this social science research project is the degree to which it is premised on the idea that any description and understanding of these events should be based on a careful consideration of the viewpoints of those people who were involved.

The methodology of the project involved using qualitative interviews to collect first-person accounts of who became involved in the riots and why. It also involved analysing databases of social media communication during the riots. So this is an example of social science engaging very directly in public debate, but doing so in a way that gives considerable weight to the viewpoints of people involved – to rioters' stories, victims' voices and the views of police, judges and others involved as well. Whatever one thinks about the merits of the arguments about the causes of the riots distilled by Campbell and Sharma, this research project illustrates an approach to social science that puts a premium on giving voice to participants in social worlds as a way of better describing and understanding their actions.

Reading the Riots is an example of social science explicitly aiming to inform and shape public debates about contentious issues, an approach that seeks to include the voices of various non-academics in its descriptions and understandings of those issues. Let us now turn to a much more assertive style of participatory social science, which seeks not just to inform but to actively shape and reshape the worlds it describes and understands.

3 Principles of participatory action research

In this section we look at some of the principles that lie behind the use of PAR in social science. Here you will find out more about the ways in which PAR has been developed in the areas of development studies and educational research, as a means of allowing local people and marginalised groups to 'have voice' through their involvement in social science investigations. We shall also look at different accounts of the value of PAR and raise the question of how PAR can and should be evaluated; this is a theme further developed in Sections 4 and 5.

Founded on the two dimensions of *action* and *participation*, PAR is often used by social scientists to solve problems or to foster change based on the involvement of those closest to the problem in question. It is thus developed by social scientists carrying out applied research that is orientated towards solving practical problems. It also often has an affinity with ethnographic research which, as you saw in Chapter 6, is based on a close, direct engagement with research participants.

3.1 The values of participatory action research

As we have already seen, PAR is associated with a particular value-orientation, and is often used to support people who are discriminated against, or in some way excluded, to express their voice and address the power relations that lead to their marginalisation. It is a social science approach that is closely connected to the social worlds it investigates. PAR can be understood as a means of intervening in the social worlds under investigation, through the involvement of research subjects in the research process itself. Writing in the field of development studies, William Foote Whyte describes PAR as rooted in both social science and the 'real world' of communities and organisations. The developments of participatory and action-orientated approaches to social research are related to the decision making of those who have a low community or organisational ranking (Whyte, 1991, p. 7). Whyte emphasises that PAR develops out of a tradition of applied research, which is designed to address practical problems such as worker participation in the areas of agriculture and industry. The specificity of PAR, he suggests, lies in the way in which it is used by social scientists to transform 'key informants' into 'active participants in the research'

(Whyte, 1991, p. 9). This is linked to what he calls the 'democratic values' of PAR researchers (Whyte, 1991, p. 10).

Figure 8.2 PAR developed out of a tradition of applied research, which addressed issues such as the marginalisation of agricultural workers from development policy

A particularly important aspect of Whyte's definition is the specific role it envisages for the social scientist involved in PAR. Rather than thinking of research subjects as sources of raw data that are analysed, interpreted and presented by the researcher, PAR presumes that researchers and research subjects share in a more 'dialogic' relationship of partnership and collaboration. Robert Chambers, one of the most important theorists and practitioners of this approach, argues that PAR thinks of researchers as facilitators, listeners and learners, not just as teachers and lecturers (1998, p. xv).

PAR is an approach developed in research fields in which describing and understanding the social worlds of poor, disempowered or marginalised people is of paramount importance. In development studies, for example, it is an important approach because, as Chambers observes, the redefinition of the role of the researcher enables 'local people, including the poor, illiterate, women and the marginalised themselves to appraise, analyse, plan and act' (1998, p. xvi). For researchers in the field of development studies, PAR is a means of facilitating the production of knowledge by local people directly. PAR researchers thus do not seek to describe and understand social worlds from the outside; rather, they seek to include participants in those social worlds in the process of investigation itself, enabling them to inform and shape the research process.

An emphasis on empowering the researched is also important in education studies, another key discipline within which PAR has emerged. Particularly influential here is the emancipatory educator Paulo Freire, who undertook community-based educational research in Brazil during the 1960s and 1970s with the objective of ensuring that 'poor and marginalised groups developed a heightened awareness of the forces affecting their lives, and then used this greater awareness as a catalyst to inform their political action' (Kindon et al., 2007a, p. 10). The aim of such an approach is to 'support people's participation in knowledge production and social transformation' (ibid.). Again, this reflects the self-consciously democratic values at the heart of PAR.

Participatory and action-orientated approaches have also been developed as a means of undertaking research into the effectiveness of educational techniques and approaches (e.g. Harris and Foreman-Peck, 2001). This research is also committed to actively involving participants in the process of producing knowledge that is orientated towards addressing problems and fostering change. Social scientists in this regard can be understood to use PAR to enact participants in social worlds as active participants in social science itself.

You will notice that these two examples of PAR in education studies have different emphases: Freire's approach is more explicitly radical in its political ambitions, whereas the assessment of education practices is a more modest project. There is no single, agreed model of how PAR should be used or for what purposes. It is possible to distinguish two broad approaches to PAR (see Cameron, 2007), defined by different ideas about what sort of action this kind of social science is meant to support:

- A *liberatory* approach, which grew out of the popular education movement of the 1960s and 1970s, is designed with the aim of improving people's circumstances, particularly 'those who experience oppressive and exploitative conditions that limit life opportunities' (Cameron, 2007, p. 207). This is PAR produced with and for subjects of marginalisation and disempowerment.

- An *institutional* approach which aims to produce recommendations for institutions to act on. This is PAR used to enhance the performance of institutions.

Figure 8.3 Emancipatory educator, Paulo Freire

These can be understood as two ideal types, though in practice there is often a significant degree of overlap between them. Whether liberatory or institutional in orientation, the emphasis on action for *change* is crucial to PAR. Questions of change inform the emphasis on 'having voice' that defines PAR, and underscore the degree to which this type of social science seeks to enact social worlds in alternative ways. This notion is captured by Chambers, who describes the importance of including research subjects in development studies research along three dimensions. Development researchers, he says, have found:

> ... that there are new ways to enable those who are poor, marginalised, illiterate and excluded to analyse their realities and express their priorities; that the realities they express of conditions, problems, livelihood strategies and priorities often differ from what development professionals have believed; and that new experiences can put policy-makers in closer touch with those realities.
>
> (Chambers, 1998, p. xv)

So, in development studies, where issues such as poverty reduction, gender inequality and rural deprivation are central, Chambers indicates three values that PAR supports:

- an *intrinsic* value of allowing poor or excluded people to express themselves
- what we might call an *instrumental* value, in helping researchers better understand the problems they are investigating
- a *practical* value, in better informing action by policy makers to address these issues.

As you can see, then, PAR is a form of participatory social science that is explicit about using descriptions and understandings in pursuit of particular values. Within this field, however, there are various views regarding what PAR should be used for, and a range of different but overlapping values that are being pursued. As you move on to the next section of this chapter, you should keep in mind these different views and the different values at stake in PAR, because they are important in debates about how best to evaluate this sort of engaged participatory social science.

4 Participatory action research in practice

As you saw in the last section, PAR has developed in a range of forms as a means of providing marginalised groups with the opportunity to 'have voice' through the research process. This approach has been particularly influential in development studies, where critical social scientists have sought to include 'local voices' in research processes. It has also been taken up more widely to involve a range of groups that social scientists define as 'marginalised' due to the unequal configuration of rights and obligations.

In this section you will look at two case studies of PAR in practice that seek to include the voices of marginalised groups. One of these is more institutionally orientated, while the other might be described as a more liberatory type of PAR. First you will consider a project in a Canadian city where PAR is used in order to involve refugees and immigrants in the effective provision of healthcare services. Second, you will look at a project involving young black and minority ethnic women from New York City, where PAR is used as a means of community empowerment in challenging processes of stereotyping.

When considering these two case studies, think about the discussion in Section 3 regarding the values that PAR seeks to put into action: these are key to how social science of this sort can be evaluated.

The two cases reflect quite different orientations in the use of social science research. The first is more attuned to *applied* social science, and the second more attuned to *activist* social science. The fundamental point about PAR, in both these types of social science, is that social scientists are not the sole or even the main actors in the PAR research in either of the cases discussed in this section. Various participants are involved in the two PAR projects you will look at here – healthcare practitioners, refugees and immigrants in the first case; and young black and minority ethnic women in the second. Before we consider the use made of PAR in policy or institutions, it is important to recognise the importance in this approach of using participatory social science methods to help people to find their own voice, to define and express themselves and the worlds within which they live. In this regard, PAR is one means by which social science helps to translate the private troubles of people into issues of public concern.

4.1 Case study 1: refugee and immigrant healthcare

The first PAR project is *institutionally orientated*, because it involves healthcare practitioners as well as local community members. The project is a community-based one, developed by a group of healthcare and welfare practitioners from various non-profit health and immigrant support service agencies in a mid-size western Canadian city. The overarching goal of the project is defined as being 'to develop resiliency among newcomers coping with acculturation stress associated with migration and settlement processes' (Van der Velde et al., 2009, p. 1294). 'Acculturation stress' here refers to the pressures that newly arriving migrants experience in living in a new culture and environment. To meet its overarching goal, the project involves more specific objectives:

- to build capacities for positive health outcomes with members from immigrant and refugee communities
- to develop institutional readiness to support community initiatives that enhance newcomers' mental health
- to create an environment conducive to productive collaboration among professionals providing formal mental healthcare services (Van der Velde et al., 2009, p. 1294).

As you can see, this is research that seeks to have very clearly defined effects on institutions and participants. It has a strong institutional leaning, though as a community project it bridges the institutional and liberatory 'ideal types' introduced in the last section. The project is one that is also *applied* in its approach to social science: it has been developed in order to solve the problem of service-user disengagement. This programme is heavily action-orientated, and thus steeped in a tradition of applied social research. There is a clear problem to be solved here – namely the current failure of healthcare provision to engage community members and to address effectively the acculturation stress of refugees and immigrants.

Crucial to the success of these aims is the involvement of representatives from diverse service-user communities. The project is designed as a means to provide 'outreach' to these groups, so a key dimension is to ensure that services are engaged by, and respond directly to, the needs of immigrants and refugees. The project is thus not orientated towards a change of organisational practice alone, although this remains an important dimension of the project.

Figure 8.4 PAR has been used to foster engagements between newly arriving migrants and healthcare providers

What is worth highlighting is that it is not social scientists directly who have employed PAR in this instance. Rather, it is the community project that uses PAR as a means of bringing together healthcare practitioners and service users in order to enhance the effectiveness of institutional practice and encourage community engagement. This is a reminder that social science approaches are often used outside of university settings, including social scientists working within various non-academic research institutions as well as those using the methods and approaches of social science research outside of a research setting. The uses of social science are, to put it simply, diverse. Consistent with the facilitative role of researchers in PAR, the health professionals involved in this project play a primarily administrative role, while a core group of individuals from different ethno-cultural communities is responsible for building links between their communities and the mental health project (Van der Velde et al., 2009, p. 1294). This example of PAR engages both institutional practitioners and local participants in the pursuit of change.

This project also included an evaluation project, undertaken by academic social scientists, to assess the degree to which the community-based PAR project has succeeded in putting into practice the theoretical emphasis in PAR on enhancing participation, knowledge acquisition, empowerment and social change among immigrants and refugees. The social scientists evaluating the project draw attention to its importance in allowing for a better understanding of the healthcare problems of refugees and immigrants. They argue that PAR allows healthcare practitioners to *understand* the specificities of these challenges, while at the same time supporting refugees and immigrants to become involved in the development of healthcare practices (Van der Velde et al., 2009). This is an example of the instrumental value of PAR: it allows refugees and immigrants to better inform practitioners regarding the development of healthcare provision.

The social scientists evaluating the project also point to the ways in which PAR allows such groups to develop knowledge of existing institutional provisions, to become empowered with regard to their healthcare, and to participate in processes of social change with regard to healthcare provision. These are examples of the intrinsic value of PAR in practice, allowing participants to express and reshape their own worlds through their involvement in the project.

In the evaluation of this community-based PAR project, then, it has been found that PAR enacts social worlds in two related ways. First, it informs changes in institutional policy and practice by bringing to bear the subjective insights of service users as well as practitioners in order to provide both a better understanding of the needs of refugees and immigrants and a better idea as to how these might be effectively met. This draws on both the instrumental and the practical values of PAR that Chambers (1998, p. xv) identifies (see Section 3.1). Second, PAR helps to enact the social worlds of the participants themselves, in so far as the involvement of refugees and immigrants in the project reshapes their own experiences and sense of self. For example, Van der Velde et al. find that at the start of the project, refugees and immigrants were engaged with as subjects of acculturation, distress and isolation from healthcare services; by the end of the project they appear as actively engaged in the policy process, using their involvement in the PAR project for a range of purposes, including the aim of effecting policy and advocating change on a broader scale (2009, p. 1300).

In this example, the evaluation by social scientists of a community-based PAR project reveals the process of transformation that such an approach can bring about. The refugees and immigrants participating in this project might be thought of as 'marginalised groups' who suffer as a result of the failure of institutional practice. But they also appear as 'empowered groups' who inform practitioners and fellow community members regarding the development of healthcare provision. It seems, then, that the participants undergo a process of change through their involvement in PAR, shaping themselves as active agents engaged in the process of developing policy and practice. This is one dimension of enactment by participation in social science that PAR facilitates, by allowing participants to 'have voice' through the research process. It is one example of participatory social science being used as a means by which the subjects of social science research are able to translate or articulate their private concerns as public issues. This is a point that you will further examine in looking at how PAR enacts subjects in the second case examined in this chapter, whose subjects are young 'womyn of color' in New York City.

4.2 Case study 2: young 'womyn of color' in New York City

The second case of PAR is a project involving a group of young black and minority ethnic women living on Manhattan's Lower East Side in New York City (Cahill, 2007). Defining themselves as 'womyn of color', these young women deploy a feminist alternative to the term 'woman', which makes no reference to a man, while drawing inspiration from the civil rights activist and social scientist W.E.B. Du Bois in deploying the term 'of color'. Calling their project 'The Fed Up Honeys', this group of young women studies the effects of gentrification on their New York City neighbourhoods, and shares the findings of their research with members of their community and the wider public through the development of a website and a local sticker campaign. Their main concern is to challenge processes of stereotyping in order to transform the experiences of young black and minority ethnic women living in their area.

Figure 8.5 Homepage of the Fed Up Honeys website

The Fed Up Honeys project was actually initiated by a student, Caitlin Cahill. She describes how the primary purpose of the project is to study and understand young urban women's experiences and interpretations of the urban environment:

> The project was developed for my dissertation research on the subject of the everyday lives of young women in the city … This

> study took a deliberately open theoretical and methodological approach in order that the objectives of the project would be determined collaboratively by everyone involved. To this end, the project adopted a participatory research approach in order to engage young women researchers in a collective process of looking critically at their social and environmental contexts.
>
> (Cahill et al., 2004, p. 233)

In setting up the research, Cahill recruited seven women between the ages of 16 and 22 from diverse backgrounds, all of whom lived on the Lower East Side. These participants were trained in social research skills, and involved in detailed discussions regarding the focus and design of the project (Cahill et al., 2004, p. 233). The group received a grant to continue their research, and decided collectively to focus on the problem of stereotyping from the perspective of young 'womyn of color'.

Reading 8.1 is a piece written by Erica Arenas, one of the participants in the project, and will give you a flavour of the Fed Up Honeys. It is a first-person, highly personal statement. But it is also a public statement, presented as part of the wider project and published on the Fed Up Honeys website and in print, as part of a broader campaign of raising awareness about racial stereotypes in public media and the urban public space.

What questions does Erica's account raise about her identity as a young 'womyn of color' in New York City?

Reading 8.1

The voice of a young womyn of color

I am an interesting young womyn who bores herself to delirium. And a comedian who can't tell a joke. I am a responsible sister and a helpful daughter. I love to be me and yet I am different around others. I am extremely emotional but want to hide my feelings. I have a hard time trusting some and put too much trust into others. This leads to hurt feelings and total vulnerability. I want to be vulnerable but it makes me feel weak. I want to feel weak but no one wants to care for me. I want to care for those I love and want them to care for me more. I never believe anyone can love me as much as I do them. I want to take care of people but don't want them to need me. I am too clingy and never see friends and family. I am a complete idiot but an intelligent person. I am lacking education. I have no communication skills and I am a good listener. I am a good listener who hates to hear people speak. I am a reader who watches way too much TV. I am a good friend and girlfriend but I have few friends and no boyfriend. I am open and bold but hold my tongue when I'm hurt. I put people in their place and yet others walk all over me. I try too hard and yet do nothing at all. I am a procrastinator but I am always early. I help and help and help, and get nothing in return. I am not where I would like to be and want to be so much further. I am very opinionated and yet know nothing about the world. I know where I want to go but I am confused. I know what I want but I am confused. I know how I feel but I am confused. I know what I mean but I confuse myself. I am boring and fun, and innocent and cruel. I am trusting. I am always here. I am always there. I am always needed. I am loved and hated. I am admired. I am spiteful but not jealous. I am very jealous. I am scared of everything. My face shows bravery. I am angry. I am in love. I am confused again … Honestly, I am too much to put into words.

(Source: Fed Up Honeys, 2004)

This is a highly personal reflection regarding the experience of one young woman living on the Lower East Side of New York City. It is presented by the project itself in this way: 'This is an example of how a young womyn describing herself manages to convey the difficulty and challenge of being a contradiction … of being many things at once' (Fed Up Honeys, 2004). Located as part of a broader attempt by the group to challenge dominant stereotypes about those who live on the Lower East Side, Reading 8.1 is an example of the use of personal testimony to raise issues of broader public concern. It is, then, an example of how this project facilitates Erica 'having voice', by providing a platform in which this personal expression is used to challenge stereotypes and raise troubling questions.

The process by which this research project developed is described by Cahill as one that was 'structured' in terms of working practice, but at the same time was designed in order to create the 'space for the unexpected to happen' (Cahill et al., 2004, p. 237). The research involved participants as equals, and sought to challenge the categories and hierarchical relationship between the researcher and the researched. This is described by one of the participants in the following terms: 'the project facilitator made us realise that we were all equal partners and our collaborative project really would integrate all of our ideas. This atmosphere of democracy and community started us out with camaraderie and respect' (Cahill et al., 2004, p. 236). This emphasis on democracy and community reflects some of the key dimensions of PAR as an approach that were discussed earlier in this chapter – inclusion, co-production and intervention.

The Fed Up Honeys project is explicitly orientated towards including and empowering the young women involved. The participants not only designed and undertook the research themselves, they were also trained in social science research methods. This provided the participants with knowledge and skills that they did not previously have, and allowed them to undertake social science research directly in the terms that they felt were important. As one participant, Tiffany, suggests, this had a transformative effect on their understanding of social science research at the same time as it featured as a tool of self-empowerment: 'I never thought of research as a tool to talk back to the community … I thought of research being used like statistics, making observations about things and only using them for big companies and businesses' (Cahill et al., 2004, p. 236).

This process of using social science research to 'talk back' to the community in which the participants live is important in three senses:

- It suggests that the involvement of participants in the research provides for otherwise marginalised groups to become active in the transformation of their experiences. This is an example of the intrinsic value of PAR.
- It indicates that the co-production of research by an academic (in this case a student) and community members (in this case young black and minority ethnic women) provides opportunities for participants to 'have voice' through the research process. This is an example of the instrumental value of PAR.

- It displays an interventionist approach in the very process of research itself, with participants not only analysing the process of stereotyping but also undertaking actions to challenge such processes through engaging in self-reflection and community activism. This is an example of the practical value of PAR.

These three dimensions are all evident in the fact that the research participants wrote up and disseminated the research results, through a website, a report and an awareness-raising sticker campaign.

This project can be understood as a liberatory type of PAR research, in so far as it allows those who are disempowered or marginalised to 'have voice' and engage in a process of change or transformation. This starts with a process of self-reflection, which refers to the development of a 'heightened awareness of the forces affecting their lives' on the part of 'poor and marginalised groups'. This is then used 'as a catalyst to inform their political action' (Kindon et al., 2007a, p. 10). This process is described in the following way by Indra, one of the participants:

> We came to the agreement that we wanted to provoke others into rethinking the standard negative stereotypes of young urban women of color … But before we could even realise that that was what we wanted to do, we had to (through angry eruptions, upset and discussions) realise that we were living under the veil of those stereotypes ourselves.
>
> (Cahill et al., 2004, p. 238)

The process of self-reflection, although difficult, is described as a productive one by the participants in the project: 'We crafted a project that made our voices the centerpiece, and were able to develop new and innovative approaches to research that are more likely to catch the attention of our peers and urge them to re-think their own self-perceptions and those of their communities' (Cahill et al., 2004, p. 239).

The activist orientation of this project is evident in the attempt to transform the experiences of community members more widely. Not only do the participants in the project redefine their own perceptions of self through the research process, but the research also challenges and reshapes the perceptions of community members more widely. This is an example of a process of transformation whereby personal concerns are articulated as public issues. In the case of the Fed Up Honeys, such a process of reshaping was explicitly orientated towards the task of challenging processes of stereotyping and enacting young 'womyn of color' as subjects with the power to transform their wider communities. The participants in the project not only gained knowledge and skills through the research process, they also found the means to express their personal troubles as wider public issues of concern to the communities within which they lived. This occurred through their production of a research report regarding the impacts of stereotyping on young 'womyn of color', and through their development of a sticker campaign to raise awareness of these issues within the worlds that they inhabit. These activities of research dissemination and the merging of research with activism were coupled with more personal recollections that were collected by the participants themselves, as a means of documenting the experiences of young black and minority ethnic women living on Manhattan's Lower East Side in New York City.

5 Evaluating participatory action research

In Section 3 we saw that PAR is an approach to social science investigation that explicitly seeks to enact social worlds in new ways, in relation to particular values such as empowerment and equality. You have seen in Section 4 how PAR is orientated towards applied and activist uses of social science research, in particular towards research that is of practical significance in terms of either institutional or wider processes of social change. For advocates of PAR, these practical and political dimensions are a strength that allows them to make the case for social science of an applied or activist orientation. It is important to recognise that advocates of participatory social science approaches such as PAR are not recommending that social scientists adopt their own biases in their research. The argument of these approaches is that social science should be done differently, in a more collaborative and participatory way – the broader claims about the value of such approaches follow from this basic methodological commitment to involving people in social science in an active fashion.

For advocates of participatory social science, PAR is commended because of the role it plays in empowering marginalised groups in engaging in the development of policy and practice. Moreover, PAR also allows for processes of self-reflection that can lead to the shaping or reshaping of the subjects and social worlds that form the focus of social science research. Indeed, PAR is often considered as allowing an amplification of voices that would otherwise be left unheard. This is regarded as important, because it allows relations of power, inequality or privilege to be challenged and potentially transformed. Nevertheless, because of its strong claims to be a means of furthering certain values, PAR is open to evaluation in relation to the ambitions it has to enact social worlds in new ways.

Some scholars argue that the use of PAR is not necessarily orientated towards change, and that its participatory approaches can actually become conservative in effect. Thus Chambers, who as we have seen is a key figure in the development of participatory social science, has argued that:

> For some, the proliferation of the language of 'participation' and 'empowerment' within the mainstream is heralded as the

> realization of a long-awaited paradigm shift in development thinking. For others, however, there is less cause for celebration. Their concerns centre on the use of participation as a legitimating device that draws on the moral authority of claims to involve the poor to place the pursuit of other agendas beyond reproach. According to this perspective, much of what is hailed as 'participation' is a mere technical fix that leaves inequitable global and local relations of power, and with it the root causes of poverty, unchallenged.
>
> (Chambers quoted in Brock, 2002, p. 2)

Here, Chambers summarises a clear division between those who advocate participatory social science and those who argue *against* its claims of furthering social justice and empowerment. Chambers' argument *for* PAR highlights the potential impacts that participatory approaches to social science research can have on policy, practice and/ or wider frameworks of thinking and acting. The argument *against* PAR that Chambers mentions raises questions about whether such approaches feature as 'a legitimisation of the activities of powerful development actors, and as a technical shift that does not challenge dominant power relations' (Brock, 2002, p. 4).

What Chambers' statement indicates, then, is that participation need not be assumed to be positive, leading to empowerment of a transformative nature. Chambers suggests that PAR does not necessarily lead to the voices of the marginalised being heard. In fact, the assumption that this occurs can risk further silencing the more critical demands of such groups. What this suggests about PAR as an approach to social science research is that it does not necessarily have a fixed use or outcome. Despite its orientation to facilitating 'voice', PAR does not automatically result in enactments that are empowering or transformative in their effect.

One of the most important critical issues in PAR and other participatory social science approaches concerns the degree to which such approaches do, despite perhaps their best intentions, still revolve around relations of unequal power between researchers and researched. While PAR is often presented as a means of empowering marginalised people, with social scientists as facilitators, it is also the case that social scientists can themselves be further empowered in the process of undertaking participatory research, since they play a key role in translating local or marginalised voices for policy makers and other public actors (Holland and Blackburn, 1998, p. 2). The researchers James Holland and Jeremy Blackburn have suggested that the types of agency that social scientists exercise in and through PAR fall into three broad types – strategic, mediating and advocacy-orientated:

- Social scientists and intermediary institutions are often politicised through their engagement in participatory research, and thus play a *transformative strategic role* in the representation of local or marginalised voices (Holland and Blackburn, 1998, pp. 2–3). This is contrasted with an action-orientated approach that is more technical and rationalistic.
- The problems of effectively engaging local or marginalised groups and policy makers have led to the development of an alternative approach, whereby researchers and intermediary institutions play a *mediating role* in 'bringing policy-makers and local people together directly'. Nevertheless, Holland and Blackburn claim that there can remain a 'gulf in the context and the language' between the two groups involved (1998, p. 3).
- The *advocacy role*, they suggest, does not so much entail a process of 'representing the people' as it involves strategic acts to 'ensure that participation itself becomes part of the policy framework' (Holland and Blackburn, 1998, p. 3).

The two case studies discussed in Section 4 have been primarily developed by participants who are not social scientists by profession, which suggests that social scientists do not necessarily hold a position of power in relation to PAR. It is nevertheless clear that social scientists do play an important role both in devising the methods and in assessing the impacts of PAR projects. They can also play a key role in the initiation and development of such projects, such as in the case of the Fed Up Honeys project.

We have seen in this chapter that participatory social science is shaped by a variety of aims and values:

- by the practical aim – in PAR this can range along a continuum from institutional to liberatory
- by the role implied for the social scientist – from a transformative strategic role to a mediating role, or an advocacy role

- by the specific value that the participation of different groups of people in social science is meant to achieve – from the intrinsic good of participation itself through to more practical or instrumental values
- by the type of enactment that is pursued – from informing policy and practice to shaping subjects and social worlds.

Any given example of participatory social science will likely combine different elements in different ways. These principles can, in turn, function as the principles of evaluation through which the aims and objectives of participatory social science, such as a PAR project for example, can be assessed.

While some argue for PAR precisely because of its orientation towards producing knowledge that is strategic, mediating and/or advocacy-orientated, others would claim that the engagement of social scientists in such roles is inappropriate. You should remember, however, that it is not just explicitly engaged, committed social science of the type discussed in this chapter that helps to enact social worlds. You have seen examples of all sorts of social science enacting social worlds throughout the chapters in this book – from psychological experiments and social surveys in Chapters 1 and 2, to predictive models and large data sets in Chapters 5 and 7. In this chapter, you have looked at people participating in social science in a range of ways – from giving their opinions and having them taken seriously, through to a much more active, engaged form of involvement in the design and execution of research projects.

Social science methodologies that have an explicit commitment to participation in research, such as PAR, not only give voice to marginal groups but also have effects on the social worlds they investigate, and indeed seek to do so. What is distinctive about these approaches is that they tend to view the public role of social scientists as helping to produce knowledge and ideas and facilitating wider participation in the process, and not just restricted to informing policy issues.

For some, social science can ideally be considered as producing knowledge that is free of political motivation or moral commitment. For others, including advocates of approaches such as PAR, social science is thought of as having an important role to play in challenging entrenched relations of injustice and inequality, including those within the research process itself. However, look more carefully, and you will see that even forms of social science that appear to be models of 'scientific' objectivity view themselves as having a role in informing and shaping not only policy but public debate too. A social science that did not, in some sense, have that ambition would not be much use at all.

6 Conclusion: enacting social worlds

In this chapter you have seen how participatory approaches to social science seek to enact social worlds in new ways, explicitly, and in relation to values such as social justice, equality and empowerment. PAR has been discussed as an example of this sort of social science because it illustrates very well the issues that arise once we recognise that social science, of all sorts, not only seeks to describe and understand social worlds, but helps to enact them as well – to inform and shape how they develop and change over time. One of the issues that PAR raises, in turn, is just how central issues of evaluation are to the assessment of social science's broad public role. This is an approach that explicitly challenges us to think about what social scientists should be seeking to do by describing and understanding social processes; it forces us to ask what it is that we think social science is useful *for*.

This chapter has not considered issues surrounding PAR because this is the approach that we should think of as the most highly recommended way of doing social science. Rather, participatory social science has been our focus here because it makes quite explicit the issues of enactment that, as we have already suggested, arise around any social science investigation. PAR helps us see that social science can enact social worlds by informing policy, public debate and institutional practice; and it can also enact social worlds by helping to shape the subjects and areas it investigates. These two dimensions of social science enactment are not, it should be said, peculiar to PAR or to participatory social science, and you may reflect on the places where examples of both aspects of social science have come up elsewhere in the chapters of this book.

On the one hand, PAR helps us see the importance of social science research in *informing policy making*, where 'policy making' is not just restricted to government policy but extends to the formal practices of all sorts of institutions and organisations. A participatory approach is considered important in informing policy, because it serves as a means of reframing knowledge in line with the descriptions and understandings of those closest to the public issues under consideration. Earlier in this chapter, this was described as the instrumental and practical value of PAR – it is an example of social science being used to help practically orientated actors better understand how things work and what to do about specific issues. PAR informs policy by bringing to bear the knowledge of those who are otherwise 'voiceless' within the policy process.

On the other hand, we have also seen that PAR is not always focused on producing policy-orientated research. It also helps us see how social science is actively involved in *shaping the social worlds* it investigates. This does not have to be thought of in grand or dramatic terms. It can take the form of something as simple as providing someone with an opportunity to publicly voice their own sense of the complexities of having to negotiate negative stereotypes through their daily lives. Or, to put it another way, it can help people 'have voice', through which their private troubles can be recognised as having public dimensions. By involving the subjects of social research in the research process, PAR allows research participants to reshape themselves as well as the worlds that they inhabit. PAR can be used to facilitate the involvement of the subjects of social science in wider movements for change as well as the research process itself. But PAR is by no means necessarily tied to activist uses of social science research, and nor does this second dimension of enactment as shaping social worlds have to be thought of as applying only to activist styles of social science.

6.1 Chapter summary

In this chapter you have learned that:

- participatory approaches in social science seek to include various groups of people in social science investigation in order to address imbalances in opportunities to participate in society – to help people 'have voice'
- participatory approaches seek to make use of the voices and opinions of participants in social processes in order to better understand their motivations, interests and interpretations, and thereby improve social science descriptions and understandings
- participatory action research (PAR) is an example of participatory social science that explicitly seeks to include marginalised people in social science practice in order to empower them as subjects and to challenge relations of power
- PAR illustrates key issues concerning the role of social science in enacting social worlds
- the value of participatory approaches can be thought of in intrinsic, instrumental, or practical terms

- PAR is a broad approach that ranges from strongly activist and liberatory approaches to more applied and institutional approaches
- by seeking to explicitly enact social worlds in new ways in pursuit of values such as justice or empowerment, PAR makes visible the issue of evaluation in assessing the uses of social science
- PAR illustrates the two related ways in which social science can be thought to enact social worlds, by informing policy and public debate and by actively reshaping the subjects and social worlds it investigates.

References

Brock, K. (2002) 'Introduction. Knowing poverty: critical reflections on participatory research and policy' in Brock, K. and McGhee, R. (eds) *Knowing Poverty: Critical Reflections on Participatory Research and Policy*, London, Earthscan Publications.

Cahill, C. (2007) 'Participatory data analysis' in Kindon, Pain and Kesby (eds) (2007b).

Cahill, C., Arenas, E., Contreras, J., Jiang, N., Rios-Moore, I. and Threatts, T. (2004) 'Speaking back: voices of young urban womyn of color. Using participatory action research to challenge and complicate representations of young women' in Harris, A. (ed.) *All about the Girl: Culture, Power, and Identity*, New York, Routledge.

Cameron, J. (2007) 'Linking participatory research to action: institutional challenges' in Kindon, Pain and Kesby (eds) (2007b).

Chambers, R. (1998) 'Foreword' in Holland, J. and Blackburn, J. (eds) *Whose Voice? Participatory Research and Policy Change*, London, Intermediate Technology Publications.

Fed Up Honeys (2004) 'Makes me mad: stereotypes of young urban womyn of color' [online], http://www.fed-up-honeys.org/MakesMeMadreport.pdf (Accessed 30 March 2012).

Harris, J. (2011) 'West Midlands riots: tense and weary residents take stock', *The Guardian*, 12 August [online], http://www.guardian.co.uk/uk/2011/aug/12/west-midlands-riots-looting-response (Accessed 7 July 2012).

Harris, R. and Foreman-Peck, L. (2001) 'Learning to teach history writing: discovering what works', *Educational Action Research*, vol. 9, no. 1, pp. 97–109.

Holland, J. and Blackburn, J. (1998). *Who Changes? Institutionalizing Participation in Development*, London, Practical Action.

Kindon, S., Pain, R. and Kesby, M. (2007a) 'Introduction: connecting people, participation and place' in Kindon, Pain and Kesby (eds) (2007b).

Kindon, S., Pain, R. and Kesby, M. (eds) (2007b) *Participatory Action Research Approaches and Methods: Connecting People, Participation and Place*, London, Routledge.

Lewis, P. and Newburn, T. (2011) 'The Reading the Riots project: our methodology explained', 5 December [online], http://www.guardian.co.uk/uk/2011/dec/05/reading-the-riots-methodology-explained (Accessed 30 March 2012).

Lewis, P., Newburn, T., Taylor, M. and Ball, J. (2011) 'Rioters say anger with police fuelled summer unrest', 5 December [online], http://www.guardian.co.uk/uk/2011/dec/05/anger-police-fuelled-riots-study (Accessed 30 March 2012).

O'Neill, M. and Harindranath, R. (2006) 'Theorising narratives of exile and belonging: the importance of biography and ethno-mimesis in understanding asylum', *Qualitative Sociology Review*, vol. 2, no. 1, pp. 39–53.

Topping, A. (2011) 'Trouble isn't over yet, says teenager who predicted riots', *The Guardian*, 12 August, [online], http://www.guardian.co.uk/uk/2011/aug/12/riot-predict-trouble-not-over (Accessed 7 July 2012).

Van der Velde, J., Williamson, D.L. and Ogilvie, L.D. (2009) 'Participatory action research: practical strategies for actively engaging and maintaining participation in immigrant and refugee communities', *Qualitative Health Research*, vol. 19, no. 9, pp. 1293–302.

Whyte, W.F. (1991) 'Introduction' in Whyte, W.F. (ed.) *Participatory Action Research*, Newbury Park, CA, Sage Publications.

Conclusion

Clive Barnett and Mark Banks

Conclusion

This book has been primarily concerned with developing aspects of the DUE framework, as explained in the book's introduction. You should, by now, be able to recognise that the relationships between description, understanding and enactment are overlapping and entangled. In practice, any given example of social science will combine all the elements of the DUE framework – making social worlds visible, making sense of social worlds, and making a difference to how social worlds work in practice.

It is easy enough to imagine that the relationship between the three elements is a linear one – as if social science first describes by surveying and measuring, then it tries to understand by explaining and interpreting, and next it enacts by being applied. The chapters in the book are arranged to mimic this linear narrative, but that is to help you grasp the distinct aspects of the whole process of using social science. In reality, the relationship is often more complex – new social scientific descriptions are often informed by prior understandings derived from previous research that have determined what counts as useful or meaningful data to collect. Similarly, enactments will influence future decisions on how we should appropriately identify and collect descriptive evidence about a particular problem, or influence the theoretical or conceptual tools that are used in developing an understanding.

You can see examples of this throughout the book. For example, while Chapter 1 is focused mainly on introducing some key issues to do with social science description, the examples used (concerning research into the effects of television on its audiences) were intimately related to enacting policy decisions – in this case, decisions about the regulation of programming on national television. Likewise, Chapter 2 shows how something as technical as a survey was quite instrumental in the development of new sexual identities; this example of social science description was intimately involved in shaping new subjects of social worlds. In Chapter 3, you saw that contested understandings of the agency of sex workers are not just important in academic social science, but are part of public debates that shape policies about crime, housing and the safety of women. In Chapter 7, the idea that 'facts don't speak for themselves', which you first read about in relation to illegal migrant workers and sex workers, is shown to be an important dimension of social science studies of elections. It is because facts don't speak for themselves that social scientists are able to play a prominent role in the enactment of elections as meaningful expressions of 'the public will'.

In these and other ways, each chapter in this book has shown how social science is used by describing, understanding and enacting social worlds. Now that you have read the whole book, you might consider going back to Chapters 1 or 2 and noticing for yourself how issues of explanation and the use of concepts are discussed there. You could also look at Chapter 7 to see how important survey methods are to the interpretation of elections, illustrating how closely connected the act of describing social worlds can be to their different enactments in the public realm. Or you might want to note, in Chapter 5, how social science understandings help to enact different visions of mobility by being used to support or challenge particular policy proposals.

One final thing you should be able to notice now is the centrality of issues of value to how social science is used. This theme was introduced in Chapter 3 and developed in Chapter 4, around the topic of work and leisure; and then further developed, for example in discussions of contested understandings, in Chapters 5 and 6, and in consideration of the values of participatory social science in Chapter 8. If you recall the discussions in Chapters 1 and 2, however, which focused mainly on the use of quantitative and qualitative methods, these too concerned highly contentious issues that were and are the focus of competing interpretations of value – questions about the appropriate conduct of children, the proper boundaries between public and private life, and the representation of marginalised sexual minorities. Social science description, in these cases, is already embroiled in wider debates that shape and are shaped by the investigations undertaken by social scientists. In reading through the chapters, we hope this book has helped you to gain a better sense of the diverse uses to which social science is put, but also that you have come to recognise that these uses are illustrations of how much social science matters.

Acknowledgements

Grateful acknowledgement is made to the following sources:

Chapter 1: *Reading 1.1*: Beckford, M. (2009) 'Playboy bunny T-shirts and pop music videos to blame for sexualisation of children, expert warns',*Daily Telegraph*, 12 August 2009. Copyright © Telegraph Media Group Limited 2009; *Reading 1.2*: Buckingham, D. et al.(2010) *Final Report, Sexualised Goods Aimed at Children*, Ref: 2008-09/01/EOC, Research conducted for the Scottish Parliament, June–December 2009, © Scottish Parliamentary Corporate Body – 2011, reproduced under Class Licence Number C01W0000065 with the permission of the Controller, Office of Public Sector Information (OPSI); *Reading 1.4*: Buckingham, D., Willett, R., Bragg, S. and Russell, R. (2010) *Sexualised Goods Aimed at Children*: unpublished interview from a report originally produced for the Scottish Parliament Equal Opportunities Committee, Scottish Parliament Equal Opportunities Committee, Edinburgh, UK. Reproduced by kind permission of the researchers; *Table 1.1*: Maccoby, E. E. (1951) 'Television: its impact on school children', *Public Opinion Quarterly*, vol. 15, Oxford University Press; *Figure 1.2*: Copyright © Graham Jackson/CartoonStock.com; *Figure 1.3*: Copyright © Albert Bandura; *Figure 1.5*: Copyright © mediablitzimages (UK) Limited/ Alamy.

Chapter 2: *Figure 2.1*: Copyright © Time & Life Pictures/Getty Images; *Figure 2.2*: Wellings, K., et al. (1994) *Sexual Behaviour in Britain: The National Survey of Sexual Attitudes and Lifestyles*, Penguin; *Figure 2.3*: Copyright © Time & Life Pictures/Getty Images; *Figure 2.4*: Copyright © Glenn Copus/Associated Newspapers/Rex Features; *Figure 2.5*: Copyright © Fred W McDarrah/Getty Images; *Figure 2.6*: Kinsey, A.C., Pomeroy, W.B. and Martin, C.E. (1948) *Sexual Behavior in the Human Male*, W.B. Saunders.

Chapter 3: *Reading 3.1*: Sourced from http://www.independent.co.uk/news/ uk/crime/drowned-cockle-picker-to-be-buried-at-home-in-china-2111728.html, Wednesday 20 October 2011; *Reading 3.2*: Burnett, J. and Whyte, D. (2011) *The Wages of Fear: Risk, Safety and Undocumented Work*, PAFRAS; *Tables 3.1 and 3.2*: Health and Safety Executive (2011) *Statistics on Fatal Injuries in the Workplace 2010/2011*, Health and Safety Executive. Crown copyright material is reproduced under Class Licence Number C01W0000065 with the permission of the Controller, Office of Public Sector Information (OPSI); *Figure 3.1*: Copyright © Lancashire Police/

PA; *Figure 3.2*: Copyright © Fran/CartoonStock; *Figure 3.3*: Copyright © David Wootton/Alamy; *Figure 3.4*: Copyright © Sandi Dobson; *Figure 3.5*: Copyright © AFP/Getty Images.

Chapter 4: *Reading 4.2*: Scott-Clark, C. and Levy, A. (2011) 'Children in poverty', *The Guardian*, 4 June 2011. Copyright © Guardian News and Media Ltd 2011; *Reading 4.5*: Eccles, L. (2011) 'Angry young girls: binge-drinking culture "creating a generation of aggressive and out-of-control women"', *Daily Mail*, 21 October 2011, Daily Mail; *Table 4.1*: Office of National Statistics (2005) *Time Use Survey*, Office of National Statistics. Crown copyright material is reproduced under Class Licence Number C01W0000065 with the permission of the Controller, Office of Public Sector Information (OPSI); *Figure 4.1*: Copyright © Bob Thomas/Getty Images; *Figure 4.2*: Copyright © Lunamarina/iStockphoto; *Figure 4.3*: Copyright © CuboImages sri/Alamy; *Figure 4.4*: By permission of Cork City and County Archives; *Figure 4.5*: Copyright © Daily Mail.

Chapter 5: *Reading 5.1*: Pooley, C. (2010) 'Landscapes without the car: a counterfactual historical geography of twentieth-century Britian', *Journal of Historical Geography*, vol. 36, Issue 3. Copyright © (2010) reprinted with permission from Elsevier; *Figure 5.1*: Copyright © Midland Aerial Pictures/Alamy; *Figure 5.2*: Copyright © Hulton Archive/Getty Images; *Figure 5.5*: Copyright © Adrian Arbib/Alamy.

Chapter 6: *Reading 6.1:* Steil, L. (2011) '"Realness": authenticity, innovation and prestige among young danseurs afros in Paris', in Toynbee, J. (ed.) *Migrating Music*. Copyright © 2011Taylor & Francis. Reproduced by permission of Taylor & Francis Books UK; *Reading 6.3*: Adorno, T. (1945) 'A social critique of radio music', *The Kenyon Review*, no. 7, 1945. By permission of the publishers; *Reading 6.4*: Reprinted by permission, Anand, N. and Peterson, R.A. (2000) 'When market information constitutes fields: sensemaking of markets in the commercial music industry', *Organization Science*, Volume 11, Number 3, March 2000. Copyright 2000, The Institute for Operations Research and the Management Sciences (INFORMS), 7240 Parkway Drive, Suite 300, Hanover, Maryland 21076, USA; *Figure 6.1*: From http://outofafricauk.files.wordpress.com; *Figure 6.2*: By kind permission of the Library of the London School of Economics and Political Science, Reference Number MALINOWSKI/3/18/7; *Figure 6.3*: Copyright © 20th Century Fox/Rogers and Hammerstein Productions/Magna Corporation; *Figure 6.4*Courtesy of Emma Baulch; *Figure 6.5*: Copyright © Imagno/Hulton Archive/Getty Images.

Chapter 7: *Tables 7.2 and 7.3*: Denver, D. (2011) 'Elections and voting' in Heffernan, R., Cowley, P. and Hay, C. (eds) *Developments in British Politics 9*, Palgrave Macmillan; *Figure 7.1*: Copyright © Keith Morris/ Alamy; Figure 7.2: Copyright © BBC; *Figure 7.3*: Copyright © Jonathan Nicholson/ Demotix/Corbis; *Figure 7.4*: Copyright © Getty Images; *Figure 7.5*: Copyright © BBC.

Chapter 8: *Figure 8.1*: Copyright © Leon Neal/AFP/Getty Images; *Figure 8.2*: Copyright © Simon Rawles/Alamy; *Figure 8.3*: Copyright © Globo via Getty Images; *Figure 8.4*: Copyright © 67photo/Alamy.

Cover image: Copyright © DrAfter123/iStockphoto.

Index

acculturation stress 327, 329
action research 312
activist social science
  and participatory action research 326, 337, 343
administrative research
  Adorno's critique of 250, 252–5
  defining 250
  The Radio Project 249–51
Adorno, Theodore 258
  critique of administrative research 250, 252–5, 256
  and The Radio Project 250–1
African music
  Parisian *musique Afro* 233–7, 239, 240–1, 246, 257
agency 148–61
  defining 148–9
  and leisure 144–6, 148, 149–61
    and class 164, 168
    as escape 149–51
    and gender 171, 172–3, 176
    as investment 151–7
    and structure 177, 178, 179
    theories of agency 157–61, 179
  and mobility
    car use 188–9
    individual mobility 190–1
  and music cultures
    Balinese death metal 246, 254
    radio music 254
  and necessity 143
  as a normative reference point 177
  and participatory action research 330, 339
  and shadow work 124, 143, 146
    sex workers 126, 131–2
  and structure 162
  theories of 157–61
  of voters 299, 303
  see also individualisation theory; rational choice theory
aggregation
  and survey research 63–4, 69
aggressive behaviour and children
  Bandura's 'BoBo' doll experiments 32–3, 34
  and television 30
agricultural work
  data on fatal injuries 111, 112
  and illegal migrant workers 105
air pollution
  and motor vehicles 217, 219
alcohol and leisure
  the temperance movement 164, 165
  young women and binge drinking 174–5
alienation
  and voter turnout 287
American Psychological Association (APA)
  report on the sexualisation of children 37–8
Anand, Bharat N. and Peterson, Richard
  on music and market information regimes 259–63
apathy
  and voter turnout 287
Arenas, Erica
  and the Fed Up Honeys project 332–3
asylum seekers
  and music 229
  and undocumented migrant workers 119, 121, 122–3
Australia
  elections and voting 282
Australia Institute
  report on the sexualisation of children 37–8
authenticity
  and music cultures
    Balinese death metal 244–8
    coupé-décalé and Parisian *musique Afro* 234–7
automobility
  and road building 210–12
autonomy
  and leisure 144, 146, 148
averages
  calculation of in survey research 65, 67–8, 74
Bailey Review (2011)
  on the sexualisation of children 37–8
Bali Hai 242–3
Balinese death metal 230, 241–8, 254, 257
  and opinion leaders 255–6

and performative vocabulary 243, 244–5, 247
and territorialisation 243, 246–7
Bandura, Albert
'BoBo doll' experiments 32–3, 34
Banks, Mark
on creative class workers 155
Banister, David
on transport policies and practices 195–6, 201, 207, 211–12, 220, 221
Bannister, Sir Roger 149–50, 151
Baulch, Emma
case study of Balinese death metal 230, 241–8
BBC (British Broadcasting Corporation)
and the Nuffield Study 23–4, 30
Beck, Ulrich
on leisure and individualisation 158–9, 166
Beeching Report
on the UK railway system 196–7, 198, 200, 203–4, 206, 221
benevolent administrative research 252, 253
BES (British Election Study) 280–1, 289
bias
in survey research
and the Kinsey survey 75–6
prestige bias 70, 93
and values 178
Billboard magazine
and market information regimes 261, 263
Blackburn , Jeremy 339
Bloch, Alice 70, 72–3, 74
bodies
and leisure as investment 152, 153–6
Bolivia 116
Bourdieu, Pierre 151, 157, 160
British Election Study (BES) 280–1, 289, 301
Buckingham, David
research on children and television 33–4, 35
Sexualised Goods Aimed at Children 20, 44–8
Bullough, Vern 77–8, 90
Burnett, Jon and Whyte, David
case study of undocumented migrant workers 119–24, 132, 134
Butler , David 272, 279–80, 290, 301–2
Cahill, Caitlin
and the Fed Up Honeys project 331–2, 333–4, 335
Campbell, Chavez
views of the 2011 riots 315, 316, 317–19, 320
capital
leisure and physical capital 152
capitalism
Marxist theory of 163
car use 212–20, 221
counter-factual analysis of 213–20, 222
children and everyday travel 215, 218
health of the urban population 217, 219
older people 215, 217, 219
suburbanisation 216, 218, 219
and travel time 214–15, 218
and road building 205–12
induced demand 206–10
and transport policies
predict and provide approach to 194, 204, 205–6, 207
railway closures 201, 202, 204, 212
unintended consequences of 187, 188–91
case–studies
and the holistic approach 116–17, 132
participatory action research
Fed Up Honeys project 330–6, 339
refugee and immigrant healthcare 326, 327–30
the Settle–Carlisle railway line 192, 198–204, 205, 206, 212, 221–2
shadow work 116–32, 133
sex workers 117, 124–32, 134
undocumented migrant labourers 117–24, 132, 134
and theory building 132
see also ethnographic research
causal relationships
and childhood intimacies 39, 49, 50
in survey research 65, 68, 74
using experiments to identify 27–9
Caves, Richard 256–7
censuses
and descriptions 6
and surveys 67
Chambers, Robert 322–3, 324–5, 329, 337–8
child abuse
and the sexualisation of children 38
child poverty
and leisure 166–8
childhood intimacies 10, 19–51
and causal relationships 39, 49, 50
debate on the sexualisation of children 19–21, 22, 37–50

effects of television on the young 21, 22, 23–36, 349
and social science descriptions 19
Chinese cockle-pickers (MorecambeBay) 104–5, 106, 119
choice
and agency 148, 161
and leisure 150, 151, 156, 168
and car travel 207, 210
and unintended consequences 187–8
Clarke, Harold D. 291, 295
Clarke, John 164
class
and the Kinsey survey 76, 80
and leisure
and agency 160
Marxist theory of 162, 163, 164, 166, 169, 176, 179
social structures and inequalities 163–9, 176
and young women 173–4
and transport policies and practices 201
and voting
class-based theory of voting 289, 290–2, 298, 299, 303
and party identification theory 292, 293, 294
voter turnout 286–7
Clifford, James 237–9
closed questions
and survey research 24, 25, 65–7, 69–70
commodities
cultural commodities as 'experience goods' 256–7
music as a commodity 229, 230, 248, 264–5
and the culture industry 255–8
Conservative Party (UK)
and the 2010 general election 276, 277, 278
and class-based voting 290, 291–2
and party-identification voting 292, 294
constraints
and agency 148
and social structures 145–6, 162
construction industry
dangers of 109
data on fatal injuries 110–12
and illegal migrant workers 105
consumerism
and the sexualisation of children 19–20, 21, 44–8
contested descriptions 135
contested understandings 11–12, 134–5, 187, 350
and future mobility patterns
debates about 191, 192
social science and contested public issues 194–204
of the mobility of music 229–30
control groups
and the Himmelweit study 28
and the Kinsey survey 75–6
'corporate paedophilia'
and the sexualisation of children 37–8
counter-factual analysis 192
of car use 213–20, 222
creative class
and leisure 155–6, 157, 158, 159
Critcher, Chas 164
Crossley, Nick 148
cultural change
and forecasting future mobility patterns 195
cultural markers
infinite variety of 256–7
the culture industry
and musical commodities 255–8
data in social science 5, 6, 13
on elections 272, 300
informational thinness of 276, 277
and voting decisions 289
generating data in survey research 69–72
and health and safety risks at work 111–14
and shadow work 103, 105, 119, 134
understanding 7
dealignment
and voter turnout 287–8
death metal *see* Balinese death metal
deaths
in the 2011 riots 315, 320
in the construction industry 110–12
and shadow work
MorecambeBay cockle-pickers 104–5, 106
murders of sex workers 128
debate, informing and influencing 8–9
democracy
elections and voting 277–8, 282
and participatory action research 322, 323
Denver, David 293
dependent variables
and qualitative interviews 48

research on children and television
Bandura's 'BoBo doll' experiments 32
the Himmelweit study 27, 28, 29
descriptions 5–6, 10, 349–50
and childhood intimacies 19, 21, 22
research on children and television 31, 36
concepts and theories 143
contested descriptions 135
and enactment 8, 9
and ethnographic research 238–9
experiments and causal relationships 29
and intimacy 10
of leisure 144
and participatory action research 312
the 2011 riots 315–18
and shadow work 103, 108–14, 133–4
sex workers 125
undocumented migrant workers 123–4
and survey research 5, 60, 65, 88, 89, 93–4
thick descriptions 230, 232, 240
and understandings 7, 11, 146
and values 350
and voting behaviour 297–9
development studies
and participatory action research 321, 322–3, 324–5
disagreement
and social science investigation 11
disciplines of social science 3–4
domestic labour and leisure 169–71, 182
drugs and sex workers 127, 129
Du Bois, W.E.B. 330
DUE framework 4, 5–13, 349–50
and intimacy 10
and work 11
see also descriptions; enactment; understandings
Dumazedier, Joffre
definition of leisure 143–4, 151, 169
Eccles, L. 175
economic growth
and transport policies 194, 212
and valence-based voting 295
Economic and Social Research Council (ESRC)
and the British Election Study (BES) 281
education studies
and participatory action research 323–4
elections and voting 12–13, 281–304, 349–50
collecting and generating evidence about 276–81
elections and data 272
electoral registration 282, 303
and enactment 271, 300–2
general elections in the UK 272–3
(2010) 271, 276, 277, 283, 284, 286, 297
and other types of elections 278–9
and the parliamentary system 278
and social science 278–81
opinion polls 273, 302
participation in 273–4, 300, 311
importance of 272
and non-participation 271, 272, 282–8
and psephology 273, 279–81
public debate on 12–13, 280, 300–2, 303
and the secret ballot 277–8
and the swingometer 301–2
thinness of data on 276, 277
see also voting behaviour
Electoral Register (ER) 72–3
and the Natsal I survey 82–3
e-Mavens 263
enactment 8–9, 12–13, 349–50
and childhood intimacies 22
research on children and television 36
elections and voting 271, 300–2
forecasting future mobility patterns 221–2
and participation 311
and participatory action research 34–3, 313, 337, 340–1
the 2011 riots 318–20
and survey research 69–70
sex surveys 60, 63–4, 89–92
and voting behaviour 297
Ericksen, J.A. 71, 78–9
ethnicity
and the Kinsey survey 76
and leisure activities 145
ethnography and ethnographic research 3, 39, 237–41
case studies of music cultures 233–48, 264
Balinese death metal 230, 241–8, 254, 257, 355–6
Parisian *musique Afro* 230, 233–7, 239, 240–1, 246
defining 230, 232
and participant observation 237–8
proximity and distance in 237, 240–1, 248
and reflexivity 239

and thick descriptions 230, 232, 240
and travelling cultures 239–41
EU (European Union) Working Time Directive 121
European Parliament elections 283–4
evaluative research
on shadow work 105
evidence in social science 3, 7
and description 5, 6, 146
interpreting qualitative interview evidence 44–8
and shadow work 103, 105, 128, 134
for voter decisions 289
exoticist portrayals of cultures 242
experiential consequences
of shadow work 123
experimental research
on children and television 21, 22, 23, 26, 27–36
and the Himmelweit study 28
sender-message-receiver model of 34–5
variables in 27–8
expert opinions
on the sexualisation of children 20
using to identify causal relationships 27–9
experts, social scientists as 301
exploitative research 252, 256

facts in social science 143
contested 134–5, 191
and data on health and safety at work 112, 114
and descriptions 7, 11, 143, 146
and shadow work 103, 106, 133–5
sex workers 128, 131
and values 178–80
Fed Up Honeys project
and participatory action research 330–6, 339
feminist social science 7
on gender and leisure 169–74, 176, 179
and sex work 125–6
Field, Julia 81
Flood, Michael 37, 38
Florida, Richard
on the creative class and leisure as investment 155–6, 157, 158
focus groups 3, 39
and music audiences 249, 250
and research on children
sexualisation of 20, 44–8
and television 35
forecasting future mobility patterns 187–223, 350
causal understandings of mobility 205–20
new realism in 211–12
predict and provide approaches to 192, 194–6, 204, 220, 221
contesting 196–202, 204
road building 205–6
uses of social science in 11–12, 191, 192, 220, 221–2
contesting public issues 192, 194–204
and counter-factual analysis 192
see also car use; railway system in the UK; road building; unintended consequences
formal economy 103, 108, 115
freedom
and agency 148
and car travel 188, 210
and leisure 144, 146, 150
as investment 156
Freire, Paulo 323, 324
gangmasters
and shadow work 104, 105
GDP (gross domestic product)
and the informal economy 115–16
Geertz, Clifford
The Interpretation of Cultures 232
gender
and leisure 144, 169–76, 179
and agency 171, 172–3
gendered uses of time in the UK 172
see also women
general elections *see* elections and voting
generalisable findings
in survey research 67
globalisation
and migrant workers 117–24
Guardian newspaper
and the *Reading the Riots* programme 319–20
Hamilton, Clive 37, 38
Harindranath, R. 313
health and fitness
and leisure as investment 152, 153–5
Health and Safety Executive (HSE)
and data collection 112–14
data on injuries and fatalities at work 110–12
and legally registered workers 118
and risky occupations 109, 133
health and safety issues
dangerous occupations 106, 109, 110–12, 115

and legally registered workers 118
health of the urban population
and car use 217, 219
healthcare
refugee and immigrant healthcare, and participatory action research 326, 327–30
Hefner, Hugh 19
Hillman, Mayer 201
Himmelweit, Hilde et al.
Television and the Child: an Empirical Study of the Effects of Television on the Young 23–4, 26, 27–9, 30–2, 34, 253
HIV/AIDS
and the Natsal I survey 59–60, 81, 85, 94
holistic approach
and case studies 116–17, 132
Holland , James 339
Home Office report on street prostitution 127–8, 129, 134
homosexuality *see* same-gender sexual activity
Honduras 116
Hutchinson, Dr Fay 37

Igo, Sarah 63, 64
illegal migrant workers *see* undocumented migrant workers
in-depth interviews 3, 37
incomes
and child poverty in the UK 167
Independent Television Authority
and the '9 o'clock watershed' 30–1
independent variables
and the Himmelweit study 27, 28, 29
and qualitative interviews 48
India 116
individualisation theory
defining 147
and leisure 158–60, 160–1, 176, 179
inequalities of 168
and valence voting 295–6
individuality
and agency 148
Indonesia
Balinese death metal in 230, 241–8, 254, 255–6, 257
induced demand
and road building 206–10
industrial workers
inequalities and leisure 163–4
inequalities of leisure 177–8
and class 163–9
and gender 169–76
infinite variety
of cultural markers 256–7
informal economy 106, 115–16
information
and description 5, 6
understanding 7
infrastructure
and car transport 189
instrumental purposes
using leisure for 148, 151–7
instrumental value
of participatory action research 325, 329, 334
interdisciplinary social science 4
internet surveys 39, 71
the interviewer effect 71
and the Kinsey survey 78–9
interviews
and childhood intimacies 21
and closed questions 24, 25, 65–7, 69–70
and description 5
face-to-face 39
in-depth 3, 37
internet surveys 39, 71
the Kinsey survey questionnaire 77–9
open-ended 24 39, 24–6
qualitative interviewing
and ethnographic research 233
and sex surveys 93
and the sexualisation of children debate 39–48, 49–50
research on children and television 35
semi-structured 40, 65
surveys and interview research 40
and voting behaviour 272
BES post-election surveys 280–1
intrinsic value
of participatory action research 325, 334
investment, leisure as 151–7
issue-based voting theory (valence politics) 288, 289–90, 294–7, 298–9, 301, 303
Johnson, Anne 81
Johnston T, Ron *see* Pattie, Charles and Johnston, Ron
Joseph Rowntree Foundation

and the *Reading the Riots* programme 319–20
Kahn-Harris, Keith 241
Katz, Elihu 255, 263
Kinsey survey 57–9, 60, 62–3, 64, 65, 67, 74, 75–80
assessing the findings 79–80
defining and measuring sexual behaviour 69, 93–4
and enactment 64
and the Natsal I survey 81–2, 83, 86
questionnaire 77–9
and the interviewer effect 78–9
and same-gender sexual activity 58, 79, 80, 89–92
sampling technique 63, 73, 75–6, 79, 255
100 per cent groups 76
and sexual identities 64, 90–1
La Nauze, Andrea 37–8
laboratories and experimental research 27
Bandura's 'BoBo' doll experiments 32–3, 34
Labour Party (UK)
and the 2010 general election 276, 277
and class-based voting 290, 291–2
and party-identification voting 292, 294
Langhamer, Claire
on women's work and leisure 170, 173–4, 175
Lazarsfield, Paul 250, 252, 255, 257, 263
leisure 11, 143–80
as an autonomous activity 144, 145
defining 143–4
as escape 148, 149–51
as investment 151–7, 158
and social structures 145–6, 147, 162–76
class 163–9, 176
gender 144, 169–76, 179
and values 146, 178–80
see also agency, and leisure; work, and leisure
Lewis, Neil 150–1
Lewis, P. 320
Lewontin, Richard
'Sex, lies and social science' 62, 93
Liberal Democrats
and the 2010 general election 277, 278
Lin Liangren 104
Livingstone, Sonia
research on children and television 34, 35, 36
London School of Economics
and the *Reading the Riots* programme 319–20
McCallum, Robert 279, 280
MacKenzie, Robert 301–2
Maccoby, Eleanor
'Television: its impact on school children' 24–6, 32, 69
Malinowski, Bronislaw 237, 238
manufacturing industries
data on fatal injuries at work 111
market information regimes
and music 259–63
market testing
of cultural products 257–8
Marx, Karl 108
on class 162, 164, 166, 169, 176, 179
mass-mediated consumer culture
Adorno's critique of 251
Merton, Robert 187
Metallica 243
migrant workers
globalisation and the UK economy 117–18
legal and illegal 118–19
see also undocumented migrant workers
migration
and music cultures 229, 240
refugee and immigrant healthcare, and participatory action research 326, 327–30
Miller, Daniel
on car culture 189–90, 209
minority ethnic women
and participatory action research 330–6
mobility 3, 4, 11–12
car use and unrestricted mobility 188–9
mobile music *see* music
shaping individual mobility 190–1
see also forecasting future mobility patterns
moral discourses on leisure 164, 165
and young women 173–6
and class 155–6
Morecambe Bay cockle-pickers 104–5, 106, 119
music 12, 229–65
audiences and markets for 230–1, 249–63, 264
Adorno on 'good music' 251, 252–3, 254
and the culture industry 255–8
early production of popular music 249
e-Mavens 263
enacting music markets 258–63
and The Radio Project 249–51
as a commodity 229, 230, 248, 264–5

ethnographic research on music cultures 233–48, 264
and migration 229
as a practice 230
social science and contested mobilities in 264–5
values of 230
see also Balinese death metal; Parisian *musique Afro*

Natsal I survey 59–60, 61, 62–3, 65, 80, 81–8, 89
assessing 86–8
and the calculation of averages 67–8
closed questions in 66
and generalisable findings 67
and HIV/AIDS 59–60, 81, 85, 94
and Kinsey survey 81–2, 83, 86
and same-gender sexual activity 59–60, 62, 74, 84–8
sampling practices 63, 72, 73, 80, 82–4, 85–6, 93
Stanley's criticism of 59–60, 62, 84, 85–6
and stigmatised behaviour 74, 85–6, 87
value of 94
natural sciences
and social science research 23
necessity
and agency 143, 151
and women's work and leisure 171
negative unintended consequences 187–8
of car use 189–91
new realism
in transport planning 211–12
New York City
Fed Up Honeys project 330–6, 339
newspaper reports
on the 2011 riots 315, 316, 317–19
on the sexualisation of children 19–20, 21
on young women and leisure 173–4, 175
normative approaches
to agency and leisure 177, 178
Nuffield Election Studies 279–80, 301
Nuffield Foundation
Himmelweit study on television and the young 23–4, 26, 27–9, 30–2, 34, 253
observation
and description 5
and ethnographic research 233
participant observation 237–8
official statistics 5
Health and Safety Executive (HSE) data 110–14, 133
oil crisis
and car transport 195
O'Neill, M. 313
Open Society Foundation
and the *Reading the Riots* programme 319–20
open-ended interviews 24, 39, 65
and the Maccoby study on television and the young 24–6
opinion leaders
and music audiences 255–6
Ortner, Sherry B. 241
Owens, Susan 207, 209, 221

PAR *see* participatory action research (PAR)
parenting
and the effects of television on the young 21
Parisian *musique Afro* 230, 233–7, 239, 240–1, 246, 257
participation 3, 4, 12–13, 311–44
defining participatory social science 311–12
and enactment 311
participant observation 237–8
see also elections and voting
participatory action research (PAR) 13, 312–13
and action 312, 321–5, 339
for change 324–5
and activist social science 326, 337, 343
advocacy role of 339
and applied research 321–2, 326, 327, 337
case studies 326–36
Fed Up Honeys project 330–6, 339
refugee and immigrant healthcare 326, 327–30
co-production in 313, 334
defining 312–13
in education studies 323–4
and enactment 313, 318–20, 337, 340–1, 342–3
evaluating 337–41
inclusion in 313, 334
institutional approach to 324, 327–30
intervention in 313, 334, 335
liberatory approach to 323
and marginalised people 311, 321, 323, 324–5, 330, 334, 335, 338–9
mediating role of 339
and participation 312, 321–5
and policy-making 342–3

and power relations 312, 322–3, 337–9
and practical application 313
and the riots (2011) 315–20
and the shaping of social worlds 342
transformation in 313, 339
values of 313, 321–5, 329, 339–40
participatory research 312
partisan dealignment
and voter turnout 287–8
party-identification theory of voting behaviour 289, 292–4, 298, 299
Pattie, Charles and Johnston, Ron
on valence politics 296, 298–9
people trafficking
and migrant workers 105
performative vocabulary
and Balinese death metal 243, 244–5, 247
personal influence
and media audiences 255–6
Peterson, Richard *see* Anand, Bharat N. and Peterson, Richard
physical capital
and leisure 152
place, connections of 3
policies
informing and influencing 8–9
policy-making and participatory action research 342–3
and qualitative research 50
and survey research 94
transport and travel 191–2
political parties
and the class-based theory of voting 289, 290–2, 298, 299
party-identification theory of voting behaviour 289, 292–4, 298
and valence-based voting 288, 289–90, 294–7, 298, 299, 301
and voter turnout 286, 287
polling organisations 300
and the British Election Study (BES) 281
and public opinion 273
Pooley, Colin
counter-factual analysis of car use 213–20
positive unintended consequences 187–8
Postcode Address File (PAF) 72–3
and the Natsal I survey 82–3
poverty
and leisure 166–8
power relations
and choice 161
and music cultures 12, 239–40, 248
and participatory action research 312, 322–3, 337–9
and shadow work 133–4
sex workers 124, 125–6, 127–8, 129–30, 131–2
undocumented migrant workers 124
practical value
of participatory action research 325
predict and provide transport planning 192–4, 204, 220, 221
contesting 196–202
and road building 205–6, 207
prestige bias
in survey research 70, 93
probability/random sampling 72–4
and the Kinsey survey 75, 79
and the Natsal I survey 82–3, 93
psephology 273, 279–81
Pultzer, Paul 290

qualitative research 3, 19
on children
sexualisation of 39–48, 49–50
and television 34–6, 49
and quantitative approaches 25–6, 49–50
Sanders' research on sex workers 129–32
and survey research 65, 71–2
see also case studies; interviews; observation
quantitative research 3, 19
and qualitative approaches 25–6, 49–50
see also data in social science; experimental research; survey research
questionnaires
and interviews 40
and surveys 63, 93
the Kinsey survey 77–9
radio music
Adorno's critique of 252–5
Radio Yudha and Balinese death metal 244, 245, 246–7, 255–6
The Radio Project 249–51
railway system in the UK 196–204
and the Beeching Report 197–8, 199, 200, 203–4, 206, 221

and the Hatfield rail crash (2000) 195
the Settle–Carlisle railway case study 192, 198–204, 205, 206, 212, 221–2
random sampling *see* probability/random sampling
rational choice theory
defining 147
and leisure 157–8, 159–60, 160–1, 176, 177, 179
inequalities of 168
and utility 157, 159
and voter turnout 286
rational risk actors
sex workers as 131–2
Reading the Riots programme 319–20
reflexivity
and ethnographic research 239
refugee and immigrant healthcare
and participatory action research 326, 327–30
religion
and electoral behaviour 292
representative descriptions
sampling and survey research 65
representative samples 59
resourceful viewer concept
of television audiences 35
Ringrose, Jessica
research on the sexualisation of children 40–4
riots (2011) 315–20
descriptions of 315–18
and enactment 318–20
the *Reading the Riots* programme 319–20
understandings of 317–19
risk society 158, 159
and inequalities 168
risks and shadow work 133
risky occupations 106, 109, 110–12, 115
sex workers 126–7, 128, 129
hierarchies of harm 131
psychological and emotional risks 130
risk management strategies 129, 131
undocumented migrant workers 104, 105, 123
road building 192, 198, 205–12
and automobility 210–12
environmental campaigns against 205, 206, 210–11
and induced demand 206–10
and new realism in transport planning 211–12
predict and provide approaches to 205–6
unintended consequences of 192
Roads for Prosperity (UK government White Paper) 205, 210
Rockefeller Foundation
The Radio Project 249–51
rural areas
effects of railway closures on 200–2
Rush, Emma 37–8
same-gender sexual activity
and the Kinsey survey 58, 79, 80, 89–92
and the Natsal I survey 59–60, 62, 74, 84–8
recent surveys on 86–7
sampling frames 72–3, 75, 93
and the Natsal I survey 82–3
sampling in survey research 65, 72–4
music audiences 255
sex surveys
Kinsey 63, 73, 75–6, 79, 86, 255
Natsal I 63, 72, 73, 80, 82–4, 85–6, 93
see also probability/random sampling
Sanders, Teela
Sex Work: A Risky Business 129–32, 134
schools
and the sexualisation of children debate 45, 47
Scottish Parliament Equal Opportunities Committee
report on sexualised goods aimed at children 44, 46
self-reflection
and participatory action research 335, 337
self-reflexivity
and individualisation 158
sender-message-receiver model
of experimental research 34–5
Sennett, Richard
on car use and unrestricted mobility 188–9
sensemaking
and market information regimes 260, 262
Settle–Carlisle railway case study 192, 198–204, 205, 206, 212, 221–2
sewerage workers
data on fatal industries 111, 112
sex surveys 10, 57, 349
criticisms of 59–60, 62–3, 93, 93–4
defining and measuring sexual activity 69
prestige bias in 70
and standardisation 70–1
and stigmatisation 74, 85–6, 87
and women 76, 80, 84, 94
see also Kinsey survey; Natsal I

sex workers 105, 106, 117, 349
  and case study research 124–32, 134
  defining sex work 125
  and feminist researchers 125–6
  indoor workers 125, 129–32, 134
  numbers engaged in prostitution 126
  and power 124, 125–6, 127–8, 129–30, 131–2
  as rational risk actors 131–2
  risk management strategies 129, 131
  risks involved for 126–7, 128, 129, 130
  and social science understandings 125, 131–2
  street prostitution 125, 127–8, 130, 134
  and values 125
sexual identities
  and the Kinsey survey 64, 90–1
sexual intimacy 57–95
sexualisation of children debate 19–21, 21, 22, 37–50
  definitions of sexualisation 38
  as a public issue 37–9
  and qualitative interviewing 39–48, 49–50
    interpreting the evidence of 44–8
    teenagers and social networking sites 40–4
shadow work 115–34
  and agency 124, 143, 146
  case studies of 116–32
  describing and understanding 104, 108–14, 133–4
  evaluative research on 105
  experiential consequences of 123
  facts, concepts and theories in 106, 108, 133–5
  inequalities and leisure 166
  and the informal economy 106, 115–16
  power and agency 124
  risky occupations 106, 109, 110–12, 115
  wages and working conditions 108, 120–2
  see also sex workers; undocumented migrant workers
Sharma, Sham
  views of the 2011 riots 315, 316, 317–19, 320
significant relationships between variables 29
Sloman, Lynn 206
Smith, Adam 187
social change
  and forecasting future mobility patterns 195
social networking sites
  and the sexualisation of children 40–4
social structures
  and constraints 145–6, 162
    of class inequalities 169
    of gender 169–76
  decline of traditional, and individualisation 158, 159
  defining 143, 162
  and differences 146, 162
  and leisure 145–6, 147, 160, 161, 162–76, 177–8, 179
    class and inequalities 163–9
  and voting behaviour 291–2, 299
social-psychological theory
  of voting behaviour 289, 292–4, 298, 299, 303
socio-economic circumstances
  and voter turnout 286–7
sociological theory
  of class and voting 289, 290–2, 298, 299
Soundscan 258, 259, 260–2, 263
South Pacific (Hollywood film musical) 242
standardisation
  in survey research 70–1
Stanley, Liz
  criticism of the Natsal I sex survey 59–60, 62, 84, 85–6, 94
statistics *see* official statistics
Steil, Laura
  case study of Parisian *musique Afro* 233–7, 239, 240–1, 246
stereotyping
  participatory action research and challenges to 326, 330, 332, 333, 335, 336
stigmatisation
  and music cultures 240
  and survey research 74
    Natsal I 74, 85–6, 87
Stokes, D. 280, 290
structure
  defining 143, 162
  and agency 148, 162
  and car use 188, 189–91
  and leisure 143, 144–6, 177–8, 179
  and sex workers 132
  see also social structures
subcultures
  and Balinese death metal 243, 244–8
suburbanisation
  and car use 216, 218, 219
Suharto (President of Indonesia) 243

survey research 57, 65–74
aggregation process 63–4, 69
calculating averages in 65, 67–8
and causal relationships 65, 68, 74
and closed questions 65–7, 69–70
and descriptions of the social world 5, 60, 65, 88, 89, 93–4
elections and voting 350
BES post-election surveys 280–1
voting behaviour 272
and enactment 63–4, 69–70
generalisable findings in 67
generating data 69–72
and the interviewer effect 71
and prestige bias 70, 93
and standardisation 70–1
and music audiences 249, 250, 255
non-responses 74
and paid fieldworkers 79, 84
and qualitative research 65, 71–2
sampling 72–4
and stigmatisation 74, 85–6
value of 94
see also Kinsey survey; Natsal I survey; sex surveys
telephone surveys 71
television
influence on elections and voting 302
research on children and 21, 22, 23–36, 49, 349
the '9 o'clock watershed' 23, 30–1
Bandura's 'BoBo doll' experiments 32–3, 34
Buckingham' study 33–4, 35
Livingstone's study 34, 35, 36
the Macoby study 24–6, 32, 69
the Nuffield (Himmelweit) study 23–4, 26, 27–9, 30–2, 34
resourceful/engaged viewers 35, 36
temperance movement 164, 165
territorialisation
and Balinese death metal 243, 246–7
theory building
and case studies 132
thick descriptions 230, 232, 240
Tombs, Steve 113
transport practices and policies *see* forecasting future mobility patterns
travelling cultures
and ethnography 239–41
two-step flow
and media audiences 255–6
Twyford Down protest 210–11
uncertainty
and music audiences 255–8
understandings 6–8, 146, 349–50
and childhood intimacies 22
research on children and television 31, 36
concepts and theories 143
ethnographic 238–9, 241, 248
of leisure 144
and participatory action research 312
the 2011 riots 317–19
and shadow work 103, 108–14, 133–4
sex workers 125, 131–2
undocumented migrant workers 123–4
and survey research 88
and voting behaviour 297, 297–8
and work 7, 11
see also contested understandings
undocumented migrant workers 105, 106, 115–16
case study of 117–24, 132, 134
and gangmasters 104, 105
health and safety issues 104, 105, 123
and the immigration system 122–3
Morecambe Bay cockle-pickers 104–5, 106, 119
unintended consequences 187–8
of transport policies and practices 191, 195
car use 187, 188–91
railway closures 201
United States
elections and voting 282
music audiences
and Soundscan 258, 259, 260–2, 263
and The Radio Project 249–51
participatory action research, and the Fed Up Honeys project 330–6, 339
see also Kinsey survey
Urry, John 210
utility
and rational choice theory 157, 159
and voter turnout 286

valence-based voting 288, 289–90, 294–7, 298–9, 301
values in social science 350
and leisure 146, 178–80
and music 230

and participatory action research 313, 321–5, 329, 339–40
and research on sex workers 125
and understandings 7, 8, 11
contested 191, 350
Van der Velde, J. 329
variables
and experimental research 27–9
significant relationships between 29
voting behaviour 274, 303
floating voters 294
social science theories of 289–99
class-based 289, 290–2, 298, 299, 303
evaluating 297–8
party-identification 289, 292–4, 298, 299, 303
valence-based voting 288, 289–90, 294–7, 298–9, 301, 303
voter turnout 274, 284–8, 303
first- and second-order elections 283–4
reasons for decline in 285–8
trends in 284–5
see also elections and voting
Wadsworth, Jane 81
wages
gender inequalities in 171
and organised labour 108
and shadow work 108
undocumented migrant workers 120–2
Waring, Amanda
on leisure as investment 153–5, 157
waste, recycling and water workers
data on fatal industries 111, 112
Wellings, Kaye 68, 81, 87
Whalley, Anne 201
White, Dr Catherine 19, 20
Whitelegg, John 201
Whyte, David
and Burnett, Jon, case study of undocumented migrant workers 119–24
research on injuries at work 113
Whyte, William Foote 321–2
women
and the Equal Pay Act (1970) 108, 171
and leisure 169–76
moral discourses on young women 173–6
and sex surveys 76, 80, 84, 94
work 3, 4, 10–11
defining 103
and the formal economy 103, 108, 115
health and safety issues 108, 109–14
and leisure 148
and class 163–9 163–4
as escape 150
and gender 169–72, 176
and individualisation theory 158–9
as investment 151–7
and rational choice theory 157–8
Marxist theories of 108
understanding 7, 11, 103
unpaid 103
see also shadow work

Yanky, Agus 244
young women
and binge drinking 174–5
and the Fed Up Honeys project 330–6